Topsy-Turvy

BOOKS BY ANYA JABOUR

Scarlett's Sisters: Young Women in the Old South
Major Problems in the History of American Families and Children
Marriage in the Early Republic:
Elizabeth and William Wirt and the Companionate Ideal
Family Values in the Old South
(co-edited with Craig Thompson Friend)

Topsy-Turvy

HOW THE CIVIL WAR
TURNED THE WORLD UPSIDE DOWN
FOR SOUTHERN CHILDREN

Anya Jabour

Ivan R. Dee

CHICAGO 2010

www.ivanrdee.com

Library of Congress Cataloging-in-Publication Data:
Jabour, Anya.
   Topsy-turvy : how the Civil War turned the world upside down for southern children / Anya Jabour.
      p. cm.
   Includes bibliographical references and index.
   ISBN 978-1-56663-632-2 (cloth : alk. paper)
   1. Children—Confederate States of America—History. 2. United States—History—Civil War, 1861–1865—Children. 3. Children and war—Confederate States of America. 4. Children and war—United States—History—19th century. I. Title.
   E585.C54.J33 2010
   973.7083'0977—dc22   2009053471

Acknowledgments

A PROJECT LIKE THIS would not be possible without the work of other scholars. Many of these are named in the footnotes and the Note on Sources, but a few deserve special mention here as well. James Marten, who has written several of his own books on children in the Civil War era, encouraged me to undertake this project, read multiple drafts of the manuscript, and offered detailed and insightful suggestions along the way. Jennifer Ritterhouse read drafts of two early chapters and urged me to think in terms of telling stories.

I owe a special debt of gratitude to the participants in the Symposium on Children and Education in the Transmission of Southern Culture. This 2007 event, organized by Catherine Jones, held at Georgia populist Thomas E. Watson's historic home, Hickory Hill, and sponsored by the Watson-Brown Foundation and the Institute for Southern Studies at the University of South Carolina, brought together a remarkable group of scholars in a tranquil setting for two truly inspirational days of intellectual exchange. Holly Brewer, Patricia Crain, Carolyn Eastman, Lorri Glover, Catherine Jones, Elizabeth Kuebler-Wolf, Valinda Littlefield, and Jennifer Ritterhouse were the best writing workshop group a scholar of childhood could hope for.

I am also grateful to my fellow panelists and the audience members who gave me encouragement and ideas when I presented early versions of parts of this project at annual meetings of the Southern Association for Women Historians in 2006 and 2009. I am thankful for the financial support of the History Department at the University of Montana, which enabled me to present early versions of my work at these conferences.

I am deeply indebted to the interlibrary loan staff of the Mansfield Library at the University of Montana, who enabled me to acquire obscure titles and dusty tomes from other institutions. The University of Montana granted me a yearlong sabbatical to bring this book to fruition. Gary Cotton and other members of the staff at the Library of Congress provided indispensable assistance in acquiring illustrations for this volume.

Two of my former students assisted me with this project. Jeneva Plumb helped me with research in the WPA oral histories, and Katie Knowles took time away from her own dissertation research to send me pertinent citations. I thank them for their help and wish them all the best in their own scholarship.

A. J.

Missoula, Montana
February 2010

Contents

Topsy-Turvy

Confederate Childhoods

Fifteen-year-old Ernest Wardwell was a schoolboy in Baltimore, Maryland, when the Civil War began. As he walked to school on April 19, 1861, Ernest observed the excitement created by the presence of Union soldiers passing through the city en route to Washington, D.C. President Lincoln had called for 75,000 troops to assemble, responding to the newly formed Confederacy's bombardment of Fort Sumter, off the coast of Charleston, South Carolina, a week earlier. As Ernest made his way to school, "the air was resonant with rumors and excitement," and the streets were crowded with Confederate sympathizers protesting the presence of "Yankee invaders" come "to pillage our city." "Everybody seemed full of patriotic fire," Ernest observed, "and warlike sentiment ran high. Knots of men, some of them carrying guns and pistols, hurried through the streets, and gave rent [sic] to loud expressions of vengeance against the 'Northern Scum.'"[1]

Although Ernest proceeded to school, he and his agitated classmates were so unruly that the principal dismissed school, advising the students to proceed directly home. "In a twinkling," Ernest and his friend Henry Cook instead made their way through an "immense crowd" to the train depot, where they found a "frantic multitude" opposing the soldiers waiting to board the train to the national capital. "It was an awful melee," as Ernest described the scene, "a wild mob of crazy men and boys shrieking with fearful oaths their desire to annihilate the hated 'Yankees,'" and hurling stones, brickbats, and "missiles

3

of all kinds" through the windows at those inside. Although from a nonslaveholding family himself, Ernest was caught up in the mood of the mutinous mob. "At first I was paralyzed with fear," he admitted, "but only momentarily." The two boys "quickly imbibed the martial spirit that pervaded," and both Ernest and Henry joined the angry mob, chasing the beleaguered soldiers through the city "like a vociferous army of howling wolves."[2]

A year after Ernest Wardwell caught war fever, a thirteen-year-old slave girl called Susie King became part of an early experiment in emancipation on the Georgia Sea Islands. When hostilities began, Susie lived in the coastal city of Savannah with her maternal grandmother, her brother, and her mistress. Susie's duties as a house slave required her to make frequent trips to the town's pumps to fetch water for her owner's household; on such trips she often witnessed the slave auctions that regularly tore apart slave families. "I remember, as if it were yesterday, seeing droves of negroes going to be sold," she wrote in her memoirs. "I often went to look at them, and I could hear the auctioneer very plainly from my house, auctioning these poor people off." With such early impressions of one of the harshest aspects of slavery, Susie learned everything she could about the great conflict that offered the promise of freedom. Having secretly learned to read and write, the slave girl garnered information about the war from newspapers as well as from her parents and grandmother, who taught her that "the Yankee was going to set all the slaves free." Disregarding local whites' warnings that Union soldiers intended to harness blacks to carts and use them as horses, Susie was eager to see the soldiers for herself: "I wanted to see these wonderful 'Yankees' so much," she recalled. A year into the war, after Union forces captured Port Royal, South Carolina, Susie "was sent out into the country to my mother." If the teenager's owner sent her away from the city to keep her from seeking freedom behind Union lines, the ploy was unsuccessful. In April 1862, two days after nearby Fort Pulaski was occupied by Union soldiers, Susie's uncle came with his seven children to take his niece to St. Catherine's Island, one of the Union-occupied Sea

Islands just off the Georgia coast. "We landed under the protection of the Union fleet," she recounted, "and remained there two weeks, when about thirty of us were taken aboard the gunboat P——, to be transferred to St. Simon's Island; and at last, to my unbounded joy, I saw the 'Yankee.'"[3]

The following year Sue Chancellor, a planter's daughter, had a very different encounter with the Union Army. In May 1863 fourteen-year-old Sue and her six siblings found themselves at the epicenter of the Battle of Chancellorsville. The Chancellors were wealthy Virginia slaveholders who had first encountered the Civil War in the form of Confederate pickets stationed nearby. Grateful for well-prepared meals and sympathetic to the widowed Mrs. Chancellor, the soldiers were attentive and kind to the Chancellor children, teaching Sue's older sisters to play cards and presenting Sue with "a beautiful white lamb" as a pet. Soon, however, young Sue encountered another side of war as refugees from the Battle of Fredericksburg began to arrive during the winter of 1862–1863, bringing with them a bewildering variety of conflicting rumors. "Everything was reported," the teenager remarked with evident exasperation. In the spring the Chancellor home was occupied by Union soldiers who laid claim to "all of our comfortable rooms" and relegated the family to a single room at the rear of the house. Despite the exchange of "mahogany furniture" for "pallets on the floor," the Chancellor home remained a magnet for refugees: "We were joined by one and another of our neighbors," Sue explained, "until there were sixteen women and children in that room." Meanwhile the main house had been converted into a military hospital; the sitting room became an operating theater, and "our piano served as an amputating table," Sue recalled. Finally, on May 2, 1863, falling shells forced the Chancellor family and their friends to take refuge in the basement overnight. While offering some protection from harm, the cellar's thick walls could not block out the sounds of the fighting: "Oh! Such cannonading on all sides, such shrieks and groans, such commotion of all kinds!" Sue wrote. "We thought that we were frightened before, but this was far beyond everything." When the basement's occupants emerged the next day, they found the house on fire, amputated limbs spilling from the sitting-room windows, and "rows and rows of dead bodies covered with canvas" in the yard. "Oh, the horror of that day!" Sue exclaimed. "Cannons were booming in every direction, and missiles of death were flying as this terrified band of women and children came stumbling out of the cellar." The scene "beggar[ed] description": "The woods around the house were a sheet of fire; the air was filled with shot and shell; horses were running, rearing, and screaming; the men were amass with confusing, moaning, cursing, and praying." Many years later Sue solemnly observed, "If anybody thinks that a battle is an orderly attack of rows of men, I can tell him differently, for I have been there."[4]

Farther south and another year into the war, teenage bondsman William Rose also had a memorable encounter with the military. William was just a "stripling lad" during the Civil War, but he vividly remembered Union General William Tecumseh Sherman's 1864 "March to the Sea" from Atlanta to Savannah. Young William was a slave on a plantation in rural South Carolina, not far from the Georgia border, and he eagerly seized the opportunity to witness Confederate soldiers mustering to confront Union forces. "Boy-like I got to see and hear everything," he recalled decades later. Accompanying his father to the local train station to collect mail for the overseer, the youngster was amazed to observe trains filled with Southern soldiers on their way to challenge General Sherman's troops, who were even then "marching tump-tump" through the neighboring state of Georgia. "What a lot of train[s]!" he exclaimed. "De air fair smoke up wid dem." William was particularly struck by what he later described as "de bravest thing I ever see." The soldiers on board the trains played instruments, sang gay tunes, laughed and shouted, and vowed to make the Union soldiers tremble. "Boys," declared one Confederate, "we going to eat our dinner in hell today." The slave child was convinced—rightly, as it turned out—that death awaited the soldiers, despite their boasts about the sharpness of their bayonets and their promises "to cut the Yankee throat." Standing on his tiptoes to watch the train pull out of the station, across the trestle, and out of sight, he soberly recalled, "De last thing I hear is de soldier laugh and sing. . . . All going down to die."[5]

By the following year the Civil War was drawing to a close. Confederate defeat and African-American emancipation were on the horizon. In February 1865 seventeen-year-old Confederate Emma LeConte spotted the United States flag floating over the state house in the college town of Columbia, South Carolina. "Oh, what a horrid sight!" she exclaimed. "What a degradation! After four long bitter years of bloodshed and hatred, now to float there at last! That hateful symbol of despotism! I do not think I could possibly describe my feelings." But Emma was not at a loss for words for long. Soon after Confederate General Robert E. Lee's surrender in April, she turned to her diary in despair: "The South lies prostrate—their foot is on us—there is no help. . . . They say *right* always triumphs, but what cause could have been more just than ours? Have we suffered all—have our brave men fought so desperately and died so nobly for *this*? For four years there has been throughout this broad land little else than the anguish of anxiety—the misery of sorrow over dear ones sacrificed—for *nothing*!" Living under military occupation and faced with formal surrender, Emma and her family despaired. "We are all very miserable," she concluded.[6]

Columbia's emancipated slaves did not share Emma's sorrow at the Confederacy's defeat. On Independence Day the town's black population held a "grand celebration" in the center of town. An "immense procession" made its way to College Hall, which had been decorated with flowers by freed children in preparation for the event, for a series of speeches celebrating freedom. Afterward, old and young enjoyed a brass band, fireworks, and a dance that went late into the night. After three centuries of slavery and four years of war, Columbia's African Americans at last "had the day to themselves."[7]

*

As these accounts of the Civil War—from start to finish—indicate, the war had a significant impact on children's lives. At the same time these different narratives demonstrate that there was no single child's experience of the Civil War. Children's experiences of and reactions to the turmoil of the Civil War era differed depending on whether they were Northern or Southern, boys or girls, black or white, slave or free, rich or poor. This book addresses the lives of children living in the slaveholding South. I focus on children living in the eleven Confederate states that seceded from the Union: Virginia, North Carolina, South Carolina, Georgia, Florida, Tennessee, Alabama, Mississippi, Arkansas, Louisiana, and Texas. Because much of the Civil War was fought in the border states, however, I also include children from the slave states that remained in the Union: Maryland, West Virginia, Kentucky, and Missouri. Where possible, I have incorporated the experiences of white Union sympathizers (African Americans, of course, were Unionists in Confederate territory).

When I speak of "children," I refer to people who had not achieved adulthood according to the standards of their time and place. Thus while I treat entering military service as a coming-of-age experience for adolescent males, I do not address the experiences of soldiers who had already acquired adult status by benefit of military service. Most of the youth included here were under the age of eighteen at the time of the war's onset, but I also include some individuals who had entered their twenties but had not yet assumed adult roles, such as unmarried daughters living at home.

For purposes of clarity for a contemporary audience more accustomed to chronological calculations of age, this study generally refers to youngsters under the age of two as "infants"; to individuals under the age of five as "toddlers" or "very young children"; to persons between the ages of five and twelve as "children" or "young children"; to youth between the ages of thirteen and eighteen as "adolescents" or "older children"; and to people between the ages of eighteen and twenty-five as "young adults." Where possible, the ages of individuals are noted; because slaves did not always know their ages precisely and because memoirists often provide only vague dates, some ages

Children living in the Confederate South witnessed the destruction of war first-hand. In this photograph, four children watch a group of soldiers approaching during the First Battle of Bull Run near Manassas, Virginia, in 1861. *(Library of Congress)*

are estimated based on internal evidence and prevailing cultural patterns.

Southern children's lives were unavoidably and irrevocably changed by the course of the war. The Civil War may have been a national tragedy, but it had an especially devastating effect on Southern soldiers, civilians, and communities. Confederate soldiers died at a rate three times that of their Union counterparts. Although civilian deaths due to hunger, disease, and violence have not been so carefully documented, one historian has estimated that the overall mortality rate for the South was greater than that of any country in World War I. Because the war was fought largely on Southern soil, parts of the

South became a "permanent landscape of war." Everywhere in the Confederacy, "death was omnipresent."[8]

Children in the Confederacy thus experienced the Civil War in an especially profound and personal way. Certainly children in the North were affected by the war: their male relatives served (and sometimes died) in the Union Army; their magazines and schoolbooks discussed the war; and their play took on a military character. But children in the South, living on the front lines rather than on the home front, experienced the war in a more immediate manner. Like Northern children, they bade farewell to and sometimes mourned the deaths of fathers, uncles, cousins, and brothers; they gathered war news from a variety of sources; and they adopted martial themes in their play. But in addition, children in the war-torn Confederacy had direct and frequent contact with military warfare. Like Ernest Wardwell, Susie King, and William Rose, they watched armies gather; like Sue Chancellor, they witnessed battles and confronted armed invaders; and like Emma LeConte, they lived under military occupation. Children in the Confederate South truly lived in a war zone.

The Civil War was a frightening—even traumatic—experience for Southern children. Psychologists define traumatic experiences as sudden, unpredictable, and overwhelming, arousing intense feelings of terror and vulnerability. Trauma victims often suffer from lingering traumatic memories, painful feelings, and visual images of trauma. The experiences of children in the Civil War South bear all the hallmarks of trauma. Southern children confronted unexpected and terrifying events beyond their comprehension or control, and these experiences had lasting effects.[9]

Sue Chancellor's intense fear during the 1863 shelling of her home seems undiminished in her retelling of the story for her descendants. "Many on both sides have passed away," she reflected many years later, "and the years have dimmed my memory for incidents and occurrences, yet the horrible impression of those days of agony and conflict is still vivid, and I can close my eyes and see again the blazing woods, the flaming house, the flying shot and shell, and the terror-stricken women and children pushing their way over the dead and wounded."[10] Young Sue's emotional disturbance was not unique. Southern children's accounts of the Civil War frequently expressed feelings of anxiety and helplessness as they encountered situations beyond their understanding or control.

Southern children adopted a variety of strategies to cope with their material and emotional difficulties. Gathering information about the Civil War—whether from observation, like Ernest Wardwell and William Rose; from newspapers and family members, like Susie King and Emma LeConte; or from rumor, like Sue Chancellor—helped reduce the unpredictability of life in a war zone. Other children in the Confederate South incorporated the crisis into their play, a common means for children to assert power over events beyond their control and thereby reduce their feelings of helplessness. And the children included here sought control over their experiences in one final way: they told their own stories, claiming narrative power that offset the powerlessness they had experienced as children in the midst of military conflict. Children in the Southern Confederacy thus found ways both during and after the war to cope with their difficult experiences and painful emotions.

While Southern children shared wartime experiences, expressed similar emotions, and used common coping strategies during the war years, they adopted different perspectives on the events and issues of the great national conflict. Susie King welcomed Union soldiers as liberators; Sue Chancellor befriended Confederate pickets; and William Rose admired the bravery of both Union and Confederate troops. Ernest Wardwell eagerly joined the riot brewing in his hometown; Emma LeConte passively observed the occupation of hers. In the slaveholding South, four key variables—race, class, gender, and legal status—shaped children's social identities and affected their daily lives. Southern children's reactions to the Civil War differed depending on these same variables. From the controversy of secession to the upheavals of the war years, to the defeat of the Confederacy and the coming of emancipation, and in the decades that followed, Southern children's responses to the dramatic events of the Civil War era varied according to their social status.

As the historian James Marten contends, there was a "children's Civil War"—that is, children experienced the national crisis differently from adults.[11] For Southern children, living in a war zone, unavoidable and frequent experience with military conflict often led to fear and anxiety. They attempted to mitigate their helplessness and vulnerability by gaining some measure of control over their circumstances through information gathering, playacting, and storytelling. Although children had unique experiences during the Civil War, their reactions to the conflict were not uniform. In the Confederate South, children's responses to the war differed depending on their place in slaveholding society. This book thus highlights both the distinctiveness of childhood and the diversity of children's lives.

CHAPTER ONE

Family and Identity

GROWING UP IN A SLAVE SOCIETY

"I once saw two beautiful children playing together," wrote the fugitive slave and abolitionist author Harriet Jacobs. Yet this seemingly idyllic scene gave Jacobs no pleasure. "One was a fair white child," she elaborated, "the other was her slave, and also her sister. When I saw them embracing each other, and heard their joyous laughter, I turned sadly away from the lovely sight." Jacobs explained that she "foresaw the inevitable blight" that would be cast over the slave girl's life. While the white child would become "a still fairer woman," whose "pathway was blooming with flowers . . . from childhood to womanhood," the black child was fated to "dr[i]nk the cup of sin, and shame, and misery, whereof her persecuted race are compelled to drink."[1]

The contrast Jacobs drew between the "two beautiful children"—one black, one white—was a keen observation on the importance of race in determining the meaning of childhood in the slaveholding South. Likewise, Jacobs's decision to choose two girls to illustrate the shame of slavery was a telling one, for gender, as much as race, shaped the experiences of children in the antebellum South. Jacobs did not comment on the role of legal status or economic class, but as the daughter of a free black carpenter she might well have noted how freedom and slavery, wealth and poverty, affected the lives of Southern children. Southern children entered the war years with identities firmly grounded in the rigid hierarchies and day-to-day realities of the Old South. These identities shaped young Southerners' expectations about their futures and their responses to the national conflict. Early childhood lessons in social identity prepared Southern children for the Civil War.

Southern children grew up in a society defined by extremes. At the two extremes of social status in the slaveholding South were planters and their slaves. Members of the planter class—commonly defined as owning twenty or more slaves—typically resided in the fertile lowlands and derived their wealth from the sale of staple crops (tobacco, sugar, or cotton, for instance) cultivated by slave labor. While only a minority of white Southerners owned enough human property to be classified as planters, the majority of enslaved blacks resided on plantations. Although they shared living and working space, white planters and black slaves were worlds apart in terms of social status. Indeed, physical proximity could actually increase social distance by offering regular opportunities to reinforce racial hierarchies. Annie Burton, who was born into slavery in 1858 and lived on a plantation with thirteen other slave children and ten white ones, recalled "happy, care-free childhood days on the plantation, with my little white and black companions." Yet even though all the children enjoyed "the great hog-killing times" and the "great sugar-cane grinding time" and relished the crispy bits of bacon and the sweet sugar-cane juice they were permitted to have on such special occasions, their "jolly time" together nonetheless revealed the stark differences between them. The former slave captured this contradiction in her postwar memoirs when she wrote: "The negro child and the white child knew not the great chasm between their lives, only that they had dainties and we had crusts."[2]

Free black and mixed-race people occupied an anomalous position in antebellum Southern society. Free people of color—especially favored former slaves who had been fathered by their owners—could enjoy considerable economic success, occasionally even owning slaves themselves. Sometimes, though not always, these slaves were family members who could not be emancipated by state law. Yet when plantation mistress Tryphena Blanche Holder Fox described the marginalization of Mississippi Creoles, a group with both European and African heritage, she indicated that even great wealth could not elevate a mixed-race group to elite status. Describing one "old mulatto man . . . worth a hundred thousand dollars" in her Plaquemines Parish home, she wrote: "His father was an Englishman, his mother a black slave. He lives with a negro woman and has several children; I saw two of the girls who came down on the boat with me. They have every thing that money can procure for the body, but no education and of course they are mere nothings, neither white or black, illegitimate and shut out from all grades of society."[3]

Keenly aware of their uncertain status, many free black families made considerable sacrifices to clothe and educate their children as well as their white neighbors did. In Natchez, Mississippi, free black barber William Johnson and his emancipated wife Ann Battles Johnson, themselves urban slaveholders, arranged for their children to be privately educated in the classics and the fine arts as well as for their sons to be trained as blacksmiths. Urban centers with significant populations of free blacks sometimes established schools for them, sometimes quite similar to those attended by planter-class youth. In Baltimore, the Oblate Sisters' School for Colored Girls offered classes in religion, French, and fine arts and enforced "Rules of conduct for Young Ladies." Hard work and higher education might set "very wealthy" free blacks above their "merely independent" neighbors. But such attempts to achieve respectability were largely lost on white Southerners, who regarded all people with African heritage as racially inferior. "On the whole I consider them as a class only one grade higher than the negroes and that owing to the little European blood in them," Mrs. Fox pronounced. Indeed, most of the American South's free people of color occupied a financially precarious and legally ambiguous status.[4]

Most mixed-race children in the slaveholding South were the result of slaveholding men's sexual relationships with slave women.

Male slaveholders or their sons or overseers often coerced or commanded their female slaves to submit to sexual activity against their will. In many cases such sexual abuse began in adolescence. In Missouri in 1850 a fourteen-year-old slave girl known only as Celia became the unwilling sexual partner of her new master, a wealthy farmer and small slaveholder. After five years of repeated sexual assaults, Celia fought back, killing her attacker and attempting to conceal the evidence by burning his body. The teenager was tried and convicted for murder and died on the gallows in December 1855.[5]

Before her death, Celia gave birth to two children. According to Southern law, the legal status of the mother was conferred upon the child; Celia's children, the product of rape, thus became the slaves of their mother's rapist. The sexual assault of slave women by slaveholders thus produced a population of mixed-race children who became the property of their fathers. Commenting on the sexual sins of slaveholding men, the escaped slave Frederick Douglass—himself the product of a slaveholder-slave relationship—pronounced: "Slaveholders have ordained, and by law established, that the children of slave women shall in all cases follow the condition of their mothers; and this is done too obviously to administer to their own lusts, and make a gratification of their wicked desires profitable as well as pleasurable; for by this cunning arrangement, the slaveholder, in cases not a few, sustains to his slaves the double relation of master and father." In some cases this "double relation" resulted in favorable treatment and ultimately freedom. More frequently, however, mixed-race children remained slaves and were viewed with suspicion by both blacks and whites. Planter wives, unable to contest their husbands' dominance or restrain their sexuality, directed their wrath toward light-skinned children. Planter men, either to pacify their wives or to avoid gossip, often sold children who too closely resembled themselves. Meanwhile the slave community, regarding mixed-race children as an unwelcome reminder of the sexual vulnerability of slave women and the social powerlessness of slave men, sometimes shunned fair-complexioned children. Small wonder, then, that Frederick Douglass claimed, "such slaves invariably suffer greater hardships, and have more to contend with, than others."[6]

Another group occupying a liminal position in the slaveholding South were small slaveholders and nonslaveholders. While this middling class might or might not own slaves—many Southern whites moved in and out of slaveholding during the course of the life cycle—the majority owned land and operated family farms. "Plain folk" in the Old South—known as "Crackers" in some localities—populated the region's up-country, farming the lighter soils to raise food and produce clothing for their own families, grazing half-wild pigs and cows in the South's pine forests to sell to planters and city folk, and augmenting the products of farm and marketplace with the bounty of the woods, rivers, and streams.[7]

Set apart from their wealthier neighbors by their pioneer lifestyle, "plain folk" children were nonetheless united with them by racial privilege. Evelyn Ward, the daughter of a minister, schoolmaster, and small farmer, frequently played and worked alongside the children of the Wards' few slaves. Yet while she sometimes referred to the children on the family's farm collectively as "all the little fry, white and black," she also revealed significant distinctions between them. When the slave cook, Silvie, made black-eyed peas, one of the children's favorite pastimes was to beg boiled peas and "pot liquor" from Silvie and to hold an impromptu picnic in the eaves of the turkey house. Yet even on such occasions, distinctions of race and status were apparent; as Evelyn observed, "the white children had earthenware mugs and the colored children had tin cups."[8]

Slaveholders often defended the racial and class hierarchies in their society by referring to yet another hierarchy: the subordination of women to men. According to pro-slavery theorists, the enslavement of African Americans by white Southerners was a reflection of—and justified by—the subjection of women to male rule. Both situations, they argued, were rooted in biology and ordained by God. Upholding male supremacy was necessary to race-based slavery; to question one form of oppression was to place the other in jeopardy. While planter-class women benefited from the privileges of material comfort, slave assistance with household chores, and higher education, these privileges did not diminish men's ultimate authority. During the Civil War, many planter-class girls lamented the limitations of their gender. Louisiana teenager Sarah Morgan, an ardent Confederate, chafed at the restrictions of Southern ladyhood. Unable to take up arms, forbidden even to nurse Southern soldiers, Sarah excoriated the status of "worthless women" and described herself as "a chained bear." "If I was only a man!" became her wartime mantra. Of course this planter's daughter, dissatisfied as she was, was far more fortunate than other Southern girls. Less wealthy free girls and women lived under male dominance without the benefits of elite status while enslaved black females suffered the double burden of race-based and gender-based inferiority.[9]

Over the past three decades social historians have called attention to the "holy trinity" of race, class, and gender. In the slaveholding South, a fourth variable—legal status—also came into play to determine if an individual was free or enslaved. Often coinciding with race—most black people were enslaved while most white people were free—legal status was less fixed than the other categories. Although it was determined at birth (recall that the child followed the status of the mother), legal status could change, either through imprisonment (for free whites) or manumission (for enslaved blacks). Individual identity—and social power—thus were determined by the intersection of these axes. Whiteness, wealth, maleness, and freedom spelled power; blackness, poverty, femaleness, and enslavement spelled subordination.

Growing up in slaveholding society meant learning to identify oneself and others according to these social categories and to act accordingly. Within the context of antebellum family life and beginning in infancy, Southern children learned what it meant to be black or white, slave or free, rich or poor, male or female in slaveholding society. Southern children would experience the Civil War differently depending on their social status. The lessons that Southern children learned before the war shaped their attitudes toward it.

*

It is a truism that family matters in the American South. Many social institutions shaped and reinforced individual identity, including the law, politics, and religion, to name a few. But for Southern children the most important day-to-day social institution was the family. One's family literally defined one's identity by determining one's race and legal status; in addition, it was in the context of family life that children were socialized into their role in Southern society.

While family was important for all Southern children, children grew up in many types of families. The most common family type for all Southerners was a nuclear family defined by a conjugal tie and linked by co-residence, yet the basic nuclear family exhibited many variations in form and focus. In addition, while the typical family was a nuclear family consisting of a husband, wife, and children living in a single shared household, the slaveholding South also exhibited several forms of extended family life in which close and distant kin shared resources, a residence, or both.

In the plantation South, slaveholders and the enslaved, while usually residing under different roofs, participated in a common household enterprise: the production of a staple crop such as cotton, rice, or tobacco. Thus even though the white slaveholding family usually resided in the "big house," which might range from simple frame structures to the mansions glorified in Old South lore, and individual slave families generally lived in several small cabins grouped together in "the quarters" between the big house and the fields, blacks and whites nonetheless were joined "within the plantation household." Indeed, wealthy planters and pro-slavery authors often cast white male heads of household as the patriarchs of "our family, black and white," and at least some mistresses regarded themselves as "mothers of the whole plantation." Most enslaved black families thus existed within the context of a larger plantation household in which white nonkin claimed both financial ownership and familial authority.[10]

Many families formed by black bondspeople also exhibited another form of extended family: the cross-plantation, or "abroad," family, in which husbands and wives lived on different plantations, children resided with their mothers, and fathers visited only occasionally. Both as a result of cross-plantation marriages and as a consequence of the division of slave families by sale, many slave households contained only a mother and her children. While most slave children had daily contact with their mothers, only a minority had even sporadic contact with their fathers.[11]

Yet another form of extended family was the multi-generational family, in which close and distant kin either shared a household or pooled their labor—often both—to achieve economic security and ensure child care. Such arrangements may have been particularly common among poor families of both races, especially in the Southern upcountry where nonslaveholding "plain folk" practiced self-sufficient farming rather than staple-crop agriculture, and in the South's urban centers, where free blacks created both tri-generational female households (grandmother, mother, daughter) and male-headed extended-kin compounds. All these types of extended family filled a valuable function for the South's middling and working classes by increasing the number and variety of workers and by providing older relatives to care for young children while able-bodied parents engaged in paid work outside the home.[12]

Wealthy planter families too valued kinship relationships beyond the nuclear family or the immediate household. Women returned to their childhood homes to give birth; families dwelling in disease-ridden low-lying areas spent entire summers with relatives who resided in healthier upland regions; and older children left home to live and attend school with their cousins. In addition to such lengthy visits and child exchanges, well-to-do Southern whites engaged in extensive family correspondence and shared resources, including slave labor. Although they did not ordinarily live under the same roof, elite whites incorporated extended kin into the life of the nuclear family in many other ways.[13]

Mothers were the most constant presence in many slave children's lives. This was especially the case in cross-plantation families, in which the parents resided on different plantations, and continued to be a common pattern for many African-American children after emancipation. Here, a female-headed family gathers in front of what appears to be a former slave cabin. This photograph, taken in 1902, was originally titled "A Happy Family." Notice that the younger children are dressed in smocks regardless of gender. *(Library of Congress)*

Black Southerners had their own version of extended relationships: "fictive kin." White owners' actions separated many black family members whose relationships were not recognized or protected legally. The sale of slaves or the division of estates after an owner's death parted families belonging to a single owner while the migration of slaveholders divided cross-plantation families. In response to the uncertainty of family life under slavery, enslaved blacks created extensive "fictive" kinship ties, manifested in the common practice of referring to elderly blacks as "aunt" or "uncle." This custom functioned as a sort of safety net for vulnerable slave families.[14]

Southerners of all backgrounds often included relatives by blood, marriage, or choice in their definition of family—and often in their household as well. Children in the slaveholding South thus grew up surrounded by many adults of both races, a situation that gave them a personal interest in the continuation or abolition of slavery and thus a real stake in the outcome of the Civil War.

Southern families differed in dynamics as well as in membership. Historians of nineteenth-century family life in both the United States and Europe have discerned at least two distinct family types: the "traditional" and "patriarchal" family, in which the authority of the male head of household was paramount; and the "modern" and "child-centered" family, in which affection replaced authority as the most important familial tie. Historians of white families in the slaveholding South find a sometimes uneasy mix of these two types. Well-to-do Southerners attracted by the ideal of "companionate" rather than patriarchal ideals of marriage and "child-centered" rather than authoritarian parenting practices nonetheless found it necessary to uphold patriarchal authority within their own families in order to justify the racial dominance they exercised as slaveholders. Meanwhile historians of slavery disagree on how to describe slave families. While some scholars contend that enslaved African Americans attempted, insofar as possible, to replicate the male dominance of the surrounding white society, others describe the slave family as "egalitarian," indicating shared authority between husband and wife, or even "matrifocal," indicating the paramount importance of the mother-child bond. Among all this variety, change, and contestation, however, there was one constant: the Southern family, however constituted or defined, served the primary function of socializing youngsters and thus shaping identities. During the Civil War the family would also become the primary site for children to learn about the issues at stake and to express their political loyalties.[15]

In the slaveholding South, one's family determined one's place in society. Individual identity and social power in the slaveholding South were clearly determined and sharply demarcated by race, class, gender,

Although a majority of slave children grew up in nuclear families, most also relied on extended kin and fictive kin for practical and emotional support. Here, five generations of a family group in South Carolina demonstrate family solidarity for the photographer in 1862. *(Library of Congress)*

and status. The circumstances of birth and the early years of life indelibly marked an individual's place in Southern society. Moreover it was within the family that Southern children learned to define themselves and others according to the markers that mattered in slaveholding society. When white Southerners fought to defend Southern independence and the institution of slavery, they also fought to defend a set of social hierarchies that were deeply embedded in family life.

*

Within their families, Southern children learned their status in slaveholding society early and thoroughly. Childhood thus created and perpetuated the slaveholding South's rigid social hierarchy, structured around the axes of race, class, gender, and status, reinforced through socialization practices such as observation, interaction, and instruction, and marked by language, education, dress, and discipline.

Beginning at birth, Southern children's daily lives were shaped by the factors that determined social power in slaveholding society. Mississippi plantation mistress Tryphena Blanche Holder Fox revealed both the stark contrast between slaves and slaveholders and the importance of early lessons in social hierarchies in her comments on her only child, Fanny, and Fanny's companion and caretaker, the slave girl Adelaide. Although born in the North, Mrs. Fox had thoroughly imbibed the values of her planter-class husband and neighbors by the time she gave birth to her daughter in 1857. Shortly after Fanny's first birthday, Mrs. Fox enlisted the oldest child of one of her slaves, Susan, to "come in & play with her." Adelaide was not a mere playmate, however, but a maid-in-training. Mrs. Fox planned to "bring her up to be faithful & smart & cleanly in her habits," so as "to make a house-girl of her." In the meantime five-year-old Adelaide served as a baby nurse. "She amuses Fanny very well & saves me a good many steps," Mrs. Fox explained. Just as important as young Adelaide's training in service were her lessons in subordination. Adelaide quickly learned to call her white playmate by an honorific, "Miss Fanny," as well as to be (or at least appear to be) "quite delighted" when called "to go wash her face & hands & come play with Miss Fanny." Referring to a toddler as "mistress" and cleaning up before spending time with her reinforced the message that Adelaide was Fanny's social inferior. Indeed, according to Mrs. Fox, Adelaide quite looked up to her young charge. "She thinks there is nobody like 'mistress,'" Mrs. Fox averred.[16]

Of all the signs of social status that Southern youngsters learned, race was the most visible and significant. According to the Baltimore slave Frederick Douglass, "it was a common saying, even among little white boys, that it was worth a half-cent to kill a 'nigger,' and a half-cent to bury one."[17]

Race was intertwined with class and status, which made it a particularly potent marker of social order. The English-born Georgia

Although black and white children grew up side by side in the slaveholding South, intimacy did not connote equality. Indeed, close contact between slave and slaveholding youngsters had the potential to reinforce racial hierarchies by highlighting the many differences in their daily lives. In this idealized illustration from the abolitionist novel *Uncle Tom's Cabin*, Eva, an angelic white child, embraces Topsy, an orphaned black child. *(Library of Congress)*

plantation mistress Fanny Kemble worried about the effects of the slaveholding South's racial hierarchy on her own daughter:

> I do not think that a residence on a slave plantation is likely to be peculiarly advantageous to a child like my oldest. I was observing her today among her swarthy worshipers, for they follow her as such, and saw, with dismay, the universal eagerness with which they sprang to obey her little gestures of command. She said something about a swing, and in less than five minutes headman Frank had erected it for her, and a dozen young slaves were ready to swing little 'missus.' Think of learning to rule despotically your fellow creatures before the first lesson of self-government has been well spelled over! It makes me tremble.[18]

As a white, free, and wealthy individual, Kemble's young daughter learned early and thoroughly that it was her lot in life to "rule despotically" over those who were black, enslaved, and poor. Yet as a girl she would also have learned that she was herself subject to the rule of males of her own race, class, and status. As the historian Drew Gilpin Faust has perceptively pointed out, elite white women were simultaneously privileged and oppressed. Beneficiaries of the South's hierarchy as white, wealthy, and free individuals, they were also subordinated as females. Even very young girls were aware of this paradox. South Carolina planter's daughter Sally Elmore Taylor, for example, rode horseback "fearlessly" and dreamed of being a missionary to China, yet she came to understand that both her present activities and her future prospects were constrained when a visiting uncle playfully hoisted her up to stand on the family mantel. "Mother's indignation was appalling," Taylor recalled. "She told him I was a lady (I was *seven* years old!)." Like seven-year-old Sally Taylor, Southern children of all ranks learned at an early age to identify themselves in terms of social standing.[19]

Southern children learned to position themselves and others through a socialization program that began in infancy. Three major forms of socialization—observation of others, interaction with others, and instruction from adults—combined to educate Southern youngsters about their own standing and that of others.

The childhood experiences of planter's daughter Fanny Fox and her slave attendant, Adelaide, offer an instructive example of the importance of simple observation in learning about one's place in Southern society. Doted upon by both planter-parents and waited upon by a slave attendant, the white child experienced lenient discipline and plentiful attention. Slave women's and children's household labor granted Fanny's mother the leisure to enjoy her daughter's prattle and to respond to her demands. "She learned 'up up' a few days ago," Mrs. Fox remarked soon after Fanny's first birthday, "& it has been the burden of her song most of the time to-day, and I am obliged to take her up to satisfy her."[20]

Well-to-do white parents in the Old South fostered intimate relationships with their children. In this antebellum lithograph, a mother affectionately reaches out to her daughter, at her right, and her son, at her left. Notice that young children of both genders wore short dresses that allowed them to play outdoors with gender-neutral toys such as the hoop carried by the girl. *(Library of Congress)*

Meanwhile Fanny's slave companion, Adelaide, just four years Fanny's senior, was responsible not only for the white child's care and amusement but also for a variety of household duties, including sewing. While young Adelaide no doubt observed Fanny's leisure time and contrasted it to her own heavy workload, she may have been struck further by Fanny's close relationship with her indulgent mother, a relationship that Adelaide and her enslaved mother, the house servant Susan, had little time or energy to emulate. Observing others, then, was a major way for children to learn their place in Southern society. In the Fox household, Fanny learned to be a pampered child; Adelaide learned to serve her.

The interactions of these two children reinforced these lessons. Although Mrs. Fox had initially brought Adelaide into the big house as a baby nurse, after Adelaide's sixth birthday her primary duties became housework and sewing while Mrs. Fox devoted herself nearly full-time to Fanny's care and entertainment. There were exceptions. "I generally keep her with me Sundays, talking to her & showing her pictures," Mrs. Fox wrote about her young daughter in 1861, when Fanny was four and Adelaide eight years old, "but to-day I let her have Adelaide to play with her, set table & dress doll-babies."[21]

When Fanny and Adelaide played together, the older girl entertained and supervised the younger one while remaining subordinate to her; while Fanny chose to spend time with Adelaide (when her mother allowed it), Adelaide was ordered to tend to Fanny's desires (Mrs. Fox "let [Fanny] have Adelaide" as a playmate). In their interactions with each other, then, Fanny and Adelaide rehearsed for their adult roles as superior and inferior. This particular interaction, which took place only a couple of months into the Civil War, was a reminder that not only the institution of slavery but an entire social order based on slavery were at stake in the conflict.

Slave boys as well as slave girls were often assigned the task of looking after their masters' children. At the age of seven, Frederick Douglass was sent from his master's plantation to the Baltimore home of Mr. and Mrs. Auld and "their little son Thomas." As Douglass described the scene, "Little Thomas was told, there was his Freddy,—and I was told to take care of little Thomas." At the moment of introduction, therefore, the slave boy learned that he existed to serve while the white boy learned that he existed to be served. Douglass's interactions with the son of a different master taught similar lessons. Douglass accompanied the white man's son hunting, serving as a kind of human retriever as he searched for the birds that "Master Daniel" shot. Such interactions taught both white and black children their places in slave society.[22] They also indicated the literal and figurative power of weaponry—reserved for white males—in slaveholding society. Guns and swords would loom large both in Southern children's wartime play and in their later accounts of the Civil War.

As both Fanny and Adelaide's and Frederick and Daniel's experiences suggest, adults—usually white, wealthy, slaveholding adults—shaped children's interactions in both subtle and not so subtle ways. Not surprisingly, then, adults often offered—and enforced—explicit instructions about children's place in slaveholding society. Adult guidance was one of the most important forms of early training in learning one's "place" in Southern society. As James Curry, who grew up in slavery, recalled, though initially he and his master's children "loved one another like brothers," their childish affection was short-lived. "The love of power is cultivated in their hearts by their parents," Curry explained of slaveholding children, "and they soon regard the negro in no other light than as a slave."[23] As the secession crisis loomed, slaveholding children's early lessons in regarding slave children as their social inferiors rather than their beloved playmates would incline them toward a pro-slavery and pro-secession position. Childhood experiences thus predisposed planters' children to become Confederate sympathizers.

Like Fanny Fox's mother and Frederick Douglass's master, many white adults maintained slave society's racial hierarchies by requiring slave children to address slaveholding children by honorifics while referring to enslaved adults and children by first names only, and often by diminutive versions of their given names. This was a common way to assert dominance and reaffirm hierarchy, often to the detriment of children's interracial relationships. Virginia slave Robert Ellett remembered his "young masters" fondly. "I played with them, ate with them and sometimes slept with them," he explained, concluding, "we were pals." The "pals" soon learned to repudiate their friendship, however, when the white boys' father (and Ellett's owner) "carried me in the barn and tied me up and whipped me 'cause I wouldn't call my young masters, 'masters.'" Thereafter the boys fought regularly because of Ellett's obstinate refusal to address the white boys "properly"—and the white boys' new insistence on their former playmate's humility. Similarly, Kentucky slave Hannah Davidson recalled that her owners' youngest child, Mayo, wanted her to address him as "Master Mayo"—an idea he surely imbibed from his parents. "I never would call him 'Master Mayo,'" she asserted, and as a result "I fought him all the time."[24]

These childhood conflicts between enslaved and planter children presaged the competing familial and political loyalties that white and black children would adopt during the Civil War. Shortly before the war began, plantation mistress Keziah Hopkins Brevard was taken aback when "a little negro girl" told her "'twas a sin for big ones like them [adult slaves] to say sir to Mass Thomas & Mass Whitfield & little [white] ones like them (T. & W.—a babe & a little boy)," children in Brevard's extended family. This unnamed slave girl understood the social significance of naming, and she criticized the requirement that adult slaves accord respectful titles to white children, a practice that contradicted intraracial standards of respect for the elderly among both whites and blacks. While white children accepted their parents' judgments about their own social standing and support for the Confederacy, black children often learned from their own parents to resent their inferior status and side with the Union.[25]

Language was a powerful marker of social place in the slaveholding South, but it was not the only one. As they were socialized to observe the distinctions in slaveholding society, Southern children also learned to recognize and use a variety of markers of social standing, including clothing, education, and discipline. During the Civil War and Reconstruction, Southern children and their parents would continue to use these markers to reinforce—and undermine—the South's social order.

Clothing both signified and displayed social standing. North Carolina slave girl Harriet Jacobs described her coarse "linsey-woolsey" shift—the uniform common to slave children of both sexes—as "one of the badges of slavery." Until they began full-time fieldwork (usually around age ten), slave boys and girls alike were dressed only in coarse linen shirts that, at least initially, fell to the knees or below. One former slave in Louisiana humorously described the "split shirt tail" he wore as a "li'l chile": "Dem was sho' fancy shirt tails dey make us wore in dem days. Dey make 'em on de loom, jes' in two pieces, with a hole to put de head through and 'nother hole at de bottom to put de legs through. Den dey split 'em up de side, so'd us could run and play without dem tyin' us 'round de knees and throw us down. Even at dat, dey sho' wasn't no good to do no tree climbin', less'n you pull dem mos' up over you head." When children grew quickly, the lack of undergarments became apparent. Northern visitors often expressed shock at the sight of scantily clad slave children waiting at table. In an amusing anecdote from his childhood as a slave in Oklahoma, Morris Sheppard explained that he wore "a stripedy shirt" made by his mother, Easter, until age eleven, when his mistress came riding by, saw the slave boy in his outgrown shift, "and nearly fall off'n her horse!" The former slave gleefully related the punchline: "She holler, 'Easter, you go right now and make dat big buck of a boy some britches!'"[26]

Although loose-fitting one-piece garments offered slave children great mobility, if limited protection from the elements, slave boys—like their white counterparts—welcomed the day they exchanged their shifts for pants. For boys of all races and classes, putting on pants for the first time, or "breeching," symbolized the achievement of maleness. South Carolina planter's son John Clinkscales recalled "glorying in my first pair of pantaloons" when he was six years old. "I was just out of my dresses," he reminisced, and "I was restless and reckless as a boy could well be." While only white boys could aspire to manly independence, all boys welcomed the moment they left behind a gender-neutral or even feminine ensemble for one that clearly announced their masculinity. As Frederick Douglass recalled his own graduation to pants at the age of seven: "The thought of owning a pair of trousers was great indeed!"[27] Boys in the antebellum South relished the opportunity to call attention to their difference from—and superiority to—girls. During the Civil War, military service would become the most important marker of masculinity, and boys of all ages—and both races—would become obsessed with all things military.

While boys from different backgrounds shared the experience of trading skirts for trousers, girls' adoption of adult attire varied. Young girls of all backgrounds dressed in shifts or slips that fell to mid-calf; elite girls' attire was distinguished by fancy needlework and rich fabric rather than by cut or length. Slave girls (and probably many nonslaveholding white girls as well) continued to wear loose-fitting dresses that enabled them to do heavy labor. Well-to-do white girls, however, adopted elaborate fashions such as ankle-length skirts and whalebone corsets that both proclaimed their elite status and restricted their movements. When Florida resident and erstwhile tomboy Sarah Pamela Williams made her debut as a proper young lady in Charleston, South Carolina, she "felt like a wild bird of the forest whose wings had been clipped and who was bound by the bars of a cage":

> My dress, my pronunciation and my very individuality were changed! I never went with a skip and a jump anywhere, not even in the backyard. My skirts were lengthened a little and when I went on the street I wore a thick blue veil over my face [and] a bonnet and my hands were encased in kid gloves. My hair was no longer in "pigtails" but braided smoothly and pinned up in the back. . . . We sat very quietly and listened to the talk of our elders and replied very meekly and modestly if we were addressed.[28]

Pamela's new dress and the new limitations on her activities set her apart both from white boys—who enjoyed increased mobility as they aged—and from slaves, who undertook greater responsibilities as they grew older. But they united her with white women who held—or aspired to—elite status.[29] Both during and after the Civil War, elite girls would continue to use their clothing to announce their high social standing.

Education also helped shape Southern children's lives and define their identities. At the two extremes of Southern society, the scions of wealthy slaveholding families attended college to prepare for advantageous marriages and successful careers while the offspring of enslaved

Elite children usually received their earliest instruction at home, from their mothers. In this 1846 lithograph, a mother holds a primer while her child points out letters of the alphabet. Literacy was an important marker of social status in the slaveholding South. Slave labor—including the labor of slave children—permitted planter-class parents the leisure to devote themselves to their children while slaves were legally prohibited from learning to read or write. *(Library of Congress)*

blacks were legally barred from learning to read and write. As the former slave John Fields, who after emancipation would seek higher education and become a physician, observed: "Our ignorance was the greatest hold the South had on us."[30] Indicating the importance of education, after emancipation the education of children would become a subject of acute concern—and sometimes conflict—for both black and white Southerners.

In the antebellum South, white children from the planting and professional classes usually received their earliest lessons at home, first from their mothers (and, less often, from their fathers) and later from tutors and governesses. In their early to mid-teens, both boys and girls frequently left home for a period ranging from a few months to several years to attend institutions of higher education, variously known as academies, seminaries, and colleges. For both boys and girls, these schools offered an education in the classics (Latin and Greek) as well as instruction in a wide variety of subjects, including mathematics, geography, physics, astronomy, history, literature, philosophy, and rhetoric. For boys, a classical education was intended as preparation for careers as lawyers or politicians. For girls, the purpose—though not necessarily the scope—of education was more limited. Girls were expected to use their schooling to prepare them to teach their own children as adults. The "ornamental" subjects that girls studied in addition to the classics, such as music, art, and dance, allowed them to display their elite status and attract wealthy suitors.[31] The importance of education for elite white children was undiminished by the Civil War. In the postwar South, while education remained an important marker of social status, it also acquired new significance as an essential avenue toward self-support for many former slaveowners.

Well-to-do free blacks offered their sons and daughters similar lessons, but with a twist: even before the Civil War, free black children understood that they would have to use their education to support themselves in the future. When the wealthy Johnson family of Natchez, Mississippi, gave their daughters lessons in music and sent their sons away to school, they imitated white elites in training girls to be accomplished ladies and boys to be classical scholars. At the same time, however, they apprenticed their sons to the blacksmith trade, one of the skilled occupations dominated by free black men, and gave their daughters a sufficient education in the basics to prepare them to become grade-school teachers, one of the few respectable occupations open to Southern women of any race.[32] Like education itself, teaching was destined to gain importance in the post–Civil War South as whites joined the ranks of wage-earning educators.

Less-privileged children of both races somewhat sporadically attended local day schools, where both boys and girls learned basic literacy and mathematics. Texas immigrant Charles Nagel learned his lessons in his native German, but otherwise his schooling in a one-room country schoolhouse was typical of Southern plain folk: "The essentials of the study course," he recalled, "were the three R's." Ernest Wardwell, the oldest child in a nonslaveholding white family, indicated both the limited scope and sporadic nature of most Southern children's formal schooling when he remarked, "I learned to 'read, write, and cipher,' shoot squirrels, and catch 'mountain trout'" in the rural Maryland village where he spent his "tender years."[33] While such rudimentary education seemed sufficient in the slaveholding South, after emancipation many white Southerners would express greater interest in educating poor white youngsters in order to shore up the faltering foundations of white supremacy.

Legally barred from learning to read or write, slave children occasionally acquired these skills from kindly owners, white playmates, or free blacks. As a child in Baltimore, Frederick Douglass developed friendships with poor white boys in the neighborhood, bartering his daily rations in exchange for lessons in reading. Virginia planter's daughter Susan Dabney Smedes claimed that she and her siblings "delighted in teaching the house-servants." In Savannah, Susie King attended a secret school at the home of a free black woman for two years. The thirty students there masqueraded as errand runners and apprentices, staggering their arrivals and departures to avoid arousing suspicion and wrapping their schoolbooks in paper to disguise them as parcels. Those few slaves who were literate also passed their knowledge to one another.[34]

For many slave children, the legal denial of literacy imbued education with tremendous importance. In his memoirs, Booker T. Washington explained:

I had no schooling whatever while I was a slave, though I remember on several occasions I went as far as the schoolhouse door with one of my young mistresses to carry her books. The picture of several dozen boys and girls in a schoolroom engaged in study made a deep impression upon me, and I had the feeling that to get into a schoolhouse and study in this way would be about the same as getting into paradise.[35]

The ability to read and write would prove useful to many slave children during the Civil War era, enabling them to gather information independently of their Confederate owners. After emancipation, educational opportunity would prove to be one of the most salient markers of African Americans' new status as free people.

For most slave children, however, lessons of survival and resistance were more important than formal education. Slave children learned to work, and work well, from an early age. Fathers, mothers, aunts, uncles, and both real and fictive kin trained slave children to fulfill their assigned tasks and avoid punishment. This early training would become especially important in the war years when slave children and adolescents assumed an ever-increasing workload. Early training in survival and resistance also served slave children well. Because they were the most constant presence in slave children's lives, it fell to slave mothers, more than anyone else, to teach their children how to maintain the delicate balance that defined American slavery: resisting slavery and retaining humanity while also submitting to authority and surviving the system. In particular, slave mothers did their best to help their daughters resist rape. Cornelia Jennings vividly remembered the lessons she learned from her own mother. "My mother was the smartest black woman in Eden," Cornelia boasted. Like other slave parents and kin, Jennings's mother taught her daughter to be a good worker: "She was as quick as a flash of lightning, and whatever she did could not be done better. She could do anything." But Cornelia learned one more lesson from her mother: "The one doctrine of my mother's teaching which was branded upon my senses was that I should never let anyone abuse me. 'I'll kill you, gal, if you don't stand for yourself,' she would say. 'Fight, and if you can't fight, kick; if you can't kick, then bite.'"[36]

Such lessons in day-to-day resistance also taught powerful lessons in self-respect—lessons that enabled slave children to adopt dissident political opinions during the war and to achieve independence following emancipation.

Slave parents' efforts to teach their children to resist abuse—and, more generally, their efforts to discipline their children—were complicated by the system of slavery. Harriet Jacobs's recollections of her childhood include a poignant example of slave children's divided loyalties. Jacobs's father was a free man and a skilled worker who taught his son, William, to "detest the name of master and mistress." But William was not only his father's son; he was his mistress's slave. As both authority figures battled for dominance in the young boy's life, William found himself confused and uncertain. As Jacobs recalled one incident:

> One day, when his father and his mistress had happened to call him at the same time, he hesitated between the two; being perplexed to know which had the strongest claim upon his obedience. He finally concluded to go to his mistress. When my father reproved him for it, he said, "You both called me, and I didn't know which I ought to go to first." "You are *my* child," replied our father, "and when I call you, you should come immediately, if you have to pass through fire and water."[37]

The divided loyalties that Jacobs described would become still more acute in the war years. While masters and mistresses celebrated the cause of Southern independence, slave parents and kin prayed for freedom. Slave children in the Confederate South, like those in the prewar years, had to decide whether to side with their owners or with their own families.

Slaveholders regularly challenged slave parents' authority over their children in the antebellum South. In the 1930s former slave Caroline Hunter recalled: "During slavery it seemed like your children belonged to everybody but you. Many a day my old mama has stood by and watched master beat her children till they bled and she couldn't open her mouth." Other masters more subtly compromised slave women's authority over their children by protecting them from punishment. When Nancy Williams refused to obey her mother, she ran to the master for protection. This probably made her mother even more furious at her lack of control over her daughter. "When she did [catch me]," Nancy recalled, "she beat the devil out of me." Either by mistreating or favoring slave children, slaveholders demonstrated the limits of slave parents' authority. When one slave woman stood up to her mistress, asserting, "If [white] folks owns [black] folks, then [black] folks owns their own children," the mistress flatly replied, "No, they don't."[38]

Both during and after the Civil War, authority over black children would remain contested. Wartime runaways escaped from slavery to reunite parents with their children, yet white refugees often divided slave families by taking only some slaves with them and leaving others behind. Black mothers and fathers in the postwar South attempted to strengthen parental control over their children, but postwar apprenticeship practices removed black children from their families and placed them instead in the power of white employers.

One of the most powerful ways in which antebellum slaveholders demonstrated their own power—and slave adults' powerlessness—was to punish adult slaves in the presence of slave children. Maryland slave Frederick Douglass vividly recalled the horrific punishments inflicted upon his principal caretaker, Aunt Hester. "I remember the first time I ever witnessed this horrible exhibition," he wrote in his memoirs. "I was quite a child, but I well remember it." The "terrible spectacle" of seeing his aunt, stripped to the waist and bound to a joist while her master lashed her until she bled, Douglass wrote, was "the blood-stained gate, the entrance to the hell of slavery."[39] Knowledge that slave parents could not protect themselves, much less their children, from the rigors of slavery was a potent reminder of slave children's inferior status in Southern society. Not surprisingly, slave children in the Civil War years both feared and revered soldiers, depending on whether they saw them as oppressors or protectors.

Disciplinary action taught privileged as well as oppressed children about the importance of one's social identity in the Old South. When one slave girl was caught stealing candy while she went about her task of cleaning, her mistress not only whipped her but required her daughter to help by placing the slave girl's head under the rocker of a chair and rocking forward on it to hold her in place. For both girls, this was a harsh lesson in the relative status of mistress and slave. Although the slave girl suffered permanent injuries—she was never able to open her mouth completely after the experience—the white girl no doubt also bore lasting psychic scars.[40]

In some cases, such childhood experiences inspired white children to question slavery altogether. Angelina and Sarah Grimké's career as outspoken abolitionists stemmed from their horror at their mother's cruelty toward the slaves in her South Carolina household. As an adult, Angelina Grimké vividly recalled the "heartbroken countenance" of a young slave boy in the Grimke household after he had been so "dreadfully whipped that he could hardly walk." Mary Grimké's brutality may have extended to her children as well as her slaves, which may have encouraged her daughters to sympathize with slave children. As a girl, Angelina kept a diary in which she commented that her mother "rules slaves and children with a rod of fear."[41] More often, however, white children learned to imitate their parents' cruelty. During the Civil War this manifested itself in role-playing games in which white "Confederates" tormented black "Yankees."

Discipline—and who had the power to administer it—helped define children's social identities and shape their daily lives. Slave parents' powerlessness contrasted dramatically with the pronounced patriarchy of most white families. Although many white Southerners fostered affectionate relationships with their children, they also taught them to regard their fathers as "the head of the household," with ultimate authority over all other family members. This pattern may have been particularly pronounced among the South's plain folk, who were less affected by trends of modern child-rearing and child-centered family life than their wealthier neighbors. Indeed, recent research on Southern yeomen suggests that plain-folk patriarchs cast themselves as "masters of small worlds," wielding authority over their wives and children much as their wealthier neighbors exercised power over their slaves.[42]

White children of all classes learned to regard their parents as sources of both indulgence and punishment. Doting mothers might pamper their children while stern fathers might demand instant obedience—or vice versa—but the paramount authorities in white children's lives were their parents. During the Civil War, white soldier-fathers attempted to maintain their relationships with their children from afar. They corresponded with older children and begged their wives to remind younger children of "there [sic] absent Father." Colonel Dorsey Pender, who left an infant and a two-year-old behind when he joined the Confederate Army, mournfully reflected: "It is a hard thing to think that our own child does not know anything about [me]; to feel that he may never."[43]

For Confederate soldiers, the Civil War created the long absences that made them fear their children would forget or never know them. For many enslaved fathers, and for some slave mothers as well, separation from their children was the norm. Judging from Harriet Jacobs's recollections, free black families recognized this as an important distinction between free families and enslaved ones, and they regarded parental—perhaps especially paternal—authority as a sign of their free status and honored it accordingly. Slave children's limited contact with their fathers thus represented and reinforced social distinctions in the American South. The Civil War offered Southern blacks an opportunity to change this situation. During the Civil War, black men who joined the Union Army declared their manhood; following emancipation, both veterans and freedmen demanded their rights as fathers. For their part, freed children looked up to their soldier-fathers as heroes and welcomed the chance to take direction from their own fathers rather than from white owners.

The vulnerability of slave families to separation by sale, migration, or estate division contrasted dramatically with both the affec-

The threat of family separation loomed over every slave child. Separations by sale may have increased during the Civil War as slaveholders sought to avoid wartime losses of human property to escape or emancipation. In this wood engraving, which appeared in *Harper's Weekly* in 1861, exhausted slave children doze in the foreground while an auctioneer encourages bids for a slave mother and infant behind them. *(Library of Congress)*

tionately indulgent, child-centered parenting that was increasingly common in planter families and the sternly disciplinary, authoritarian child-rearing that prevailed among plain folk (and possibly free black) families. John Fields, who was born a slave in Kentucky, offered an account of family separation made particularly poignant by his matter-of-fact description. When Fields was six years old, his master died, and Fields and his siblings—twelve children in all—were divided up and distributed among the heirs. "We slaves were divided by this method," Fields explained the process: "Three disinterested persons were chosen to come to the plantation and together they wrote the names of the different heirs on a few slips of paper. These slips were put in a hat and passed among us slaves. Each one took a slip and the name on the slip was the new owner." This entirely impersonal exercise resulted in all twelve of the children being separated from their mother. Seven children went to Charleston, (West) Virginia; two to Lexington, Kentucky; and one to Harford, Kentucky; Fields and one brother remained behind in Owenburg, Kentucky. "My mother was later allowed to visit among us children for one week of each year," Fields continued, "so she could only remain a short time at each place."[44] While free children of both races were of course orphaned and adopted, their care was assigned to relatives, family friends, or orphan asylums; only slave children were so cavalierly parceled out to entire strangers. Families, then, not only provided the site for socialization into slaveholding society but also replicated Southern hierarchies, with family security serving as yet another marker of social status.

It is therefore not surprising that both during and after the Civil War, first runaway and then freed slaves relished the opportunity to reunite their families and to reduce outside interference. Indeed, one of the most interesting developments of the postwar period was African Americans' insistence on protecting black children from apprenticeship to white employers, even to the extent of taking in distant kin and unrelated orphans. The denial of family security under slavery increased the importance of family unity in freedom.

*

Families taught Southern children their place in slaveholding society and thus shaped their responses to the Civil War, which imperiled the established social order. They also served as the primary source of information about the looming crisis of war. Just as they learned the importance of race, class, gender, and legal status within their families, Southern children also learned about slavery, secession, and the Civil War from family members. Even when they gleaned information from other sources, Southern children evaluated that information in the context of their familial relationships. For Southern children, family membership and political beliefs would be closely intertwined.

CHAPTER TWO

Taking Sides

CHILDREN'S PERSPECTIVES ON
SLAVERY, SECESSION, AND CIVIL WAR

Lucy Paxton Scarborough, the daughter of Louisiana slave-holders, was only three years old when the Civil War began. Nearly six decades later she recalled that "in those days her three great terrors were Yankees, run-away niggers, and booger-bears." Young Lucy's "three great terrors," combining the timeless fear of monsters under the bed with the immediate concerns of a war over the future of slavery, raises the question of how—and what—Southern children learned about the major issues dividing the nation: slavery, secession, and the Civil War.[1]

Children's attitudes toward the national conflict were shaped by their families and their identities. Not surprisingly, most children of slaveholders were stalwart supporters of slavery and secession while children of slaves quickly learned to regard the Civil War as a battle for freedom and family. The attitudes of free black and poor white children are more difficult to trace, but, like other children, youngsters from these strata of Southern society probably adopted the attitudes of their elders. Just as family was an important determinant of children's social status, it was also a major factor in children's political opinions.

43

Children's political loyalties differed most dramatically by race. Most white children supported the Confederacy while the majority of black children sided with the Union. Children of all backgrounds agreed that the central issue of the Civil War was slavery. White children occasionally referred to abstract notions of states' rights, Southern independence, or divine favor, but the concrete issue of slavery—and the day-to-day hierarchies and personal interactions it underlay—meant much more to them. Both family membership and social identity inclined white children to support the Confederacy and the continuation of slavery. Black children also understood that slavery was at stake in the conflict. Moreover they drew a close connection between family and freedom. Their parents and other adult slaves taught them, both by example and precept, to support the Union; equally important, their childhood experiences exposed them to the many ways in which slavery endangered family members and family life. The prospect of emancipation and the influence of slave elders alike inspired black children to support the Union and seek "Liberty and Freedom," as one slave boy expressed it.[2]

While political loyalties divided according to race, the ways that children expressed their politics differed depending on gender. Boys of all backgrounds expressed admiration for soldiers and a desire to enter military service; girls, excluded from this option, sought other ways of demonstrating their interest in the issues. Class and legal status also shaped wartime politics. Class tension often was behind divisions between Unionists and Confederates. Southern states or portions of states populated largely by nonslaveholding whites or small slaveholders sometimes became pockets of Unionist sentiment and occasionally fostered resistance to the Confederate government. While they generally did not mention class divisions, white children were often deeply troubled by political wrangling in their communities and families.

Legal status, closely intertwined with race, became important in a new way in the Civil War era. Well before the war broke out, slaves circulated rumors that Northern whites intended to free them; after the Emancipation Proclamation of 1863 granted liberty to slaves in Union-occupied Confederate territory, such rumors acquired new validity, and increasing numbers of slaves openly expressed their support for Lincoln and the Union. Slave children, despite their early training in secrecy, were especially likely to reveal the extent of slaves' support for Lincoln's armies. Older slave children sometimes became openly rebellious.

Children relied on adults both for information about the Civil War and for cues on how to interpret that information. Yet children's attitudes did not simply mirror those of adults. Children filtered the information they received through their own lenses, with their concerns for familial relationships, childhood friendships, and personal identity shaping their responses to the conflicts that surrounded them. Southern children thus adopted unique—though by no means unified—views that reflected their family membership and social standing. Regardless of their family background and political views, the children of the Confederacy were political actors who sought political and military information, made independent judgments, and demonstrated political loyalties in the Civil War South.

*

Perhaps more than Northern children, Southern children became aware of sectional conflict well before the secession crisis of 1860–1861. Virginian Kate Virginia Cox Logan claimed to have been "fed on political questions since early childhood."[3] Logan's references to being "fed" are appropriate since white children seem to have learned about politics primarily from their parents and other relatives, who impressed their views on slavery and secession upon their offspring to good effect. Nine-year-old Letitia Dabney, for instance, recalled that she repeated the political views of her father and uncle "like a little parrot." For the most part, white children took their political cues from the adults around them, with the addition of an atmosphere of "wild interest and excitement" that seems to have especially infected the younger set, even when they were "very unknowing" about the details of the debate.[4] Most white Southern children, from an early age, learned by example to defend slavery, revere the South, fear abolitionists, favor secession, and support the Confederacy.

This process could begin quite early both in children's lives and in the history of Southern sectionalism. As early as the mid-1850s, nine-year-old Susan Bradford remembered the incursions of Northern abolitionists into her Florida plantation community as "when the serpent entered Eden." As a girl, Susan, who read and denounced Harriet Beecher Stowe's anti-slavery novel *Uncle Tom's Cabin* as a pack of lies, frequently overheard conversations between her planter father and his neighbors about "the Abolitionists; looked upon, evidently as a kind of bug-a-boo or a first cousin to the devil." It was difficult for the youngster to acquire solid information about these "bug-a-boos," the nine-year-old wrote in her diary in 1855, because "the grown folks keep very quiet when we children are around and if they are talking when we come into the room they stop right away." Susan, who noticed that "the grown-up folks all look troubled," grew concerned. One night she dreamed that "the Abolitionists were after me and they were like the Devil . . . with horns and cloven feet."[5]

By the time Susan entered her teens she had a more thorough understanding of abolitionist doctrines, though she retained her contempt for critics of the South and its "peculiar institution" of slavery. When she was only eight years old, Susan had been presented with a slave girl, Frances, as her special charge. As she wrote in her diary in 1854, "Mother says she is my Re-spon-si-bi-li-ty. Isn't that a big word?" Mrs. Bradford explained to Susan, "I was to be patient with my little maid; I must not get mad with her; I must not strike her; I must not say hard things to her and if she was so bad I could not stand it I must bring her to mother to be corrected just as she corrects us." Young Susan was overwhelmed with her new responsibility. "I will try to do my best," she wrote, "but I wish she did not belong to me."[6]

As she grew older, Susan built on this attitude, thoroughly imbibing the pro-slavery doctrine that enlightened white people had a responsibility to ignorant blacks, and that while slavery was perhaps a misfortune, it was a misfortune for the slaveholders more than for the slaves themselves. When Susan was twelve years old, her mother told her that "the white people are the real slaves." Her father gave her several volumes of writings by pro-slavery author John C. Calhoun and "said I could come to him if there was anything I did not understand." Susan immediately adopted a thoroughly sectional position. From her father she learned "of the strong, deep feeling of dislike and mistrust, which existed between the North and the South"; from her reading she learned "the doctrine of State's Rights," which she said was "very clear, perhaps . . . because I have so often heard it discussed by Father." This white youngster's political sentiments, though clearly modeled on her parents', also were affected by her close relationship with her black nursemaid, Lulu. Mrs. Bradford may have adopted a gradual emancipation outlook, favoring colonization, but Susan wrote in her diary, "I do not want to give up my Lulu, nor do I want her to be sent to Liberia."[7]

As young Susan Bradford's diary and reminiscences suggest, white children's daily lives before the secession crisis predisposed them to accept pro-slavery arguments and adopt sectionalist politics. Having been brought up in secure homes by loving parents, the children of slaveholders found it easy to accept the notion that blacks were better off under benevolent Christian masters than left in ignorance and savagery in an unknown heathen country. With limited contact with Northerners, Southern born-and-bred whites also readily learned to hate and fear Northerners as fanatical abolitionists who would endanger Southern slaveholders' financial futures and physical safety in their efforts to free African Americans. And having grown up attended by slaves who doubled as their own servants and playmates, planter-class children likely found the notion that blacks were divinely ordained to render service to whites both logical and comforting. Filtering limited information about slavery and secession through their own childhood experiences, white children embraced the Confederate cause early and completely.

Slave children, growing up in such close contact with their white playmate-masters, also gleaned information about abolitionism and sectionalism well before the secession crisis. As Susan Bradford expressed it, "of course, the negroes knew of the strong feeling against the abolition movement among their 'white folks.'" While some of the family's retainers betrayed the slaves' secret "midnight meetings" to the Bradford family, the fact that there were such meetings indicated that enslaved African Americans did not share their masters' and mistresses' disdain for "the fanatical Abolitionists." How slaves learned about the sectional controversy is less clear. According to Susan, "every Northern newspaper contained expressions, either for, or against the abolitionist doctrines"; yet as a largely illiterate population, most slaves would not have had access to this form of news. Many no doubt learned about the issue in the same way, if from a different perspective, as Bradford herself—that is, by overhearing "remarks, dropped here and there" by white adults. As small slaveholder's daughter Evelyn Ward sagely commented, "Children, you can learn a great deal if you will only keep still and listen."[8]

At least some slaves learned about the ongoing debate over the future of slavery from Northern abolitionists and then shared the information with one another. According to Susan Bradford's diary and memoirs, journalists, visitors, and teachers alike moved to the South from the North in the 1850s, bringing "strong Abolition sentiments" with them and attempting to incite local slaves to seek freedom. When she was only four or five years old, Susan overheard a conversation between her black nursemaid, Lulu, and one of these outsiders, who told the slave girl, "'If you will listen to me, as soon as you cross Mason and Dixon's line you will be free.'" Afterward Susan asked her father, "What does *free* mean?" While the resulting contretemps resulted in the expulsion of this particular abolitionist, and Lulu herself disavowed any interest in seeking freedom, one can imagine the reverberation of such inflammatory information "in de quarter," where Lulu spent that evening "with the other young negroes" on the plantation.[9]

For slave children as for white children, the most common way to gain information was to overhear adult conversations. Isaac Adams,

God bless you massa! you feed and clothe us. When we are sick you nurse us and when too old to work, you provide for us!

These poor creatures are a sacred legacy from my ancestors and while a dollar is left me, nothing shall be spared to increase their comfort and happiness.

Southern white children were reared to regard slavery as a beneficent institution. In this 1841 image created by a Northern apologist for slavery, an attractive and affluent slaveholding family is depicted in the foreground with apparently contented African-American slaves dancing in the background. The white family's son gestures toward an elderly black couple with a small child resting at their feet, while the elderly slave man proclaims the benefits of slavery: "God Bless you massa! You feed and clothe us. When we are sick you nurse us, and when too old to work, you provide for us!" The master responds, "These poor creatures are a sacred legacy from my ancestors and while a dollar is left me, nothing shall be spared to increase their comfort and happiness." Planter-class children, who imbibed these messages from infancy onward, became stalwart supporters of slavery, secession, and the Southern Confederacy. *(Library of Congress)* born a slave in Louisiana, later recalled, "The first I knowed about the War coming on was when Mr. Sack [his owner] had a whole bunch of whitefolks at the Big House at a function. They didn't talk about anything else all evening." Similarly, Barney Alford remembered that his master and other men "wud cum to de big house an' stan' round under de trees" and talk politics before the Civil War. Meanwhile the adult slaves gathered secretly at night by the creek "an' pray for to be sot free." Barney, who was probably a fairly young child, knew about these gatherings but did not join in, "fur I wus 'sleep at dat time."[10] At a young age and well before the war's outbreak, this slave child knew that the future of slavery was in question and that a war might be fought to settle the issue. Moreover he understood that his owners and his own community held widely divergent political views, and he comprehended the importance of slaves' secrecy when it came to the inflammatory issues of slavery and freedom. Slave children could learn a great deal by eavesdropping on Southern adults of both races.

Slave children, like white children, had ample opportunities to learn about the debate over slavery and sectional politics well before the start of the Civil War. Many slave children evidently were both fully cognizant of the impending crisis and aware that the institution of slavery was in jeopardy. Adeline Blakely of Arkansas, who was ten years old when the war began, was particularly well informed about midcentury political debates, perhaps because her master, Mr. Parks, did not initially support secession. Decades later she explained prewar sectional politics to an interviewer: "If you didn't go with the popular side [i.e., secession] they called you 'abolitionist' or maybe 'Submissionist.'" And black children also understood that slavery was at stake in the coming conflict. Wade Owens of Alabama, who was only a toddler during the war, recalled, "Marsa said war was comin' an' thought hit was to free us."[11]

Mothers, who had played such an important role in teaching self-respect before the war, fostered subversive views during the secession crisis. Tom Robinson, who had been born a slave in North Carolina but was separated from his mother and sold into slavery in Texas at the age of eleven, cherished the memories he had of his mother. "I can just barely remember her," he stated decades later. "But I do remember how she used to take us children and kneel down in front of the fireplace and pray" for freedom. Tom's recollections indicated the importance of both his mother's evident desire for freedom and the extent of slave women's nonviolent resistance through prayer. "She'd pray that the time would come when everybody could worship the Lord under their own vine and fig tree—all of them free. It's come to me lots of times since," he reflected. "There she was a'praying, and on other plantations women was a'praying. All over the country the same prayer was being prayed. Guess the Lord done heard the prayer and answered it."[12] Whether God was listening or not, Tom clearly was. His love for his mother inspired his hatred of slavery.

Just as Southern white youngsters' childhoods prepared them to become loyal Confederates, black children's youthful experiences laid the foundation for Union sentiment. Black children knew from keen observation and lived experience that slavery meant harsh punishments for disobedience, servile submissiveness to white authority, and potential separation from family members. Despite all the ways in which slavery undermined parental authority and threatened family unity, slave children also learned to respect their own parents and other kin and to take their cues from them. Thus when the secession crisis reached its climax, slave children unhesitatingly adopted an anti-slavery and pro-Union stance.

Black and white children alike adopted pro- and anti-slavery stances that accorded with those of their parents well before the Civil War. As sectional politics heated up, however, Southern children were subjected to a growing barrage of alarmist propaganda. As Donald Reynolds has found in his study of Texas newspapers, editorials and letters to the editor kept anxiety about the possibility of a slave uprising at fever pitch in the years and months leading up to the war. Troubled by evidence of slave resistance, yet insistent that slaves were content with their lot in life, slaveholders reconciled this seeming contradiction by blaming slaves' unrest on Northern abolitionists.

Both the possibility of slave rebellion and the threat of Northern abolitionism gained credence in 1859 when the charismatic and fanatical abolitionist John Brown and a handful of followers occupied the federal armory in Harpers Ferry, Virginia, intending to provide rebellious slaves with weapons and provoke an armed insurrection. Although the raid proved unsuccessful, it inspired a wave of hero-worship among Northern abolitionists and a corresponding panic among Southern slaveholders, who became increasingly concerned that Northern whites were determined to bring death and destruction to the South. After John Brown's Raid, white Southerners grew more suspicious of Northerners and other outsiders. As Reynolds explains: "The distrust that southerners had habitually harbored toward northerners now gave way to something like a siege mentality, and white citizens throughout the slave states exercised heightened vigilance, for fear that other John Browns were lurking in their midst."[13]

Because schoolteachers in the antebellum South often came from the North, schoolchildren's lives were directly affected by the growing panic as communities expelled suspected abolitionist educators and banned "anti-southern" schoolbooks. Some states passed laws requiring teachers to be native Southerners, and several communities burned "incendiary books" in public conflagrations. Southern schoolchildren could hardly avoid the all-encompassing atmosphere of suspicion and fear that such actions both reflected and promoted.[14]

For many Southern schoolchildren, then, one of the first signs of trouble came when a teacher was dismissed for harboring the dangerous doctrine of abolitionism. Teenager Sarah Lois Wadley was terribly disappointed to learn that she could no longer take lessons from her previous teacher. "They say he is an abolitionist," she explained to her diary in October 1860; "at any rate, he has not come back, and his house is for sale." Despite her liking for her erstwhile teacher, this sixteen-year-old evidently took her cues from local adults, devoting long passages in her diary to the subject of abolitionism. Her reflections indicate how thoroughly—if not precisely how—white children and adolescents imbibed pro-slavery and pro-secession principles:

The Abolitionists have sowed the seeds of dissension and insurrection among us, those seeds are fast ripening and a bloody harvest seems impending; they have burnt our homesteads, killed
our citizens, and incited our servants to poison [sic] us, think
they that we will submit to continual disturbances, oft repeated
wrongs, much longer, no! they shout Freedom and Union, but
they would take away our freedom and give it to the negro, they
would sap the foundations of that Union which our ancestors
labored amid bloodshed and tyranny to found. . . . I shudder
to contemplate a civil war. . . . Better far for us would be civil
war than this dreadful incubus which hangs over us now, this
continual wrangling and bitter malediction with which we are
persecuted.[15]

Both black and white children were affected by public discussions
of abolitionist activity and the heightened awareness of slave resistance that followed John Brown's Raid. Older white children were
sometimes directly involved in family and community responses to
suspected slave insurrections and Northern spies. Boys who had used
their guns and knives only on squirrels and frogs now might have to
use them on rebellious slaves and Northern abolitionists. Virginia
planter's son Benjamin Fleet, who was only fourteen years old when
the Civil War began, set out one dark night with "my Bowie knife &
Pa's Colt's Revolver" in search of an abolitionist rumored to be in the
neighborhood. "With a cocked pistol," he searched a church and a stable by candlelight, but to no avail. When rumors of a slave insurrection inspired the formation of an ad hoc slave patrol among the rural
neighborhood's adult men, Benjamin, who was the oldest son living
at home, was charged with defending his mother and younger siblings
in his father's absence. Once again the teenager was well armed, with
"three guns, a pistol and two clubs" at his disposal.[16]

Younger children were more likely to observe than to participate
in vigilante violence. More than one Southern child recalled the horror of executions of suspected spies and rebellious slaves before and

during the war. Ten-year-old Susan Snow's master forced her to view African Americans on the gallows "to see what dey done to a Nigger dat harm a white man." Such sights were memorable and terrible for both black and white children. Nearly seventy years later, white Richmonder Benjamin Wilkins, who was only five years old during the secession crisis, still shuddered at the memory of the "gruesome sight" of the bodies of seven executed slaves dangling from a large scaffold erected on a hillside outside the city, "where they could be seen for miles around."[17]

Adolescent slaves occasionally ran afoul of local vigilance committees. In July 1860 a Texas slave named Bruce alerted his master of a fire in the barn, asserting that three unknown white men had set the building ablaze. Under questioning he admitted to setting the fire himself. Subsequent investigation convinced local whites that a "general revolt of the slaves, aided by the white men of the North in our midst," was imminent. Accounts of this alleged conspiracy were widely circulated, and in its wake other Southern communities heightened their vigilance, questioning slaves under duress until they "confessed . . . under the lash." Children were not immune from such treatment. In Mississippi a slave girl's report of a plot led to the arrest of more than thirty alleged slave conspirators. In Galveston, Texas, a slave boy met his death at the hands of local vigilantes after being seen "near the premises" of a burned structure.[18]

Whereas black youngsters were depicted as potential arsonists in newspaper coverage of alleged conspiracies, white youngsters were identified as defenseless victims. As Edmund Drago remarks in his study of white children in Civil War South Carolina, South Carolinians "made children central to why they seceded and went to war." Letters to the editor throughout the South justified the questioning, torture, expulsion, and execution of Northerners and slaves in terms of protecting homes, families, and children. While this was certainly in part an effective rhetorical device, children may indeed have been frightened by the oft-repeated assertion that they were the intended targets of a violent uprising. One resident of Marshall, Texas, asserted,

"Women and children have been so frightened by these burnings and threatened rebellion of the Negroes, that in several instances they have left their homes in their fright, and when found were almost confirmed maniacs!" Letters like this one, widely reprinted throughout the South, proved to be self-fulfilling prophecies. Another citizen claimed, "All is alarm and excitement with our children."[19]

When news of John Brown's Raid reached the Bradford plantation, young Susan Bradford described it as a "horrible, horrible time" of uncertainty; "our whole world seems turned topsy-turvy." Most disconcerting of all was the realization that "we can trust none of the dear black folks who, before this, we had relied on at every turn." Children were not immune to this tension. On the contrary, an exchange between Susan and her young charge, Frances, suggested that slave children were perhaps more likely than adults to reveal their true feelings. While the adult slaves on the Bradford plantation did not seem "disturbed," Frances asked her young mistress, "Do you understand what all this is about?" When the older girl replied that she did not, but that she and her parents would soon know more, Frances "laughed, a crazy kind of laugh, and said: 'Yes, you will; you white folks will know a heap you ain't never knowed before,' and then she ran out of the room."[20]

Many white children remembered an atmosphere of dread and foreboding in the months following the raid on Harpers Ferry and leading up to the election of 1860. Virginian Constance Cary recalled, "there was the fear . . . dark, boding, oppressive, and altogether hateful. I can remember taking it to bed with me at night, and awaking suddenly oftentimes to confront it through a vigil of nervous terror of which it never occurred to me to speak to any one." Seven-year-old George Robertson likewise remembered "an oppressive feeling of solemnity" that affected people of all ages. "It was as if half the people were attending the funeral of the other half," he soberly remarked.[21]

The charged atmosphere was intensified, in many cases, by children's ignorance. While adults no doubt intended to protect their children by shielding them from the possibility of civil war, their silence sometimes led children to imagine the worst. In Texas, farmer's son Charles Nagel described the situation: "The air became tense with apprehension. . . . Our own parents spoke guardedly in our presence, and when they were most serious made sure that we were not within hearing." Shut out from the adults' conversations, eleven-year-old Charles and his brothers nonetheless heard rumors of conscription and imagined they would be seized and forced into service at any moment. "Our young minds were filled with visions of riders coming down upon us and taking away whom they could find," he remembered.[22]

Anxieties grew as the hotly contested and highly symbolic election of 1860 approached. The two-party electoral system dissolved under the strain of sectional disagreements over slavery. The Democratic party divided into rival sectional groups, each with its own presidential candidate; Southern moderates, including members of the defunct Whig party, ran a candidate on a vaguely defined platform of "Constitutional Union"; and Abraham Lincoln, who had gained a national reputation during a series of debates over the future of slavery in the western territories in 1858, emerged as the Republican party's choice for president. A divided Democratic party could not hope to win the election; nor could a neophyte party like the Constitutional Union party. Southern slaveholders thus faced the very real prospect that Lincoln would become the next president with no Southern votes and no political obligations to the slaveholding states. Despite his public pronouncements that he had no intention of meddling with the institution of slavery where it existed, and his assertion that he did not support "the social and political equality of the white and black races," Lincoln's public denunciation of slavery as "an unqualified evil" and his famous declaration that "a house divided against itself cannot stand" convinced many that the Illinois lawyer posed a serious threat to slaveholders' interests within the Union.[23]

Many white Southerners assumed that Lincoln's election would lead inevitably to civil war. Shortly before her sixteenth birthday, in October 1860, Mississippi teenager Sarah Lois Wadley recorded "great excitement here concerning the coming election" adding,

"God grant that it may not be the cause of breaking up our glorious Union." Like other white Southerners, Sarah believed that Northern abolitionists would leave Southern slaveholders no option but civil war if they elected Lincoln to office. White Southern children, adopting their parents' political perspectives, regarded Lincoln as a fanatical abolitionist who would, if elected, summarily end slavery and render slaveholders paupers. As Lucy Buck, who was eighteen years old when the war began, put it, Lincoln was an "arch-fiend" whose election would usher in "a despotism as atrocious as ever the fair sun shone upon." The election of an abolitionist despot, naturally, would leave no alternative to secession and war.[24]

Enslaved Southerners likewise regarded Lincoln's possible election as a harbinger of war—but they regarded this eventuality in a positive light, as an avenue to emancipation. As they had before, slaves continued to gather information from their owners but to adopt their own perspectives as they disseminated knowledge within the slave community. Robert Glenn was working in the fields under an adult slave's supervision (and was therefore probably in his early teens) when he learned about the election and its potential impact on slavery from the elderly woman assigned to his care. "The woman who looked after Henry Hall and myself," he explained, "told me she heard marster say old Abraham Lincoln was trying to free the niggers."[25]

While older slave youth like Robert Glenn kept their own counsel, younger slaves sometimes could not restrain their excitement. Frank Patterson, a North Carolina slave who was ten years old at the time, recalled shouting "Hurrah for Lincoln" during the presidential campaign of 1860. When his mistress asked him why, he replied, "Because he's goin' to set me free."[26]

Even slave children too young to comprehend the issues became enthusiastic supporters of Lincoln as the candidate for freedom. As Mississippian Susan Snow, who was eleven years old when the war broke out, explained, "I didn' know nothin' 'bout Abe Lincoln, but I hear'd he was a-tryin' to free de Niggers an' my mammy say she want to be free."[27]

With war and slavery hanging in the balance, it is small wonder that, on November 6, 1860, twenty-two-year-old Virginian Fannie Page Hume wrote in her diary: "This is the long talked of & much dreaded 'election day.'"[28] After adults cast their votes, children anxiously awaited the results. Evelyn Ward's favorite brother, twenty-one-year-old Will, rode out in the middle of a rainstorm to collect the mail, hoping to learn the election news. The entire family apprehensively awaited his return with the results. Evelyn, then seven years old, was tense with anticipation and fear:

> As it began to grow dusk he came in with the news. Lincoln was President! What a stir and buzz of talk! Now there would certainly be war, the grownups were saying. I looked at Mother. She was saying nothing, but looked—I couldn't tell you how she looked. War! And Will would have to go! All the raw chill of the outside came into our pleasant room. I sat by the window watching the cold rain run down the panes. Big drops were running down my cheeks. . . . I sat there, a poor little frozen-hearted thing, seeing misery come to take the place of our happy life.[29]

Although white children's family loyalties and political loyalties generally reinforced each other, the coming of war meant that political beliefs might endanger family members. Fear—for their own safety, for their male relatives, and of the unknown—began to be mixed with excitement in the final months before war was declared.

Immediately following the election, Southern opinion-makers sprang into action to push for secession. According to one Virginia planter's daughter, as early as December 1860 "the newspapers were full of secession talk and the matter was eagerly discussed at our tables," quickly transmitting information from adults to children.[30]

Southern children might not fully understand the reasoning behind secession, but they nonetheless caught secession fever. North Carolinian George Robertson, who was only eight years old when the war began, later recalled: "The newspapers had been filled with war talk and some of the leaders of men made inflammatory speeches. I recall one which I heard but did not altogether understand. Governor Foote of Mississippi made such a talk in the largest church in town. . . . I did not understand all this speaker said, but I felt he was for fighting and I was too."[31]

Pro-slavery ministers joined the propaganda campaign. Shortly after the election of 1860, Fannie Page Hume heard "an excellent sermon" in which the minister "plainly set forth . . . the danger of *compromise*," a strong pro-secession stance. Children in rural areas received such sermons in printed form, after the fact, often via older family members. Sarah Lois Wadley's father brought home a newspaper containing the pro-slavery sermon of a New Orleans pastor and, apparently, read it aloud to the family. According to Sarah, the minister presented "incontrovertible arguments that slavery is providential and *right*, that the slave being by nature incapable of self government is dependent upon his master for protection and that it is the duty of the master to extend that protection to him."[32]

Slave children also learned about the outcome of the election and the possibility of war from sermons. Texan William H. Adams recalled that shortly before war broke out, a white preacher came to his plantation to urge the slaves to "pray fer de South to win," warning them that if the North was victorious and slavery ended, the slaves would be homeless and hungry. Emancipation, the minister explained, would leave blacks "free to roam roun', without a home, like de wil' animals." Clearly, as the war loomed, slaveholding adults sought to inculcate slaves with the same pro-slavery messages that their own children already embraced. Just as clearly, slave children learned both Unionism and secrecy from adult slaves. On William Adams's plantation, for instance, when the visiting white minister demanded a show of hands for supporters of the South from the assembled slave congregation, "we all raised our hands 'cause we was skeered not to, but we sho' didn' wan' de South to win." Afterward the slaves held a night meeting "down in de hollow" in which they agreed to put on a front of support for the South while secretly planning to "turn de tray roun' and pray for de North to win."[33]

Children of both races learned much the same information about the politics of slavery, and they acquired this information in very similar ways. But because they were strongly influenced by their parents and other kin, black and white children adopted different perspectives, with black children learning to desire freedom while white children learned to defend the South's "peculiar institution." Those too young to understand the issues at stake nonetheless wished to please their parents, and they quickly learned to tailor their actions (and likely their beliefs as well) to earn adult approval. Decades later, the former slave Adeline Blakeley remembered what happened when the young son of her master and mistress unintentionally ran afoul of his family's Confederate loyalties:

> The little Blakeley boy had always liked to play with the American flag. He'd march with it and carry it out on the porch and hang it up. But after the trouble began to brew his mother told him he would have to stay in the house when he played with the flag. Even then somebody saw him and scolded him and said 'Either burn it or wash it.' The child thought they meant it and he tried to wash it. Dyes weren't so good in those days and it ran terribly. It was the awfulest thing you ever saw.[34]

The little Blakeley boy, like other children in the Civil War South, learned the importance of conforming to his family's beliefs.

Precisely because of children's dependence on adults for information and guidance, when adults disagreed, children found their loyalties divided. This dynamic was acute for white children and adolescents in the border states between Lincoln's election in November 1860 and the official declaration of war in April 1861. Only weeks after Lincoln's election, South Carolina seceded from the Union in December 1860. By February 1861, Georgia, Alabama, Mississippi, Louisiana, Texas, and Florida had followed suit, and a provisional Confederate government was established in Montgomery, Alabama. While most white Southerners espoused pro-slavery views, some, especially in the upper South, initially opposed secession and hoped for a peaceful settlement of sectional differences. These "reluctant Confederates," as one historian has dubbed them, took the lead in Virginia, North Carolina, Tennessee, and Arkansas, which remained in the Union but threatened to secede if armed force were used against the South. Even after these states joined the Confederacy, significant portions of their populations retained Unionist sympathies. The border states of Maryland, Missouri, and Kentucky, which remained in the Union, had important slaveholding interests and pro-secession adherents.[35]

Southern children were thus exposed to competing attitudes about secession and war as well as to potential damage that ideological differences might wreak on personal and familial relationships. Henry White, who lived on a plantation outside Baltimore, recalled that his family was fraught with strife throughout the secession crisis: "Hardly a day passed that I did not hear one or more such discussions [arguments about secession vs. union], during which the parties thereto frequently lost their tempers, and ended, some of them, by not speaking to each other."[36]

In Virginia, which did not join the Confederacy until April 1861, the secession crisis tested the loyalties—and the tempers—of the Fleet family. Benjamin Fleet, a politically savvy youngster who regularly served as a poll watcher in his rural Virginia community, initially had strong Unionist leanings. After attending a February 1860 Whig convention in nearby Richmond, the thirteen-year-old pronounced: "John Minor Botts is my choice for the Presidency!" Botts, a Whig lawyer from Virginia who favored sectional compromise, became a favorite for the presidential nomination in the American party, which in 1859 succeeded the foundering Whig party. Botts was a strong Unionist who urged caution and compromise. After Lincoln's nomination, Botts publicly countered claims that Lincoln was an abolitionist and urged his fellow Virginians to remain calm rather than join the Deep South in seceding from the Union, which he deemed an unwarranted, illegal, and ill-advised rebellion against the federal government. "There is no danger of disunion," he declared in October

1860. "First, because there is no necessity; second, because there is no right; and third, because there is no power." After Virginia seceded, Botts retired from public life and began work on a critical history of the Confederacy; he was arrested, jailed, and held under house arrest for Unionism during the Civil War. After the war he published his memoirs under the long yet pointed title *The Great Rebellion: Its Secret History, Rise, Progress, and Disastrous Failure. By John Minor Botts, of Virginia. The Political Life of the Author Vindicated.* Young Benjamin's support for Botts's candidacy—which he marked by naming a new colt after the Unionist politician—indicated his own loyalty to the Union and his opposition to secession.[37]

In May 1860, when the Whigs, reconstituted as the Constitutional Union party, convened in Baltimore and nominated John Bell and Edward Everett as pro-Union presidential and vice-presidential candidates, respectively, Benjamin threw his support their way. His namesake colt, John Minor Botts, had died when it was only a few days old; undaunted, young Ben expressed a wish that a neighbor would name her newborn son either John Bell or Edward Everett. In August he "paid fifty c[en]ts for my picture of those Gallant Men," which he hung in his bedroom.[38]

Benjamin's stalwart Unionism caused tension in his relationship with his older brother Fred, three years his senior, who was attending school at the University of Virginia. The university was a hotbed of secessionist sentiment: William Lowndes Yancey, a fiery advocate of secession, spoke at the university, and Fred's roommate, Pat, purchased a picture of John C. Breckinridge, the Southern Democrats' choice for president after the party split along sectional lines over the issue of slavery. The portrait was "tacked up on the mantelpiece" of the dorm room. "What do you think of it?" Fred teased his younger brother about his well-known "Whiggery." Ben retorted that he wanted his brother to "buy a picture of Bell and Everett in opposition to Pat," while the boys' mother counseled, "let politics alone, and save that 50 c[en]ts."[39]

The sibling rivalry intensified as the election neared. From the University of Virginia, where students too young to vote held a mock contest a few days before election day, Fred reported the college's election returns: "The vote was this, for all the states, Breckinridge 245, Bell 232, Douglas 26, [and] for Virginia: Bell 162, Breckinridge 157. What do you think of it?" At home, Ben confided to his diary, "I only hope and pray to *God* that Bell and Everett may be elected." Skipping school the next day to attend the polls, he recorded the local votes in his diary: Breckinridge was the victor with 112 votes; Bell and Everett followed with 82 votes; and the Northern Democrats' candidate, Stephen Douglas, won a single vote. Ben immediately wrote a letter to his brother to inform him of the local results, but in his next diary entry he was forced to concede that in the national election "Lincoln is elected certainly without doubt."[40]

From the University of Virginia, where students sported Confederate cockades, formed military companies, and threatened to withdraw from the university if the state remained in the Union, Fred wrote home urging immediate secession. "We must all be a united South," he declared. "What are the opinions of Pa & you & other Bell men upon this question?" At home, family members gathered to hear "Pa" read aloud from the newspapers. Dr. Fleet remained steadfast in his Unionism, writing, "Even though Lincoln's election is a fixed fact, the Union need not of necessity be dissolved." At the same time, however, he conceded that "if the South secedes, he goes with the South heart and soul." Although Ben was engaged in molding bullets—"we are preparing for the 'Yankees,'" he wrote in his diary—he continued to oppose secession. Closely following the selection of electors for the state convention that would vote on secession, he was incensed when his older brother attributed the younger boy's Unionism to his "ignorance of the state of affairs." Ben replied with a two-page letter that he described as a "*schorcher*."[41]

Only after shots were fired at Fort Sumter did the Fleet brothers see eye to eye on sectional politics. "War has really commenced!!!"

Ben wrote in his diary following the engagement. A few days later he noted that "an overwhelming majority" of the Virginia Convention had voted to join the Confederacy. Like many other border state residents, Benjamin Fleet quickly abandoned his Unionism once the first shots of the Civil War were fired. "I have been for the Union all along until the first Gun was fired at Fort Sumter," he remarked. He served as a poll counter during the popular vote held in May to ratify the state convention's secession vote. "I kept the polls for Secession," he proudly wrote in his diary, adding with satisfaction, "Everybody that voted, voted for Secession."[42]

Political disagreements like these were commonplace in the Upper South, and children often were caught up in conflicts over secession. When thirteen-year-old Maryland schoolgirl May Preston's mother sent a Confederate flag in a package of treats, she also warned her against allowing it to become "the cause of unpleasantness between you and any of your young companions, or of disobedience and punishment between you and your teachers." Indeed, political disagreements might produce "unpleasantness" among white children of all backgrounds. At St. Anthony's Orphanage in Baltimore, the inmates, all boys, quarreled and fought over secession. In an effort to forestall similar disagreements among the girls in their charge, the nuns at St. Joseph's Academy banned songs, speeches, and compositions on "any political topics."[43]

Political differences among whites also sometimes arose in the Deep South. Nine-year-old Letitia Dabney, a resident of Mississippi whose parents hailed from Virginia, recalled that her father and uncle were at first "violently opposed to Secession," a situation that created friction between the Dabneys and their pro-secession neighbors. More troubling for children, political differences sometimes disrupted family harmony. In Texas, where German immigrants maintained strongholds of Unionist sentiment, eleven-year-old Charles Nagel was troubled by disagreements among kin. "Even old and close relations in some cases became strained," he later recalled.[44]

Eliza Frances Andrews, who turned twenty-one the year the Civil War began, reported "awful family rows" in her Georgia household. All the children were "determined Rebs," the father was a staunch Unionist, and the mother attempted in vain to maintain family harmony by imposing a rule of avoiding political discussions at home. "I am afraid all this political turmoil has something to do with father's illness, and my heart smites me," the young adult wrote in her journal. "I don't want to be disrespectful," she worried, "but [my brother] Henry and I are born hot-heads, and never can hold our unruly tongues."[45]

While disagreements among family members often caused white children confusion and distress, contrasting opinions between white owners and black slaves do not seem to have caused slave children similar angst. Rather, slave children simply adopted the views of enslaved adults, which revolved around the desire for freedom. As Barney Alford of Mississippi recalled the conversations among his elders, "Sum uf de slaves wanted ole man Abe [Lincoln] to whip de south an' sum uf dem was for de south beatin', but all uf 'em wanted to be sot free."[46]

Slave children who were isolated from other slaves, however, took their cues from the only adults with whom they came into contact: their owners. Katie Phoenix, the only slave of a widowed mistress, explained, "When de war broke I didn't know what it was for. . . . Mrs. Harris was hatin' the North and I was hatin' the North too. I thought the North was kind of like a spider in a dream that was going to come and wipe away de house and carry me off."[47] For the most part, though, slave children do not seem to have suffered from divided loyalties. When forced to choose between the desires of their parents and the politics of their owners, they invariably chose family ties over the bonds of slavery.

Slaves of all ages usually were careful to conceal their political knowledge—and their Union loyalties—from whites. Children, however, were sometimes less cautious than adults. It was after an exchange with "a little negro girl" in early April 1861, shortly before the first battle of the war, that slaveholder Keziah Goodwyn Hopkins Brevard concluded, "our negroes are far more knowing than many will acknowledge." The youngster's assertion that "negroes hated white folks" caused the mistress considerable anxiety: "Now if black children have this talk what are we to expect from grown negroes," she worried.[48]

Brevard did not have to wait long for an answer to her question. After Lincoln's election, events progressed toward secession and civil war with almost blinding speed. The tentative peace was broken on April 10, 1861, when President Lincoln sent a naval expedition to Fort Sumter, a federal military base that South Carolina Confederates had seized in February. Before the federal ships reached land, on April 12, Confederates fired on the fort. After a thirty-four-hour bombardment, federal troops trapped inside the fort surrendered to secessionist gunmen. Lincoln called for 75,000 soldiers to put down the rebellion; Virginia, North Carolina, Tennessee, and Arkansas seceded; and the Civil War had begun. Evelyn Ward recalled: "As the winter drew toward spring there was more and more drilling, and more and more war talk. I know now what was happening. I don't know that I understood it then. I did know when Mr. Lincoln called for troops from all the states, and when Fort Sumter fell. How excited everyone was!" The excitement and high spirits of the adults around her eased the youngster's earlier fears of war. "It didn't seem to me that anyone was sorry about it except Mamma," she commented.[49]

Like Evelyn Ward, most white children quickly, if only temporarily, forgot their anxieties once secession occurred and war broke out. For many Southern children, the coming of war seemed inevitable if not positively desirable. When the first shots of the Civil War were fired, the Charleston Battery was "thronged with spectators of every age and sex." Youngsters gravitated to the waterside to witness the official onset of hostilities. One toddler, not yet able to speak clearly, imitated the cannons' booming. Another child, a boy just entering his teens, attached himself to the Palmetto Guards and fired seventeen shots.[50]

The first shots of the Civil War were fired at Fort Sumter, off the coast of Charleston, South Carolina. Southerners of all ages gathered on the Battery to view the destruction, pictured here in an 1864 photograph. *(Library of Congress)*

One of the most dramatic accounts of youngsters' response to the start of hostilities was Sophia Haskell Cheves's reminiscences of "M[ada]me Togno's Establishment for young ladies—the fashionable Charleston boarding school in 1860–61." Apprised of the Confederate demand that the Union evacuate Fort Sumter, just off the coast of Charleston, or be fired upon, the "half frightened" and "wildly excited" schoolgirls stayed awake all night, waiting for the "bombardment." Just as dawn was breaking, she concluded, "one deep awful boom resounded through the air, and we knew that the battle had begun."[51]

Although not all Southern children had the kind of front-row seats that Sophia Haskell Cheves described, white children almost universally reported catching war fever—what Louisianan Kate Stone called "the excitement in the air"—once hostilities began. Thirteen-year-old South Carolina schoolboy T. G. Barker vividly recalled the moment when he was informed by the headmaster of the firing on Fort Sumter. Spontaneously he and his classmates rose en masse from their desks, cheering, "Hooray! Hooray!" In the new Confederate capital, the aftermath of the firing on Fort Sumter was "a time of wild excitement," according to Benjamin Wilkins, who was five years old at the time. In his later memoirs he wrote that most of Richmond's whites were "crazy to get a chance to whip the 'damnyankees' and show them that no nigger loving abolitionist should ever come into the South and tell them what to do."[52]

Enslaved children also welcomed the war. Mothers, whose influence over their children continued to be paramount, were particularly important in encouraging slave children's support for President Lincoln and their enthusiasm for a war they identified as a fight for freedom. Fifteen-year-old Mattie Jackson and her mother were enslaved together in St. Louis when the war broke out. "My mother used to sit up nights and read to keep posted about the war," Mattie explained in her memoirs, and she kept a picture of President Lincoln, clipped from the newspaper, on the wall of her room. Booker T. Washington, only six years old when the war began, likewise learned about the Civil War, the Union president, and the possibility of freedom when he awakened to find his mother "kneeling over her children and fervently praying that Lincoln and his armies might be successful." Thereafter he carefully followed the adults' "whispered discussions" about the war's progress, gleaned from the slaves' "grapevine" telegraph.[53]

Southern children eagerly followed war news and enthusiastically took sides in the conflict. Although she had earlier been tearful at the prospect of her older brother going to war, when war was declared Evelyn Ward was jubilant: "The War had actually begun! I didn't

Although slave youth learned about the secession crisis and the Civil War from many of the same sources as their white counterparts, they adopted dramatically different perspectives. Many slave children participated in—or eavesdropped on—hushed conversations about the possibility of emancipation within the slave community. In this 1864 drawing of a Virginia slave cabin, three women and four children gather away from white supervision. This drawing also suggests the central role slave mothers played in slave children's lives and their important influence on slave children's political views. *(Library of Congress)*

feel afraid now. It was very interesting to watch the drilling in the study and then the drilling in the streets, both cavalry and infantry." In the excitement the Virginia girl forgot her earlier concerns about her brother's welfare. When she and her siblings watched a cousin ride off to the front, she was thrilled rather than frightened. "It stirred our blood to see that young fellow riding to gallantly for his life," she wrote. "We were beginning to know something about war."[54]

By the spring of 1861 nearly all children in the South knew "something about war," gleaning war news from conversations with family members, newspaper accounts, pro-Confederate sermons, correspondence from the front, and neighborhood gossip. As Tennessean Alice Ready put it in 1861: "The War is the all absorbing topic of conversation and of letters."[55]

Just as they had shaped their children's attitudes toward slavery, white parents continued to influence their offspring's understanding of the war. In the first year of the war, twelve-year-old Virginian Sallie Bird received regular updates from the front from her soldier-father as well as overhearing "warm" discussions of "the Yankees and the war" between her mother and grandparents. In addition, her mother encouraged her to "read the papers and keep up with the current events." Both of Sallie's parents frequently used the hardships of war as an object lesson for their preteen daughter, reminding her that "a ready cheerful obedience and an earnest desire to do [her] duty" would ease her parents' loneliness and anxiety. After a visit to her husband's camp, informing her daughter that her father was "in great peril," Mrs. Bird also impressed upon her that her dear "Papa" was eager to have Sallie be "a *good* girl, honest, true, obedient, and affectionate." When young Sallie suffered from a swollen, painful face as a result of scarlet fever, her mother admonished: "Oh, my little daughter, as you suffer pain in your face, think of the horrible torture of our poor soldiers." Combining affection, guilt, and politics, Sallie Bird's parents waged an effective campaign to train their daughter to regard Confederate loyalty and filial duty as closely linked and equally important.[56]

With their parents' encouragement, Confederate youngsters followed war news closely. Many teenagers' diaries became digests of war news. Benjamin Fleet, who was fourteen years old when hostilities commenced, was especially well informed. His family lived close enough to Richmond to get information from the Confederate capital. His father made almost daily trips to collect newspapers from local merchants, and his brother Fred joined the Confederate Army and sent regular correspondence from the eastern front. Ben, who often could hear the sounds of cannons at the family's plantation, Green Mount, eagerly sought out "war news" throughout the conflict. The former Unionist was now an ardent Confederate. Receiving news of Confederate victory at the first land battle of the Civil War, fought at Big Bethel Church near Hampton, Virginia, he succinctly but firmly indicated his loyalties in his diary: "*Good.*" In other entries Ben denounced "those rascally Yankees," mentioned accompanying his father to the store to get newspapers, joyously recorded "glorious news" of Confederate victories, anxiously awaited letters from his brother, despondently recorded "bad news indeed" about Confederate losses, noted giving money "for our soldiers" at a prayer meeting, mourned the death of a family friend at the Battle of Antietam, and celebrated the "tremendous thrashing" that Confederates gave federal soldiers at the Battle of Chickamauga. In addition to acquiring information from his father, his brother, and his neighbors, Ben himself subscribed to several newspapers. "The papers are very interesting now," he commented.[57]

Sixteen-year-old Louisianan Sarah Lois Wadley included war news in nearly every entry of her diary in 1861. Her reports suggest that on the western front, word of mouth was the most important (if not the most accurate) source of information. Sarah's use of phrases such as "it is said" or "we have received news" offer little detail about the origin of war news; more striking is her repetition of rumor as fact, particularly when the rumors were of Confederate victories. For instance, in late August 1861 Sarah wrote, "We have heard of victories won by our soldiers in Western Virginia, Missouri and Texas. It is reported, and believed, that at Leesburg three hundred Federalists were killed and the rest (one thousand five hundred) taken prisoners; in Missouri Gen'l Lyon is killed and Siegel reported wounded." In a rare show of skepticism she added, "I hope all these good reports are true, it is almost incredible that at Leesburg only six of our men were killed and nine wounded." More frequently, Sarah approvingly and unquestioningly repeated news—from sermons, newspapers, her father's conversations with other Confederates on his frequent trips to nearby Vicksburg, or unknown sources—of Confederate successes and Union failures. Confident of divine favor and military might, she declared, "God seems to aid us," and predicted, "we are on the rapid road to success[.]"[58]

After a series of victories in 1861, Confederate forces suffered an increasing number of defeats. But Confederate children could turn defeat as well as victory into pro-Confederate and anti-Union propaganda. Sarah Wadley excoriated Union troops for "their disregard for humanity" and failure to practice "civilized warfare," and she compared "Lincoln and his parasites" unfavorably to "our hero statesman," Confederate President Jefferson Davis. She described Davis as "just in council, cool, brave, and gallant in battle; firm, energetic and instant in the performance of his executive duties"—indeed, "a second Washington." Denouncing Union officers as "military dictators" and Northern soldiers as "the vandal horde," she filled her diary with "heartrending accounts" of wartime "atrocities" followed by confident assertions of God's favor and ultimate victory. "Oh, if there be a retributive justice what shall be the fate of those wicked men who have sent their myrmidons to bathe our land in the blood of its children," she mused in April 1862.[59]

Although not necessarily as eloquent as Sarah Wadley, white children of all ages eagerly sought out war news, celebrated Confederate successes, and mourned Union victories. Evelyn Ward recalled political news as an occasion for family gatherings: "We used to get the Richmond papers," she explained. "Somebody would read the news aloud. All the rest of us would gather around to hear." While the family was saddened by finding "the names of friends" among "the lists of the killed and wounded" that "were always read" aloud, the Ward children—ranging in age from one to twenty-three years old at the start of the war—offset their sorrow with pride: "We felt thrilled through and through by the accounts of the brave fighting our dear people were doing," she wrote. In the Ward household, as in many other Southern homes, "war talk" was a constant backdrop to everyday "life and lessons."[60]

Although Evelyn Ward did not comment on black children's presence or response, it is likely that they also overheard the ritualistic reading of newspapers, complete with accounts of battles won and lost. Julius Jones later testified that the slaves on his Tennessee plantation "couldn't get much news 'bout what was going on" because "the white folks . . . didn't let no information out," but Felix Haywood, who lived far from the front in Texas, indicated that he and his fellow slaves had no difficulty gathering information. "Oh, we knowed what was goin' on in it [the war] all the time," he declared, "'cause old man Gudlow [his master] went to the post office every day and we knowed. We had papers in them days jus' like now." During Sherman's March to the Sea, one soldier recounted meeting a young black woman who "knew about Burnside, McClellan, and Sherman, also the fall of Atlanta, and even the recent unsuccessful rebel attack there." Intentionally or not, slaveholders shared information about the progress of the war with those they held in bondage. As Robert Glenn explained his ability to track military engagements from his plantation in Unionist Kentucky: "The war news kept slipping through."[61]

Although they may have gleaned war news from their owners, slaves adopted a dramatically different perspective. Mattie Jackson observed: "The days of sadness for mistress—who worried that Niggers and Yankees were seeking to take over the country—were days of joy for us." When news of Union victories reached James Johnson's plantation, he recalled, "the only happy folk were the slaves, the whites were in distress."[62]

Slave children were essential to the transmission of information about the war's progress. Given that many slave children's and adolescents' work duties as waiters, maids, and general errand runners kept them near white family members, it is probable that youngsters were the first members of the slave community to learn war news. One Tennessean remembered that on her plantation it was the slave children who "would go round to the windows and listen to what the white folks would say when they was reading their papers and talking after supper." House servants' greater opportunities to overhear news about the war may have accounted for the difference that Kate Stone observed between the "lazy and disobedient" domestic workers and the field hands, who proceeded with their work "without trouble" in July 1861. If so, children's "double-agent" role as errand runners for their owners and news bringers for the slave community may have played an important role in affecting slave discipline, or lack thereof, in the Civil War South.[63]

Slave youth appear to have been particularly rebellious in the Civil War South. In Virginia a sixteen-year-old slave girl killed her mistress by hitting her with a fence rail and then choking her to death rather than submit to a whipping. In Texas frustrated slave mistress Lizzie Neblett found her two teenaged male slaves, Tom and Bill, to be especially obstreperous and increasingly insubordinate, despite—or perhaps in response to—the harsh punishments she authorized her overseer to administer. "Tom grows worse each day," she wrote in 1864; by that time he had been punished repeatedly for shirking his work, stealing chickens and firewood, and running away. Bill, too, "has got to be so lazy & trifling & pays so little heed to what I say that I don't see how I can stand him," she grumbled. Neblett believed—perhaps correctly—that the slave youth on her plantation were "trying all they can . . . to agrivate me." Although the slave mistress complained that the two young slaves "hav[e] no care about the future," a more accurate assessment might be that as Union victory became increasingly assured, African-American youngsters hoped for a future in which they were no longer subordinate to white authority.[64]

From the very beginning of the war, slaves believed it would bring freedom. North Carolinian Mary Anderson indicated the scope, though not the source, of slaves' knowledge of the conflict's implications for slavery in her memories of the war, recorded many decades later: "The war was begun and there were stories of fights and freedom. The news went from plantation to plantation and while the slaves acted natural and some even more polite than usual, they prayed for freedom."[65]

Nineteen-year-old planter's daughter Kate Stone breathed a sigh of relief when July 4, 1861, passed "without any trouble with the Negroes." She explained in her diary: "The general impression has

Enslaved African Americans knew from the beginning that the Civil War was about the future of slavery. Their hopes were borne out in January 1863 when the Emancipation Proclamation took effect. This *carte de visite* depicts a gathering of black men, women, and children at a "watch meeting" on December 31, 1862, "waiting for the hour" of freedom. *(Library of Congress)*

been that the Negroes looked for a great upheaval of some kind on that day. In some way they have gotten a confused idea of Lincoln's Congress meeting and of the war; they think it is all to help them, and they expected for 'something to turn up.'" Once Independence Day had passed without incident, the teenager hoped that the slaves' restiveness would dissipate. "I hope the house servants will settle to their work now," she concluded.[66]

But slaves' hopes—and rebelliousness—grew throughout the war, particularly after the Emancipation Proclamation. Two years into the war, President Lincoln issued the proclamation, freeing slaves in the Confederate states that did not return to Union control by January 1, 1863. Although the executive order could be enforced only in areas under Union control and did not apply to the border states of Kentucky, Missouri, and Maryland, which had not seceded, or to Tennessee, which was largely under Union control at the time of the order, news of the possibility of freedom spread like wildfire among Southern bondspeople.

In western Tennessee, "in the year 1863," despite his master's best efforts to keep the slaves ignorant of wartime events, sixteen-year-old Julius Jones heard that Lincoln had "held a council" in which "he 'greed to take all the colored people. Said if they fought on his side he would set them all free." While not fully accurate, Jones's information caught the essence of the Emancipation Proclamation, which also permitted the enlistment of freed African Americans in the military. Although the proclamation did not actually apply to the young Tennessean, he immediately left the plantation to join the Union Army.[67]

On Sarah Wadley's plantation the slaves had a particularly festive Christmas celebration in 1862, shortly after Sarah and her family received news that Union troops had entered their region of Louisiana. Sarah appeared oblivious to any connection between the slaves' joyous revelry and the Union Army's advance: "They are having a merry time, thoughtless creatures, they think not of the morrow," she commented. Of course, given that the Emancipation Proclamation, issued a few months earlier, was scheduled to take effect in only a few days, and that the liberating army was in the immediate vicinity and coming closer each day, the glee of the Wadley slaves probably reflected their hopes for the future rather than their disregard for war matters.[68] The reflections of this teenaged Confederate indicate how much Southern children's reactions to wartime events differed depending upon race.

Gender also shaped children's responses to the war. Southern newspapers were filled with accounts of heroic Confederate children, like the "Brave Virginia Boy" who prevented "Black Republicans" from vandalizing the docks in his hometown, or the "angelic" Georgia girl who came to the aid of a Confederate soldier who had lost his leg in battle. Such stories offered gender-specific models of behavior to Confederate children; girls won praise for their compassion while boys were celebrated for their bravery. Small wonder then that, as one historian puts it, "Boys were rabid secessionists." Yet girls too eagerly embraced the Confederate cause as their own. In Charleston, South Carolina, three little girls went to bed without supper in 1862 in order to donate money to the Ladies Gunboat Campaign; the following year a ten-year-old girl raffled off her dollhouse to raise money for soldiers. Boys' and girls' different contributions to the war effort—male courage, female self-sacrifice—would be a major theme throughout the Civil War. While white children of both sexes almost immediately became "very enthusiastic little 'rebels,'" as ten-year-old Mary Boykin Williams described herself and her siblings, the meaning of Confederate nationalism was very different for boys and girls.[69]

For white boys and young men, military service became an important coming-of-age ritual, a marker of both manhood and adulthood. Evelyn Ward highlighted the significance of soldiering for young men when she recalled that when her oldest brother, twenty-one-year-old Will, joined the Confederate army, he "looked big and strong in his . . . gray uniform" and had "grown a little mustache, too."[70]

Universally, white males in the Confederacy were anxious to don uniforms, drill in the streets, march to war, and claim adult manhood as their birthright. Louisianan Kate Stone's brothers—ranging in age from thirteen to twenty-one when the war broke out—were "wild to be off" to the front. Her oldest brother, who enlisted in 1861, was "in extravagant spirits" while her younger brothers were "disgruntled because they cannot go too." At least the younger boys had the prospect of being permitted to go if the war continued for a time; women, girls, and disabled male youths were permanently excluded from the action. This was an exclusion felt keenly by adolescents and young adults of both sexes. When her brother and uncle departed for the front, twenty-year-old Kate mourned her own helplessness as much as she feared for their safety:

> They go to bear all hardships, to brave all dangers, and to face death in every form, while we whom they go to protect are

lapped safe in luxurious ease. But oh! The weary days of watching and waiting that stretch before us! We who stay behind may
find it harder than they who go. They will have new scenes and
constant excitement to buoy them up and the consciousness of
duty done.[71]

Charles Leverett, a "feeble" young man from South Carolina, likewise expressed chagrin at his inability to participate in the defining
events of the day in 1861. "If there is anything that galls me it is to
be so goodfornothing in such grand times as these," he wrote. "Everybody is working or fighting or doing something except me! I feel like
Prometheus Vinctus," he lamented, comparing himself to the Titan of
Greek mythology who was chained to a rock to have his organs eaten
by eagles.[72] Being excluded from military service was a bitter pill for
young Confederates of either gender.

For those white males who were old enough, and strong enough,
to enlist, military service brought new stature as adults and as men.
Indeed, the Confederate draft literally defined manhood by limiting
enlistment to males at least seventeen years of age. For adolescent
boys, local and state militias provided an opportunity to engage in
military service even sooner. Both slave patrols and militias permitted
and sometimes required sixteen-year-old-boys to sign up. Some boys
joined military groups at still younger ages.[73]

Virginian Benjamin Fleet, who was only fourteen years old at the
onset of the war, immediately began training in a "military class"
held at his local school. Ben already had a gun, but he acquired a new
knife, "a splendid weapon," as he described it in his diary. He joined
a local militia company for "home defence," served as a scout for his
district, took part in searches for suspected abolitionists and runaway
slaves, and at one point even single-handedly detained a deserter from
the Confederate Army. Yet young Ben still wished to join the army
like his older brother, Fred, with whom he had earlier quarreled over
secession. Knowing the dangers of military service did not dampen
his ardor; even after learning that a seventeen-year-old neighbor had

been killed in his second day of service when "a ball went through his arm & thru his neck, broke both & he died instantly," Ben still longed to enlist. He chafed at the restrictions of his youthful age and small size, which prevented him from being "in the Service of my Country" until 1864, when the Confederacy reduced the minimum age of military service from eighteen to seventeen. On his seventeenth birthday in September 1863, he regretfully recorded: "Can't help wishing that I was born an year sooner & then I wd: be in the Army." Although only 110 pounds, he added, he was "pretty strong."[74]

By the end of the year Ben was "resolved . . . to go with [John S. Mosby] in the summer." Ben's determination to join "the gallant Mosby" as one of Mosby's Rangers, who were known for their daring raids and guerrilla tactics, indicated how thoroughly committed he had become to the Southern Confederacy, but it ultimately proved disastrous. On February 29, 1864, shortly after the Confederate government adjusted the age of enrollment, Ben exuberantly informed his friend William Taliaferro that he had purchased "a splendid Canadian horse" to ride to war and that William should address future correspondence "somewhere in the Army of Northern Virginia, Col. Mosby's Command." Two days later, Ben was dead. His bereaved father recorded his son's death in the family Bible:

> Benjamin R. Fleet was murdered by the Yankees on Wednesday 2nd March 1864 in King Wm Co: near Mr. Anderson Scott's, whither he had gone as a Scout, where he met the Advance Guard of the Enemy dressed in Confederate Uniform, and was killed by them. Aged 17 yrs, 5 months & 1 day.[75]

Despite the danger, white adolescent boys in the Civil War South were enthusiastic about joining the Confederate Army. As one historian has observed, "underage boys . . . knew instinctively that military service . . . was an opportunity to manhood, freedom, and glory they could not reject."[76]

Reflecting both the significance of military service and the frequency of underage soldiering, Evelyn Ward recalled a time when she

and her family met a "little fellow dressed in a blue uniform" who
turned out to be a member of a local Virginia unit, the Westmoreland
Blues:

> "What are you doing with the Westmoreland Blues?" my
> Mother asked. "I'm one of 'em, Ma'am," he answered proudly.
> "What! You! You are nothing but a child." "I'm fo'teen, Ma'am."
> "You? Fourteen?" answered my Mother. "You don't look it."
> "Yes," he said regretfully, "I'm little, but I am tall enough to
> stick a Yankee in his breadbasket." "Oh!" cried mamma, "you
> horrid little creature!" The boy grinned as though to say, "Yes,
> you are a woman, and that is the way you should feel. But I am
> a man."[77]

Older sons in plain-folk families found that military service
offered economic mobility as well as manly status. Among small-
slaveholding and nonslaveholding families, teenage sons often served
as substitutes for their fathers. In the South Carolina up-country, for
example, sixteen-year-old Warren Pursley took his father's place in the
army so that the older man could continue to farm corn and wheat to
support the other children in the family, including nine-year-old Martha. In situations like these, race, age, class, and gender combined to
offer white male adolescents unparalleled opportunities to claim new
status and privilege. As one Floridian recalled, "Those were halcyon
days for boys."[78]

Eager to enlist, many adolescent boys either overcame their parents' objections or simply ran away from home in order to join the
army. Generational as well as gender differences came to the forefront
as white Southerners took sides in sectional conflict. Amy Murrell
Taylor's study of "divided families" in the border South suggests a
common pattern in which Unionist fathers tried in vain to dampen
their Confederate sons' ardor for secession and war. Civil War diaries and memoirs offer many variations of this generational conflict,
even in families united in Confederate sympathies. In Virginia one
eighteen-year-old youth claimed adult independence by enlisting

against his father's wishes. The tale, which circulated widely among the neighbors, was a thorough coming-of-age drama. It began when the young man announced, "Father, you know I am eighteen. I am going into the army." At first, as one neighbor girl recorded the story, "his father fumed and blustered. He 'would hear none of such nonsense.' He bade his wife get 'the Boy's' clothes ready" for college, not for war. But the young man persisted, saying, "'But, Father, you know I am not going [to school]. I am going to join the army.'" The father was forced to relent and to concede his son's adult ability to make decisions about his own life: "Poor old man! He knew 'the Boy' was right."[79]

A similar dynamic sometimes emerged between mothers and sons. In Kate Stone's household, her brothers' eagerness to join the Confederate Army and her mother's reluctance to permit them to do so caused ongoing tension. While Mrs. Stone permitted the older boys to join the army, the younger boys remained at home, picking fights with neighbor boys to vent their frustration. Kate highlighted the importance of both gender and generation when she complained that her seventeen-year-old brother, Johnny, was "in a dreadful humor. . . . Boys of Johnny's age," she observed, "are generally self-willed and disobedient."[80]

While boys were more inclined to oppose their parents' wishes than girls, adolescent girls occasionally also challenged parental, even paternal, authority. Eliza Frances Andrews, for example, secretly sewed a Confederate flag in her father's Unionist household and often spoiled his dinner by relaying war news—complete with her violently anti-Yankee sentiments—at suppertime. "Poor, dear, old father," she reflected late in the war, "my conscience hurts me to think how I have disobeyed him and gone against his wishes ever since the war began."[81]

Girls' rebellion was less successful than boys', however, in large part because autonomy and independence squared with Southern notions of manhood and mastery while they conflicted with Southern ideals of womanhood, which revolved around dependence and

submissiveness. Louisianan Sarah Morgan used her diary as an out-
let for her frustration with her limited role in the conflict. Denied
even the option of nursing ailing soldiers, twenty-one-year-old Sarah
demanded, "What is the use of all these worthless women, in war
times?" adding plaintively, "Why was I not a man?"[82]

Unable to participate directly in the war effort, teenage girls and
young women nonetheless kept close tabs on what Georgia resident
Anna Maria Green called "the great national events that are now
transpiring." Writing from "the quiet of Glen Alpine," her family's
up-country plantation, in 1862, Virginian Sally Munford described
herself and her family as "completely excluded from all this commotion." Nonetheless Sally and her sisters kept abreast of developments
by reading the newspapers. Although the girls spent their time "with
our books and writing," their thoughts were occupied differently.
"Our minds are so completely absorbed in the war," she explained,
"that we think of nothing beyond the arrival of the mail, and the news
which the papers may contain." Over and over again, girls indicated
that the coming of the Civil War had a profound impact on their
outlook on life. "The war and public matters occupy my thoughts so
much," wrote seventeen-year-old Louisianan Sarah Wadley in 1862,
"that I scarcely think of noting down the events of our quiet life."[83]

Even schoolgirls were caught up in the excitement. Although
some girls' academies were converted into hospitals, abandoned in the
face of approaching troops, or closed for lack of funds, many young
women continued to attend school during the war. Raleigh, North
Carolina's St. Mary's School, for instance, operated for the duration
of the war. Like other academies, the school was a popular choice
for parents who hoped to spare their daughters the hardships of war.
Attending boarding school, however, did not exempt young women
from the changes wrought by the war. At many schools, as at Athens, Georgia's Lucy Cobb Institute, "the progress of the war was the
main topic of conversation." Atlanta resident Sallie Clayton claimed
that "war news" was one of the most important things she learned at
the coeducational school she attended. From his perch on the fence

rail next door to the Presbyterian church where classes were held, the neighbor boy, five-year-old Willie Williams, read aloud from the newspaper each morning before the bell sounded to call the pupils to their places.[84]

Some teachers, capitalizing on girls' interest in war news, made the secession crisis and the progress of the war topics for student compositions. Even when their teachers tried to keep them to their lessons, Civil War–era schoolgirls persisted in their political interests; at schools in New Orleans, students drew secession flags in their books. While parents may have sent their daughters to school to protect them from the ravages of war, they could not isolate them from the politicization of the era. As a student at Missouri's Danville Female Academy expressed it, "During the War we had some very exciting times for school girls."[85]

Slave children, too, responded to the war according to their gender. Masculinity, adolescence, and slavery all factored into older slave boys' responses to the "exciting times." African-American young men, much like their white counterparts, regarded military service as an important coming-of-age ritual. For black adolescents who were denied the usual routes to manhood such as legal marriage, paid work, and political activity, military service may have been even more important than for white youth. This may explain why Wesley, the teenage slave selected to accompany Kate Stone's brother Will to the front in 1861, was "very proud of the honor." When Wesley "promised faithfully to do his best" to serve his young master, he may have seen an opportunity to enact adult manhood even within the constraints of slavery and the Confederate Army.[86]

Other older slave boys chose to escape to Union lines and fight in the Union Army. Kentuckian John Fields, who was fifteen years old when the Emancipation Proclamation was enacted, ran away with his brother to join the Union Army. Although his brother joined up, John was judged "too young" and was turned away. Determined to enlist, the teenager crossed the state line into Indiana and attempted to enlist three more times—in Evansville, Terre Haute, and Indianapolis—but in vain. John's persistence reflected the multiple meanings of military service for black youth: adulthood, masculinity, and freedom. In Tennessee, when a seventeen-year-old youth prepared to run away to join the Union Army, his mistress appealed to him to remain, reminding him of how she had nursed him through a serious illness. "And now," she charged, "you are fighting me!" The boy's response indicated that he viewed the Civil War as a war to end slavery, and that he intended to be a part of it. "I ain't fighting you," he told his mistress. "I'm fighting to get free."[87]

Whether they spent the wars years seeing "Yankees, run-away niggers, and booger-bears" in every shadow or "fighting to get free," children in the Civil War South were thoroughly politicized. Southern children were, in historian James Marten's phrase, "little politicians" who enthusiastically engaged the great issues of the day: slavery, secession, and the Civil War. Indeed, the children of the Confederacy had little choice but to become politically conscious and militarily informed, for the war's progress would affect every aspect of their lives.[88]

CHAPTER THREE

Play and Work

CONTINUITY AND CHANGE IN THE CONFEDERATE SOUTH

In the summer of 1862 a Confederate woman reported eavesdropping on two young girls engaged in "playing ladies." "Good morning, ma'am," said the first girl. "How are you today?"

"I don't feel very well this morning, her four-year-old playmate responded, adding, "*All my niggers have run away and left me.*"[1]

The girls' play reflected both their accustomed privileges as elite white females and the new circumstances brought by the war. At the same time the girls' reference to runaway slaves indicated the greater importance of work for all Southern children in the new social order.

Southern children's work and play exhibited both continuity and change during the upheavals of the Civil War era. In their play, children adapted old patterns to new situations, as when one young girl from a slaveholding family, deprived of her dolls by the dislocations of the war, crafted new lady dolls from flowers and used nuts to design brown "mammies" to serve them. Children also used play to engage with the most pressing political and military issues of their time. Virginia mother Margaret Junkin Preston observed that her children's games were "almost wholly of a military character."[2] Play, however, did not encompass all of children's daily activities. For enslaved and plain-folk children, work had always been a part of life.

The demands of wartime made productive labor more important for these traditional workers while also drawing privileged white children into the world of work, often for the first time. Thus even as children's play reinforced traditional divisions of race, class, gender, and status, children's work crossed these boundaries and became universal in the Civil War era.

Both before and during the war, Southern children's play and work helped socialize them into their assigned status as well as prepare them for their adult roles. During the war years, however, both play and work acquired new meanings. Play allowed children to grapple with the realities of war while children's work responsibilities increased under the exigencies of wartime. Thus play and work—already important in children's lives—took on added importance during the Civil War.

The Civil War had a profound impact on Southern children's play. In the occupied town of Lexington, Virginia, Margaret Junkin Preston's two young sons, four-year-old George and two-year-old Herbert, created an entirely new set of role-playing games reflecting the military conflict. George dressed himself up as a soldier, with a stick for a sword, and solemnly bade his mother farewell "with entire gravity," explaining that "his furlough is out and he must go to his regiment again." The youngster also built hospitals out of blocks, turned chairs into ambulances, and carefully tended rag dolls "laid up in bed as sick and wounded soldiers." Meanwhile George's younger brother, Herbert, who was just learning to speak, joined in the older boy's games and confided to his mother that he killed "Lankees." Both boys played with "paper soldiers" who marched, drilled, fought, took prisoners, and even attended balls with their "ladies"—though George's shout of "The enemy—the Yankees—they are coming! Your guns! Your guns!" interrupted the celebration, and the soldiers were rushed off to battle "in hot haste," leaving the paper ladies behind. "It is amazing, and sorrowful too, to see how the language, operations, &c. of war are understood and imitated by the children," remarked the boys' mother. "Almost their entire set of plays have reference to a state of war."[3]

As James Marten observes in his study of children during the Civil War era, "one of the most basic responses to the politically charged and sometimes dangerous war environment was to mimic the responses of their elders." Children in many times and places have incorporated military conflict and mock violence into their play. According to Marten, "children easily adapt war into their play and development because they accept it as just another trauma among childhood's normal stresses and strains." For very young children, the destruction of war also may dovetail with a "destructive" phase of development and trigger a "primitive excitement" that results in either mock or real violence. Contemporary studies of children and trauma also indicate that children use play to manage their anxieties.[4] Thus for Southern children play was a natural and perhaps even necessary response to the turmoil of the Civil War. Southern children's wartime play enabled them to express their political sensibilities during a period of conflict, to reestablish—or reinvent—their roles in a social order under siege, and to reduce their sense of vulnerability amid the violence of wartime.

Children's play serves both psychological and social purposes. An indispensable part of children's cognitive development, it is also an important part of the process by which children are socialized into their expected roles. In the Old South all children engaged in play, and certain types of play were common to all children. But children's play also reflected their identity and status, and thus childish amusements carried social significance as they reinforced or undermined the social order of slave society. Once the South seceded and the war began, children's play acquired new dimensions and importance: it became a way for children to express their political allegiances. Southern children continued to mimic adult behavior and to mirror the world around them in their play, but they also used play to manage their anxieties about the war, exerting the control in their leisure activities that they did not have in their daily lives.

Play can include structured activities, such as games with clear rules, and unstructured activities, such as roaming the woods and fields. Play can also be either competitive, with winners and losers, or cooperative, advancing group goals. Play can involve toys, such as dolls or trucks, or it can involve interacting with the natural environment, including plants and animals. Finally, play can allow children to practice for adulthood in role-playing games, such as "playing house" or "playing soldiers." Role-playing games like these would acquire additional importance during the Civil War, when girls and boys practiced gender-specific responses to military conflict by protecting their make-believe families and fighting mock battles.

Popular children's games (structured play) in the slaveholding South included marbles and mumblety-peg, both of which were games in which participants competed for prizes, as well as such games as Blind Man's Buff, Fox and Geese, Hide and Seek, Capture the Flag, and I Spy, which were similarly competitive though more active games involving physical and mental challenges (finding playmates by touch, running faster or hiding better than one's peers, using logic to solve problems). Other popular games included horseshoes, hopscotch, jump rope, and a wide assortment of ball games. Such games—many of them still popular today—allow children to develop physically and mentally and prepare them for a competitive society in which adults vie for social position and work for material goods. Texan Charles Nagel experienced his "first conscious feeling of personal triumph" when playing a game called Black Man's Out, in which players on one team attempt to reach the opposite team's base without being tagged out by a member of the opposing team. As "a fast runner and a good dodger," the youngster excelled at this game of speed and agility.[5] Although Nagel did not call attention to the game's name in his memoirs, calling the losing player a "black man" in a game played by an all-white group of boys in a nonslaveholding community reflected the pervasiveness of white supremacy in the slaveholding South. In the Civil War era this would become a dominant theme in white children's play.

Although Southern children played a wide variety of games, they engaged in more unstructured than structured play, interacting with

the natural environment, inventing their own games, and construct-
ing their own toys. Like Marylander Ernest Wardwell, most Southern
children were "familiar with every brook and stream within a five
mile radius"—and with the woods and fields as well. Virginia farmer's
daughter Evelyn Ward recalled that she and her siblings, often accompanied by the children of the family's slaves, spent their free time
frolicking in the woods and streams, catching minnows, gathering
berries and flowers, and swinging on grapevines. Annie Burton, a
young slave child who lived on a plantation with thirteen other slave
children and ten white ones, reported that she and her "little white
and black companions" spent their days "roaming about from plantation to plantation." Charles Nagel, the son of German immigrants to
frontier Texas, reminisced: "Nature was wild, and we were getting out
of it all the fun it offered." Emily Dixon, a former slave in Mississippi
who was interviewed in the 1930s about her early life, emphasized
the importance of nature to nineteenth-century Southern children's
play when she demanded, "Did yo' eber take time ter think jist what
a hickory-nut tree is to chillun?" Without waiting for a reply from the
interviewer, she continued: "Deir's de shade ter play under, de tree ter
climb, de big limbs ter hang swings from, de leaves ter pin tergether
wid pine straw ter make dresses an' hats, de nuts ter eat. . . . Den
yo' can hid' hind de trunks in playin' hide an' seek, or hab hit fer de
base." She concluded, "I hab my fun under de ole hickory-nut tree."
Southern children were truly, as one slave boy expressed it, "chillun
o' nature."[6]

Southern children of all backgrounds commonly made playthings
from found objects. One slave boy remembered playing "horse" with
a tree limb while a slave girl recalled using acorns to fashion tiny
cups and saucers for tea parties. Slave girls and boys alike used rags,
clay, and string to make their own balls, marbles, and dolls. Although
white children were more likely to have ready-made toys, they too
made frequent mention of found or homemade toys. Charles Nagel
and his brothers used their pocketknives to good effect, whittling
everything from homemade baseball bats to bows and arrows. Evelyn

Ward and her siblings constructed "rag babies," carved chestnut whistles, wove "dearly prized" rings from horsehair, and used mosses to construct "fairy cups." Georgia slave John Van Hook was typical in finding entertainment outdoors and making his own toys, if atypical in his engineering prowess, when he carved soapstone to make "a little toy mill," powered by a local stream, "that worked just fine."[7]

Southern children's play emphasized imagination and independence. As former Mississippi slave Salem Powell explained: "We made up de things us played an' what us played wid."[8] The self-contained nature of children's leisure activities enabled them to design their own games without adult guidance, and the prominence of imagination in their play allowed them to integrate new themes easily. Once the Civil War began, the importance of these qualities became increasingly apparent as Southern children created new games revolving around the Civil War and its impact on social relationships.

Children from all levels of Southern society engaged in similar types of play, enjoying the outdoors, creating their own games, and making their own toys. Children of different social backgrounds also played together. Particularly before age ten or so, when work responsibilities increased for certain groups of children, Southern children played with one another regardless of race, class, gender, or status. Evelyn Ward recalled that "all the little fry, white and black" on her family's Virginia farm engaged in both structured and unstructured play. Boys and girls also played together, fishing and swimming in the summer or sledding and skating in the winter. And "poor white" and enslaved black children also became "regular playmates," roaming the woods, fields, and streams in search of climbing trees and grapevine swings, interesting flowers and insects, and edible nuts, berries, and roots. Sarah Pamela Williams, who hailed from a nonslaveholding white family, did not distinguish by race, class, gender, or status when she recalled that "as children, we enjoyed many simple pleasures, such as fishing, fruit harvests, excursions into the woods, boating and swimming."[9]

Although children of varying statuses often played together, their play was not necessarily egalitarian. Rather, children's play served as

Southern children took advantage of their rural surroundings in their play and enjoyed making pets and playmates out of farm animals. Many children in the slaveholding South engaged in leisure activities that included different races, genders, and generations. Such play often reinforced the hierarchies of slaveholding society rather than mitigating them, however. In this midcentury lithograph by Currier & Ives, a black man plays a banjo while an African-American boy dances. A white farmer and two children, a white girl and an infant, look on while pets and livestock indicate the rural setting. In this image the stereotypical imagery of the two African-American figures as well as their role as entertainment for white onlookers indicates prevailing notions of black inferiority. (*Library of Congress*)

yet another marker of social identity in the slaveholding South. This was most apparent in role-playing games, in which children practiced their adult roles and enacted their social status. As Wilma King has concluded in her analysis of slave children's play, "games that required decisions about who filled a specific role were more open to race, gender, and age discrimination than games of chance or skill." This was true for free children as well. Southern children's role-playing games highlighted gender roles, racial hierarchies, class differences, and the significance of being slave or free, thus reflecting and reinforcing the social hierarchies of slaveholding society.[10] When the Civil War threatened the social order, Southern children both reaffirmed and challenged the norms of slaveholding society in their play.

While girls and boys often engaged in similar unstructured outdoor activities, they also played gender-specific games in sex-segregated groups, reflecting their awareness of their different futures. As Charles Nagel put it, "the girls and the boys each followed their own kinds of play." While boys played such competitive, rowdy games as "soldiers" and "Injuns" or "hoss" (horse) and "wagoner," for instance, girls were more likely to play cooperative, sedate games such as "playing house" or "playing church." Such gender differences were apparent for both white and black children, whether they played together or separately. Girls of both races and all ages pretended to keep house, cook food, serve meals, and care for children. Fanny Fox, the three-year-old daughter of wealthy slaveholders, and her seven-year-old slave attendant, Adelaide, together held tea parties and played with dolls. Candis Goodwin and her fellow enslaved playmates used pine needles of different colors to designate a "play house" and its lawn. One slave girl from Arkansas remembered that she and her master's daughter, at the ages of six and seven, had "a play house back of the fire-place chimney" where they played with handmade dolls or acted out mock church services.[11]

Boys were more likely to spend their leisure time hunting or fishing. Lumberjack's son Ernest Wardwell learned to shoot squirrels and catch trout at an early age; "although but a boy," he boasted, he was "considered an expert" fisherman. Similarly John Van Hook, who grew up as a slave in Georgia, reminisced at length about "gigging" fish and proudly recalled the day he landed "a big old fighting fish" that measured "2 feet and 6 inches long." Catching this fish was especially gratifying, he explained, because while smaller fish were "plentiful and easy to catch . . . they did not give you the battle that a salmon or a red horse could put up and that was what it took to make fishing fun."[12]

Girls' play, then, prepared them for a life of domestic service while boys' play prepared them for a life of outdoor activity. In addition,

Play reinforced gender roles as well as racial hierarchies. When girls played with dolls, they practiced for domestic responsibilities in child care and home production. Dolls might be commercially produced, with wax or porcelain hands, feet, and heads, or homemade from rags, cornhusks, and clay. In this antebellum daguerreotype, a well-dressed little girl poses with an expensive doll. *(Library of Congress)*

while girls' play tended to emphasize cooperation, boys' play centered on competition. Thus girls practiced for relationships while boys prepared for achievement.

Children's play also reflected distinctions of race and class. While girls of all ages, races, and classes engaged in domestic play, certain types of play were reserved for elite white girls. Only planter-class girls reported playing "Ladies go a visiting," for instance, a game in which well-to-do girls imitated their elders in paying social calls on one another. Moreover when elite and nonelite girls played together, markers of social status were apparent in the roles each individual assumed. For instance, when the slave girl Adeline "played church" with her master's daughter, "Miss Fannie was the preacher and I was the audience." Social hierarchies also shaped the material culture of girlhood. While both free white and enslaved black girls played with dolls, for example, the former were much more likely than the latter to have expensive dolls with porcelain or wax heads, hands, and feet rather than simple homemade dolls constructed from rags and corncobs. Free black and nonslaveholding white girls were also unlikely to have the range of toys available to elite white girls. Four-year-old Fanny Fox's "very pretty doll" sported an elaborate dress of "dotted white Swiss muslin *tucked*, over a blue cambric skirt," and her mother promised to sew "some black morocco shoes & a pretty black silk cape" to complete the doll's ensemble. In 1861 plantation mistress Gertrude Thomas's three-year-old daughter Mary Bell received "a dining sett of china," "a sett of parlour furniture," and "a wooden tea sett" for Christmas, among other gifts.[13] Planter-class parents spared no expense in furnishing their daughters with material goods that demonstrated their elevated social status as well as their expected gender role, even in the midst of the Civil War.

Boys' toys also reflected social differences. The case of two Georgia boys, both between the ages of eight and ten, is instructive. Turner Thomas, the son of slaveholders, received a pistol, a knife, and a windup horse-drawn buggy as Christmas gifts while his enslaved counterpart, John Van Hook, fashioned his own rifles, pistols, and "all sorts of nice playthings" out of soapstone.[14] Both boys enjoyed play with objects representing mastery or even violence, the hallmarks of masculinity in the slaveholding South, yet their access to those objects varied according to their socioeconomic status. Significantly, too, toy guns could be fashioned out of virtually anything. During the Civil War, boys' keen interest in playing with guns became a near obsession.

Boys' play also reinforced racial hierarchies and legal status. When white and black boys played horse-and-wagon games, for instance, white boys were the riders or drivers while blacks were the "two-legged horses." Such play reflected not only racial subordination but also the realities of slave society, since the white boys frequently carried whips. One master-class boy relished cracking the whip "over the backs, and sometimes *on* the backs," of his slave steeds. Other games displaying slaveholding white boys' dominance over enslaved black boys included Soldiers and Indians, in which "de whites was de soldiers an' . . . de slave boys was de Injuns," who were vanquished by the white boys, who carried wooden guns and pretended to first shoot, and then scalp, their captives. During the Civil War, in games like Confederates and Yankees, scenarios of dominance and submission, complete with acts of mock violence, would become increasingly common in interracial play.[15]

Slave children's play with each other also reflected their awareness of their inferior legal status and vulnerability to sale, injury, and death. Slave children held mock slave auctions in which older children "sold" younger children to the highest bidder and staged mock funerals complete with handmade hearses, make-believe horses, and "last respects." Some slaves played a whipping game called Hide the Switch, in which players sought a concealed switch and the finder claimed the right to use it on the other participants if they did not successfully evade the switch wielder. Eda Harper from Arkansas explained, "if you found it, the others all run to keep from bein' hit." A variant on this game known as Warm Jacket, which boys played in both racially integrated and all-black groups, involved boys whipping one another until the pain became unbearable.[16] Given slave children's keen and early awareness of the grief and violence inherent in the system of slavery, it is small wonder that during the Civil War they adopted pro-Union sentiments and expressed them in their play.

In addition to reflecting the hierarchies of slaveholding society and children's awareness of the difficulties of life as a slave, slave children's leisure activities also enabled them to maintain a sense of self-worth, resist slavery, and protest enslavement. In his history of childhood, Steven Mintz claims that "play instilled a sense of self-worth that was vital in resisting slavery's humiliations" by allowing slave youth to demonstrate their skills and strength both to themselves and to the white children they served. As Felix Heywood expressed it, "we was stronger and knowed how to play" competitive games that "white children's didn't."[17]

Even before the Civil War, then, slave children challenged prevailing racial hierarchies through their play. One way to do this was by co-opting white children's pursuits. In Mississippi, Ebenezer Brown and another slave boy were "whup'ed" for shooting "china berries" from a hand-fashioned popgun. Although in later life the youngster believed that he and his playmate were punished because they "made de shots hit de udder chaps," his master may also have objected to slaves assuming the white privilege of sportsmanship, even in play. Similarly, fellow Mississippian Ann Drake and her enslaved companions subverted the social order when they dressed in their mothers' clothing (perhaps handed down from the mistress) "an' play lak we wus fine ladies," complete with make-believe parasols constructed of broken shrubbery.[18]

Slave children's play offered youngsters practice in subtle forms of daily resistance common to adult slaves: slowing the work pace, breaking tools, pilfering food, and so on. Annie Burton recalled that she and her fellow slave playmates helped themselves to sweet potatoes, peanuts, sugar cane, and corn in the course of their explorations "from plantation to plantation" as well as plundering the supplies of food they were supposed to deliver to the adult slaves working in the field. Barney Alford chased the chickens on his plantation and nearly set the tail of one of the horses on fire before being intercepted by the overseer. Emmaline Sturgis and her younger sister stole away from the fields to play in the woods. Slave children not only engaged in their own acts of daily resistance but also aided and abetted adult slaves who subtly undermined slaveowners' authority. Slave boys in Mississippi stretched grapevines across the road to trip up the "paddyrollers," white men who patrolled the roads for slaves who left their plantations without permission. And Richard Carruthers served as a sort of singing lookout for the adult slaves on his Texas plantation. In the overseer's absence, when the adult slaves slowed their work pace, young Richard disguised rebellion as play when he sang to warn the older slaves of the overseer's return to the fields.[19]

Slave children used music to protest slavery as well as to undermine productivity. Although white and black children often sang the same tunes, the specific songs that the slave boy Elias Thomas mentioned—"Crossin' over Jordan" and "Bound for the Promised Land"—were hopeful spirituals that promised a better life in the next world and hinted at slaves' desire for freedom in this one. Evelyn Ward's black nursemaid, Amy, taught her young charges "darky hymns." One such spiritual was a thinly disguised paean to emancipation, substituting the word "home" for "freedom":

> Little Chillun, you'd better believe,
> 'Tis a long time wagging up the cross-roads.
>
> Little Chillun, you'd better believe,
> 'Tis a long time wagging up the cross-roads,
> We'll go home by'm bye!

Many years later the meaning of this song remained a mystery to Evelyn. "As for the hymn beginning 'Little Chillun,'" she wrote in her memoirs, "I can't yet think what it did mean, but it sang beautifully." One can only imagine the satisfaction the teenage slave girl must have taken in teaching white youngsters such subversive verses.[20]

Black children also sang openly rebellious songs in their own peer groups. One slave child recalled singing a tune that protested slavery and damned slaveholders to everlasting punishment:

> My old mistress promised me,
> Before she dies she would set me free.
> Now she's dead and gone to hell.
> I hope the devil will burn her well.

Of course children also sang purely for pleasure. North Carolina slave youngster Elias Thomas remembered having "a good time in general . . . laughing, working and singing." Singing affirmed slaves' basic humanity and lightened their burdens—psychological as well as physical.[21]

*

Once the Civil War began, children's singing acquired new political significance. "Shouting" and "hollering" were common forms of political participation for mid-nineteenth-century adults as well as popular activities for children of all ages. Thus verbal expression—including but not limited to song—was one of the most frequent and important ways for children to express their political views.

Children in the Confederate South expressed their political loyalties in both popular and original song. While white children sang pro-Confederate songs such as "Bonnie Blue Flag," "Maryland, My Maryland," and, of course, "Dixie," slave children gleefully caroled out the lyrics of popular anti-Confederate songs such as "Hang Jeff Davis to a Sour Apple Tree." They also composed pro-Union songs of their own. As one slave girl explained, "De young folks used to make up a heep o' songs, den."[22]

Some songs sung by slaves during the Civil War combined antebellum millennialism with contemporary politics. In Georgetown, South Carolina, slave children joined adults in singing an anti-slavery spiritual:

> We'll fight for liberty
> Till de Lord shall call us home;
> We'll soon be free
> Till de Lord shall call us home.

One fifteen-year-old slave boy who heard the song and then ran away to join the Union Army explained that, now that the Civil War had begun, slaves no longer depended entirely on divine intervention: "'De Lord' meant for say de Yankees."[23]

Other wartime songs were completely new and entirely secular. Frank Patterson, born a slave in North Carolina in 1850, recalled several pro-Union songs when he was interviewed in the 1930s, including one with the martial lyrics:

Here's my little gun
His name is number one
Four and five rebels
We'll slay 'em as they come[24]

Southern children used music to incorporate political rivalries into their play. Black and white children sometimes engaged in what amounted to musical warfare, as revealed in an anecdote related by Mississippi slave Susan Snow many decades after the Civil War. "I's gwine tell dis story on myse'f," she began:

De white chillum was a-singin' dis song:

Jeff Davis, long an' slim,
Whupped old Abe wid a hick'ry limb.

Jeff Davis is a wise man, Lincoln is a fool,
Jeff Davis rides a gray, an' Lincoln rides a mule.

I was mad anyway, so I hopped up an' sung dis one:

Old Gen'l Pope had a shot gun,
Filled it full o' gum,
Killed 'em as dey come.

Called a Union band,
Make de rebels un'erstan'
To leave de lan',
Submit to Abraham.

Just as they had used music to protest slavery before the war, slave children now used music to express their support for Lincoln and the Union.[25]

Slaveholders, who had often overlooked the subversive features of slave children's play, fully comprehended the political implications of song in the Civil War South. On Eda Harper's Mississippi plantation, the master required the slave children to sing the Confederate anthem, "Dixie," sometimes for hours at a time. "I tell you I don't like it *now*," she exclaimed, more than sixty years later. "But have mercy! He make us sing it."[26]

Most slave children, who learned the importance of secrecy early in life, limited their subversive play or practiced it in secret. Failing to do so could bring trouble. Susan Snow, who was eleven years old when the war broke out, did not realize that the adults had been singing pro-Union songs "in dey sleeves," or in secret. Her mistress was standing nearby when young Susan expressed her loyalties in song. "She grabbed up de broom an' laid it on me," Susan recalled, adding, "She made *me* submit. I caught de feathers, don't you forgit it." Like other slave children, Susan Snow learned the importance of hiding her true feelings from whites.[27]

Confederate children expressed their political sympathies more openly. In April 1861, when the presence of Union troops called up in response to the firing on Fort Sumter instigated a riot in Baltimore, the pro-Confederate mob of "crazy men and boys" hurled "fearful oaths" as well as "missiles of all kinds" at the soldiers. Teenagers Ernest Wardwell and Henry Cook, though initially intimidated, soon "caught the frenzy and became as noisy as the others." "We boys . . . shouted imprecations with the best of them," Ernest wrote in his memoirs.[28]

Girls as well as boys raised their voices in support of the Southern Confederacy. Twenty-year-old Lucy Buck and her younger sisters and female cousins made up a "merry party" as they rode in an open wagon across a contested region of Virginia in 1862, cheering for Confederate leaders, singing "traitorous songs" such as "Maryland" at the top of their lungs, and punctuating the whole with "gleeful burst[s] of laughter" in the face of danger. In the occupied town of Vicksburg, Mississippi, seventeen-year-old Victoria Batchelor took revenge on the local Union soldiers by inviting them to call on her and then singing "Dixie" to them.[29]

Confederate children in occupied cities often used music and other forms of vocal play to express their Confederate sympathies and challenge federal control. When Union General Benjamin Butler (a Southerner) and his troops occupied New Orleans in 1862, for example, children retaliated by singing the Confederate song "Bonnie Blue Flag" in his presence. Children also used wordplay to criticize Union policies regarding prisoners of war. After his father was taken prisoner, young Jeff Davis entertained the women at his Savannah hotel with his rebellious play. Mounting a Newfoundland dog, he brandished a switch in one hand and held a bridle in the other while shouting "Bully for Jeff! Bully for Jeff!"[30]

Just as slaveholders comprehended the political significance of slave children's wartime play, Union officials recognized the rebelliousness of Confederate children's play, including singing and shouting. In South Carolina, after hearing a child singing a pro-Confederate song to the tune of "Yankee Doodle," one Union officer pondered, "How can we expect to restore the Union when even the children hate us so?" Sharing this officer's concerns, some Union soldiers punished Confederate children for their vocal rebelliousness. In Winchester, Virginia, Cornelia Peake McDonald was incensed that Union officers reportedly employed spies to prevent children from hollering in support of Jefferson Davis. In New Orleans, schoolchildren reportedly were beaten for cheering for Davis, while in Frankfort, Kentucky, a fourteen-year-old boy allegedly was shot for a similar offense.[31]

Play was a potent weapon in the battle of wills between Union soldiers and Confederate children. In Baltimore, federal officers found it difficult to maintain loyalty when little girls insisted on dressing their dolls in Confederate colors. In Winchester, Virginia, occupying soldiers attempted to maintain order by preventing young children from playing with Confederate flags. In South Carolina a youngster gained approval from the adults around him when he screwed up his face in a gruesome imitation of General Benjamin Butler. Seemingly innocent children's playthings could serve the Southern Confederacy in unexpected ways; at least one Southern family used a doll's hollow china head to smuggle medicine behind Confederate lines.[32]

In Winchester, Virginia, captured by Union forces in 1862, the play of Cornelia Peake McDonald's two oldest sons—fourteen-year-old Harry and thirteen-year-old Allan—exemplified Confederate children's rebellious play. Harry and Allan engaged in "seizures of arms on the sly," assembled their own "repository" of swords and pistols in the attic, and caused an explosion by building and firing homemade guns and cannons. Frustrated by their mother's refusal to allow them to join the Confederate Army, the boys begged permission to observe the town's decisive battle firsthand. After spending all day at the battlefield, they returned home "very grave and sorrowful" at the bloodshed they had witnessed, and "disappointed, too," at the Confederate troops' loss and retreat. Thereafter the boys engaged in a battle of wills with the occupying Union troops. On one occasion they joined a mob of boys throwing snowballs at Union soldiers; another time the pair recruited their younger brother, ten-year-old Kenneth, to stage a mock battle in front of their house while soldiers conducted a search of the residence. The three McDonald boys fought "two against one"; when one attacked, two retreated. When a curious soldier paused to inquire why two ran from one, the retreating boys pointedly replied: "We are obliged to run, we are the Yankees." "I have to be constantly on the watch for fear of my boys doing something to provoke the persecution of the Yankees," the boys' mother remarked.[33]

Like other children in the Civil War South, the McDonald boys used play to express their political views. They also engaged in perhaps the most universally popular form of wartime play: playing soldier. According to James Marten's study of children during the Civil War, "one of the most ubiquitous forms of play" was "playing army." This was clearly the case in the Civil War South. According to one "small boy's recollections of the Civil War," mock drilling was "where the small boy found the keenest enjoyment." George Robertson, who was only eight years old when the war began, explained: "While the soldiers were being drilled we had our company, too, and our flag. For guns we had pieces of plank cut in the shape of a gun and we had our full quota of officers, and Boys, we drilled." Boys of all ages and classes formed militias, drilled and marched, and engaged in mock battles. Some went further. In Union-occupied Winchester, Cornelia Peake

"Playing soldier" was a ubiquitous form of play in the Civil War South. In this 1862 *carte de visite*, a young boy is pictured wearing a military uniform, holding a crop, and resting one arm on a drum. *(Library of Congress)*

McDonald's two oldest sons, just entering their teens, built and fired a functional battery on top of the cistern "supplied . . . with guns they had manufactured out of musket barrels cut into lengths of eight or nine inches, and bored for a touch hole, then mounted on carriages of their own make."[34]

It may come as no surprise that boys would be eager to imitate their elders by playing soldier. After all, as Marylander Ernest Wardwell revealed in his memoirs, he and his playmates had played soldier even before the Civil War, sharpening sticks for spears, building snow forts, and carrying flannel pennants in imitation of "the knights of old." In the style of Napoleon, Ernest's particular hero, the adolescent and preadolescent boys staged elaborate battles for territory. After "the preliminaries of demanding surrender and being defied," Ernest and his companions "began the bombardment," finally "charging the garrison" and "placing our flag upon the demolished ruins." At the conclusion of each successful campaign, Ernest, the self-proclaimed captain, emerged victorious and empowered. "I felt indeed a hero," he recalled, "and medaled and promoted myself and officers with lavish hands."[35]

This teenager's recollections indicate the tremendous appeal of "playing soldier" for white boys, who could achieve manly independence through play several years before they might achieve it in reality. During the Civil War, however, Southern children of all backgrounds engaged in this quintessentially white male form of play. Perhaps most surprisingly, there are numerous recorded instances of black children—both boys and girls—pretending to be Confederate soldiers. In Charleston, for instance, according to one local paper, "a band of woolly headed juvenile darkies" engaged in "a lively marching and counter-marching . . . to the jolly strains of Dixie Land" while a North Carolina slave girl remembered beating tin pans and marching to another Confederate tune, "Wheeler's Cavalry." Much later in life, Kentucky slave Madison Brinn recalled his fierce desire to be a soldier. "I didn't care what side," he explained; "I jus' wants a gun and a hoss and be a sojer." When slave children pretend-drilled and played soldier, they imitated not simply adults but slaveholders. One young slave boy, only five years old when the war began, remembered watching his master drill with the local Confederate home guard. "When I got home, I tried to do like him."[36]

White girls too were caught up in the excitement, replacing peacetime play with "drilling, marching, [and] fighting." The students at Georgia's Wesleyan Female College formed a student "company" that held military drills. At the Atlanta Female Institute the schoolgirls not only practiced drills but engaged in "a drilling match" with the local cavalry—and won. Virginian Evelyn Ward attested that she and her sisters "learned to keep step beautifully" by imitating the men who drilled in her father's study. "We could shoulder arms, carry arms, right-about-face, guide right, and guide left, right wheel, left wheel, march, double-quick," she boasted, adding that the girls came to prefer drilling to their peacetime play. The appeal of pretending to engage in military conflict, then, appears to have been nearly universal in the Civil War South. As one Confederate mother wrote, "the children . . . are all soldiers here."[37]

Playing soldier both affirmed and challenged the established social order. As in the antebellum era, children in the Civil War South used play to practice adult roles. Such mimicry usually supported the social hierarchy of slaveholding society. Occasionally, however, either by valuing skill over status in competitive games or by reversing roles in playacting, children in the Old South subverted the social order. During the Civil War, when children of all backgrounds played soldier, they muted distinctions of race and gender. As in peacetime, children's play mirrored adult reality. The Civil War threatened the institution of slavery while the wartime absence of so many men forced white women to take on new responsibilities. Children's play reflected these wartime challenges to the social order. At the same time, however, children's play reaffirmed the status quo by reasserting social differences and reinforcing social hierarchies.

Although some historians have highlighted women's expanded responsibilities during the Civil War, in children's wartime play gender roles were often more exaggerated than in peacetime. White girls mimicked—and often joined—their brothers' military play, but they also engaged in other forms of political play that reflected their antebellum role as keepers of hearth and home—adapted for wartime. Confederate girls engaged in role-playing games in which their responsibility was to protect the family and preserve domestic harmony. Nannie Belle Maury's mother, for example, overheard the four-year-old sturdily defending her make-believe home and family with the words, "'Upon my word an' honour, Sir, there are no letters and papers in this trunk at all'"—using the precise words that her mother had used in a confrontation with a Union soldier a few weeks earlier. Several girls hid or buried their dolls while "play[ing] Yankee," defending their make-believe families from all-too-real threats.[38]

While elite girls played at being stalwart matrons, their male counterparts practiced being brave soldiers. In 1861 Gertrude Clanton Thomas of Georgia reported that her seven-year-old son, Turner, "already shows great military spirit" and spent a great deal of time riding his pony and "going through the different cavalry tactics." While Mrs. Thomas regarded this as an "amusing" pastime, her son clearly saw it as practice for adulthood. "He expresses himself as being anxious to engage in the war," she concluded, "only wishes he was large enough. . . ." While only older boys could translate this type of play-practice into actual military service, such activities affirmed both white male privilege and patriarchal responsibilities for protecting the family. Parents often encouraged such patterns by adjuring sons to act as "the man of the house" in their soldier-fathers' absence. Mrs. Thomas, for instance, whose husband was an officer in the Confederate cavalry, regarded "teaching my boys to be proud of their father's example" as a maternal imperative—a message that no doubt heightened the significance of military play for young Turner.[39]

Although black children and white girls also played soldier, they were not rehearsing for independent manhood in the same way that Turner Thomas was. This was reflected in the fact that in mock battles, slaves and girls were often cast in supportive or subordinate roles—as common soldiers rather than as high-ranking officers, for instance, or as captured Yankees submitting to Confederate forces. Evelyn Ward remembered that when she and her siblings "played soldier" with the slave children on her Virginia plantation, it was with "the whites as officers in the front rank, the blacks coming behind." The slave Candis Goodwin pronounced, "'Course de whites was always the 'Federates," who were routinely victorious over their black "Yankee" foe.[40]

White children probably found it reassuring to play games featuring conventional gender roles and unequal race relations. By recreating familiar settings and predictable relationships in their imaginary worlds, Confederate children may have reduced their anxieties about the tumultuous present and the unpredictable future. Slave children had a rather different experience. Interracial play in the slaveholding South had always incorporated themes of dominance and submission, but during the Civil War black and white children's play together became overtly violent. When Evelyn Ward, her family, and their house slaves were forced to take refuge in the home of another slave-holding family, the Shacklefords, the "Shackleford young people," who delighted in "pranks," entertained themselves by threatening to "shut up our little black Maria in a large screen and . . . press her flat." Although Evelyn's sisters came to the rescue "of their little black friend," preventing any actual harm, it seems likely that under the stressful circumstances of the war other white children also may have targeted their black playmates for retribution. One Virginia slave recalled that in the popular game of Yankees and Confederates, the white "Confederates" terrorized the black "Yankees": "They'd make us black boys prisoners an' make b'lieve dey was gonna cut our necks off; guess dey got dat idea f'om dere fathers," he commented sagely.[41] Combining old patterns of hierarchical interracial interactions with new themes of violent military conflict, Southern children's wartime play aggressively reasserted the social order of slaveholding society.

Racial violence was only one dimension of the pervasive violence that saturated Southern children's wartime play. Military violence was omnipresent. In the besieged city of Winchester, six-year-old Rob McDonald and his four-year-old brother Donald played outdoors in the yard while cannonballs went "whizzing over the house." During the siege of Vicksburg, small children "laughed and defiantly clapped their hands as they saw the missiles fail to hit their targets," making a game of the shelling of their hometown. In Charleston, as Confeder-ate troops withdrew and Union troops advanced, "small boys rejoiced in scooping up handfuls of the [gun]powder and tossing it on cotton bales that departing Confederate soldiers had set afire." Their prank resulted in a deadly explosion that killed more than a hundred people. In Asheville, North Carolina, two rival gangs of older boys—the "Baconsoles" to the north and the "Pinchguts" to the south—staged battles, took prisoners, and built miniature cannons from sawed-off muskets. The skirmishes between the two groups were "war," ten-year-old George Robertson averred, "much like the big war that had been going on so long." In South Carolina two little girls "playing Sherman" destroyed all their toys, even biting the head off a doll.[42]

Remarkable as these occurrences may seem, in some ways the real and mock violence of children's wartime play was a predictable response to the all-encompassing atmosphere of military violence in the Civil War South. Southern children's violence both reflected their situation and allowed them to adapt to it. Studies of children in war zones suggest that children use play to manage their anxiety about uncertainty and danger. This was clearly the case for William Lord's daughters, residents of Vicksburg, Mississippi. During the six-week siege in the summer of 1863 that forced residents to take refuge in caves surrounding the embattled city, the Lord girls amused them-selves with a set of miniature knives and forks carved from a minié ball—thus literally domesticating the war—and composed original words to a traditional tune: "Then let the big guns boom if they will, We'll be gay and happy still." Both the familiarity of the old tune and the optimism of the new lyrics must have been profoundly comfort-ing to children made homeless by the war. Similarly, when Virginian Lucy Buck's brothers spent their time "exploding bombshells in the field" for entertainment (a popular pastime for preteen boys during the war), it must have been a relief to be in control of the destruc-tion rather than a helpless victim of it. For some young children, like the South Carolina toddler who played hide-and-seek with his aunt in January 1865, playing games offered a welcome distraction from violence and fear. As one historian of children in the Civil War South has observed, "The world of play allowed children . . . a respite from the impending doom."[43]

*

Although play and work are often understood as polar opposites in contemporary America, labor and leisure were intertwined in the antebellum South. For all but the most privileged children, work was an integral part of daily life. In order to find time for recreation, then, most children found ways to mix play and work. On Evelyn Ward's Virginia plantation, for instance, "the children of the place, black and white," gathered cherries and raspberries to make jams and jellies, pared apples and peaches for preserves, and shelled and sorted beans, peas, and seeds to dry for storage. While all these tasks had economic importance, the children of Bladensfield gave them entertainment value as well. "We had a way of playing with the beans as though they were people," Evelyn recalled; "we laughed and sang and had great times." Similarly, plain-folk farmer's son Charles Nagel explained that until he and his brothers entered their teens, their work had been "half play." As a teenager Charles continued to combine work and play. Fishing, hunting, and trapping, for instance, provided the family with meat and hides, but these were also enjoyable activities. "Riding the prairies" to locate the family's free-range cattle was one of Charles's favorite activities because it allowed him to ride—and race—the family's mule. In this way, what might be called work-play prepared children not only for their social roles in Southern society but also for their work responsibilities.[44]

Although work was an important part of life for nearly all children in the slaveholding South, it was a central part of life for slave children. As workers and potential workers, slave children sustained the system of racial slavery in the American South. By 1860 more than half the slave population was under the age of twenty. Moreover the American slave population was unique in that, of all the places in the New World where black slavery was practiced, only in the United States could the slave population perpetuate itself through natural increase: the birth of new children into slavery. Thus the presence of so many slave children was essential to the very existence of the institution. As one Virginia slaveowner explained the situation: "The Children must be particularly attended to, for rearing them is not only a duty, but also the most profitable part of plantation business."[45]

Slaveholders clearly viewed slave children as workers. In late 1857 Mississippi plantation mistress Tryphena Blanche Holder Fox was delighted to get "an excellent bargain" when she and her husband purchased a slave woman with two daughters and a third child on the way. The Foxes viewed both the mother, Susan, and her daughters, ages five and three, as sources of household labor; Mrs. Fox planned to train the oldest girl, five-year-old Adelaide, to be a house servant. Even if the Foxes chose instead to sell the family, the children reckoned in their calculations of profit. Having paid $1,400 for the pregnant woman and her young daughters, Mr. Fox declared that "he would not sell her & the children for less than $2,000." As it turned out, however, both Susan and her children proved their worth in the Foxes' plantation home rather than on the auction block. By the time Adelaide was six years old, her mistress judged her to be not only "old enough to take care of herself" but also able to do "a great many useful errands around the house."[46]

Slave children began to work as soon as they learned to walk. Hannah Davidson, who was born a slave in Kentucky in 1852, recalled from the vantage point of the 1930s, "that's all I've ever known— work." For many children, early experiences with work involved personal service to the master, mistress, or one of their children. Margaret Hulm, "a house girl" in Tennessee, "waited on my mistress and her chillun, answered the door, waited on de table and done things like that." Both boys and girls worked as house servants. Henry Bibb was responsible for cleaning floors, polishing furniture, and doing whatever else his mistress asked. "She was too lazy to scratch her own head, and would often make me scratch and comb it for her. She would at times lie on the bed, in warm weather, and make me fan her while she slept, scratch and rub her feet," he recorded in his memoirs.[47]

One of the most common work responsibilities for slave children was to serve as companion-caretakers to white children. It was customary for each child in a slaveholding family to be assigned a slave child of the same gender and approximately the same age as both a playmate and a servant. As we have seen, such work responsibilities served not only practical purposes, by protecting slaveholders' children from harm and training slave children to work, but also psychological ones, by teaching both planter-class and enslaved youth their respective roles in slave society.[48]

Slave boys and girls alike served as personal attendants and general errand runners. On the Louisiana plantation Brokenburn it was the responsibility of a ten-year-old slave girl, Sara, "to stand or sit on a low footstool just behind [the mistress's] chair, to run errands and carry messages all day long, and to pick up the threads and scraps off the carpet." Likewise, James Monroe Abbott, at the age of seven, was responsible for fanning flies away from his dying master's bedside. In the late 1930s he still remembered that when the master died, and Abbott was told he could go out to play, he was overjoyed. "By God, he's daid," Abbott told everyone on his way out the door. For both boys and girls, personal service was both an early introduction to work responsibilities and a constant reminder of their own status as servants. Judging from slaves' reminiscences of such work, regardless of gender, personal service was also an unending and unpleasant work assignment.[49]

As they grew older, slave children's tasks might be differentiated more by gender. Slave boys extended the scope of their duties to the outbuildings and the fields. By age seven, Frederick Douglass was driving the cows home in the evening as well as running errands for his mistress. Both boys and girls learned gender-specific tasks from their adult counterparts. Douglass described a father-son team—"old Barney and young Barney"—who worked together in a Baltimore stable while plantation dweller Kate Stone recalled that a "half-grown little darkie, Charles" was assigned to Webster, the coachman and waiter, to help "rub the knives, do errands, [and] help clean the boots" of visitors. Slave girls learned to help their mothers but might also receive training in certain tasks—especially sewing—from their mistresses.[50]

While boys and girls in urban or particularly wealthy households might undertake increasingly specialized—and gender-specific—tasks, most slave children on Southern plantations worked in the

fields without regard to gender. Planters calculated slaves' labor contributions—and distributed food and other supplies—by referring
to "hands." An able-bodied adult male was a "full hand"; a nursing
mother was a "three-quarter hand"; a disabled slave or a young child
was a "half hand," and so on. Children began their working life in the
fields at around age six or seven as "half hands" in the "trash gang,"
a group of children, pregnant and nursing women, and elderly slaves
assigned to clearing brush. As they grew older and gained experience,
preteen and teenage slaves progressed to cultivating and harvesting
crops in the main field as "three quarter hands" and finally, in their
late teens, as "full hands."[51]

One former slave described the gradual transition to full-time
labor this way: "Us chillen start to work soon's us could toddle. First
us gather firewood." When they were a "li'l bigger" they would "tend
de cattle and feed hosses and hogs. By the time us good sprouts, us
pickin' cotton and pullin' corn." When children were ten or twelve
years old they worked full-time in the field. Slave youth thus made
up a significant portion not only of the slave population but also of
the enslaved workforce. In 1859 a planter named Alonzo Mial told
a friend: "I made with 14 hands mostly women and small boys and
girls two more of the latter to make a hand 93 bales of cotton averag-
ing 400 lbs." While work assignments varied by age and, to a lesser
extent, by gender, all slave children learned that life consisted of what
Hannah Davidson called "work, work, work."[52]

Plain-folk children, like slave children, were workers. Texan
Charles Nagel's description of his gradual assumption of responsibilities on his parents' farm was remarkably similar to slave children's
experiences. As a young child, Charles was responsible for tending
livestock, cultivating the vegetable garden, churning butter, and
gathering nuts and berries in the woods that surrounded his family's frontier home. "The demand upon our work grew with us," he
recalled, and by the time he was twelve years old Charles had added
the tasks of hauling water, splitting wood, and milking cows to his
chores. By the time he entered his teens, Charles was working in the

Slave children were workers from an early age. In this Civil War–era photograph, a group of children sort cotton to prepare it for the gin. *(Library of Congress)*

fields, hoeing corn and picking cotton alongside the adult workers. This plain-folk youth spoke from experience when he observed, "there are a hundred ways in which a youngster can help" with household production and farm work.[53]

Like Charles Nagel, most children in nonslaveholding or small-slaveholding families regularly engaged in productive labor. Raising crops, herding livestock, and harvesting nature's bounty all demanded extensive labor, and children played a key role in all these activities. As Floridian Sarah Pamela Williams explained, "Many hands were required to help and we children were always ready to assist." The Williams children augmented the family's stores of food by gathering and preserving plums, okra, tomatoes, peaches, and huckleberries; they also accompanied the family's few slaves "moss hunting" for

Spanish moss, which the Williams family used to stuff mattresses. While white children's work sometimes overlapped with the work of slaves—Virginia farmer's daughter Evelyn Ward recalled that she and her siblings worked alongside the family's slave children clearing fields for planting, for instance—white children's labor benefited their own families. Perhaps for this reason, children from the middling classes often recalled their work as a pleasurable activity. Sarah "delighted" in the work she performed, which often mixed easily with play. When Sarah and her brother Ned accompanied their father on fishing trips, for example, Ned assisted in netting fish while his sister admired the water lilies. For Sarah, another favorite time was haying season, when she reveled in the sight of her father working with a scythe, the smell of the drying grass, and the excitement of being "tossed on top" of the great haystacks and then "laughing and rolling" down.[54]

Elite white youngsters were the only Southern children for whom work—defined as necessary and productive labor—was the exception rather than the rule. Although three-year-old plantation daughter Fanny Fox's daily activities—including setting the table for tea, playing with her dolls, and sewing in imitation of her slave caretaker and companion, Adelaide—allowed her to rehearse for her adult responsibilities for entertaining, child care, and textile production, she undertook these activities for pleasure rather than for profit. Older girls in slaveholding families often sought entertainment in the kitchen, prevailing upon slave cooks to boil molasses for taffy pulls, share scraps of dough to mold small pastries, or give "tastes" of the food being prepared for meals to use for picnics. Such activities may have prepared well-to-do adolescents to supervise slaves at their work, but they did not give them much practical experience in meal preparation. Likewise, when elite boys went hunting they were shooting for sport rather than for sustenance. Thirteen-year-old Benjamin Fleet often "went squirreling" in his rural Virginia neighborhood. After a day spent in the woods and by the mill pond in August 1860, Ben returned home with his trophies: a string of "Frogs & Squirrels" dragging behind his horse. Although he proudly counted his kills, almost certainly this wealthy planter's son did not intend to eat his prey.[55] With the exception of planter-class children, however, all Southern children were familiar with the world of work well before the Civil War.

The demands of the war years made productive labor more central to all Southern children's daily lives. For the children of slaveholders, work became necessary to immediate survival rather than simply preparation for the future, as slave labor became less reliable and wartime shortages demanded higher levels of productivity. For the children of nonslaveholding whites, free blacks, and African-American slaves, for whom work had always been an important fact of life, labor became even more essential than before. Many goods no longer available for purchase had to be manufactured or replaced, and children were often the workers charged with finding substitutes for scarce commodities. While play continued to mark and make differences between children of different backgrounds, then, work became an increasingly important commonality among all children in the Civil War South.

Elite children's labor became essential to their family's survival for the first time during the Civil War. Wartime shortages, the absence of adult male family members, and the loss of escaped slaves' labor all combined to increase elite children's work responsibilities. In May 1863 Lucy and Nellie Buck, ages twenty and eighteen, respectively, assumed responsibility for their younger siblings when the house servants were reassigned to field labor. Thirteen-year-old Samuel Steel recalled that the departure of the slaves from his family's plantation "made a great difference" in his daily life. "Think of it," he exclaimed. Before the war, he elaborated, slaves were responsible for the many chores of rural life: "As the sun was setting and the cows were lowing at the gate, and the pigs were squealing for the corn, and the tired mules were lazily going to the stable or rolling in the dust, it was 'Tom, milk the cows,' 'Dick, feed the stock,' 'Harry, cut the wood,' 'John, do this,' 'Charley do that.'" Once Union soldiers neared and slaves began to escape to freedom, however, the situation changed, and slaveholders' children undertook new responsibilities: "Then it was 'Sam, milk the cows; Sam feed the stock; Sam, cut the wood; Sam do this; Sam, do that; Sam, do everything.'"[56]

Elite children of all ages and both sexes assumed new tasks. Like slave children before the war, the young children of slaveholding families acted as general helpers and errand runners, dusting furniture, making beds, setting the table for meals, and herding livestock to and from pasture. Also like their less-privileged counterparts before the war, slaveholding children often made play out of work. Evelyn Ward recalled that she and her siblings, charged with driving the cows, pretended that "we children" were Confederate soldiers and that the cattle were "Yankees." "I am afraid we didn't always drive them as slowly as our Father wanted them driven," she jested.[57]

Within the general pattern of increased work responsibilities, gender differentiation was apparent. In elite families, boys took on responsibility for outdoor work. Virginian Cornelia Peake McDonald mourned the necessity of sending her two oldest sons, thirteen and fourteen years old, to cut wood to provide necessary fuel for heat and cooking during the winter months. "Poor little fellows," she wrote in late 1862, "they have been for weeks cutting and hauling a supply of wood for our use," for "there was no other way to get it." With no firewood available for purchase, this "rough hard work" fell to the oldest sons.[58]

Parents also assigned the task of taking goods to market to their sons. Thirteen-year-old Samuel Steel, who grew up on a plantation near Memphis, made repeated trips to town with the wagon to sell cotton, buy salt, and smuggle cloth. This work was difficult and dangerous, but it also connoted both masculinity and adulthood. South Carolinian John Clinkscales, who was only six years old when the war began, reveled in the attention he received for driving farm supplies to town to trade for salt and coffee. Upon his return home, his mother praised him: "'Mama's little man; God bless you, my son.' And I was happy." Virginia planter's son Benjamin Fleet, who was fourteen years old at the onset of the war, traded schoolbooks for bookkeeping. Ben frequently traveled to Southern marketplaces to buy and sell goods during the war, once all the way to Charleston, South Carolina. Making independent decisions about purchases and sales, he became adept at negotiating prices and confident in his abilities. He also gained his father's respect. In a letter to his older brother Fred, he remarked, "Pa . . . seems to think more of me now as I have been all the way to Charleston by myself," adding, "you know I am a pretty good manager." Ben's marketing experience translated into adult masculinity. On his sixteenth birthday he wrote in his diary: "This morning 16 years ago a man was born, & I am he."[59]

Oldest sons also became responsible for supervising slaves at their work. Benjamin Fleet assumed managerial as well as marketing tasks during the Civil War. Although Dr. Fleet was exempted from military service, both his chronic alcoholism and his wartime medical practice rendered him incapable of managing the fifty slaves who worked at Green Mount. Fourteen-year-old Ben, who had previously cared only for a small flock of chickens, assumed sole responsibility for directing all of the three-thousand-acre plantation's varied operations, including growing, harvesting, and threshing wheat; raising and butchering cattle, hogs, and sheep; growing and processing sugar, cotton, and tobacco; maintaining vegetable gardens and orchards; tending chickens, ducks, and geese; taking grain to be milled; and operating the family's granary and ferry. "I am in charge at home on the farm now," Ben informed his brother Fred in the fall of 1861; "give orders without Pa's knowing anything about it often." Ben repeated this information in his diary, suggesting the importance he attached to his new duties. "I am 'boss' on the farm now," he boasted.[60]

As Ben's pride suggested, supervising slaves, like taking goods to market, was another job that connoted both adult responsibility and manly respectability. In January 1865 Georgia plantation mistress Sallie Bird remarked that her acquaintances were amazed by her fourteen-year-old son Bud's increased maturity when he accompanied his mother on a visit to his soldier-father in Richmond after a three-year absence. "The little man," as she now referred to him, had taken over as "overseer" at the family's plantation, Granite Hill, where he supervised more than forty slaves at their work tending, picking, and processing cotton.[61]

While planter-class boys learned slave management, planter-class girls assumed greater domestic responsibilities. Just as supplying firewood fell to boys, producing textiles fell to girls. As early as 1862, Louisianan Kate Stone found it necessary to learn the "unaccustomed work" of weaving cloth. Although elite girls had learned both basic sewing and fancy needlework before the war, during the war the manufacture of knitted socks and gloves and homespun cloth and clothing took precedence. Rose P. Ravenel, who was only eleven years old at the war's outbreak, remembered that she was "made to knit one or 2 p[ai]r of socks for the Soldiers every month," and that even her lessons did not interfere with her work: "Read french aloud every day to Mamma," she later recalled, "made to knit while I read." While Ravenel, like other elite Southern girls, knitted for the benefit of Confederate soldiers, girls also used their new skills in the service of family members. As Atlanta teenager Sallie Clayton explained, "At first socks only were knitted for the soldiers but in course of time when we had to think also of ourselves, came stockings, plain and clocked, gloves, comforters, caps, hoods, shawls, capes, jackets, undervests, etc.," as well as crocheted hairnets, gloves, and hats. With so many items dependent on female labor, all the girls in the Clayton family—even three-year-old Almyra—made knitting a daily chore. In Virginia, teenager Sally Munford recorded in late 1863 that her "Fall work" consisted of "patching, mending, and turning old clothes" to extend their usefulness. Ten-year-old Atlanta resident Carrie Berry recorded sewing, knitting, and quilting in her wartime diary. During the Civil War, textile production—spinning, knitting, and sewing—became a daily chore for elite girls of all ages.[62]

General household maintenance and the care of younger siblings also devolved upon planter-class girls, particularly upon older daughters. Eleven-year-old Virginian Katie Wallace "washed & combed" her younger brothers and helped them dress while teenagers Emma and Carrie Holmes became "accomplished chambermaids" in their New

Confederate women relied on their children for emotional and practical support in their husbands' wartime absence. Both sons and daughters took on new responsibilities for household labor during the Civil War. Boys in particular were often adjured to be mindful of their roles as the "men of the family." Here, a Maryland woman poses with her two young sons for an 1862 photograph. *(Library of Congress)*

Orleans home. Many of these tasks were familiar ones, yet they became more frequent and intense during the Civil War with the departure of household slaves. After her family's domestic servant, the slave girl Mary, ran away to follow General Sherman's army, ten-year-old Carrie Berry of Atlanta commented, "I will have to go to work to help Mama." Thereafter she spent her days "cooking and cleaning house and waiting on Mama and [newborn] sister Maggy." The three oldest daughters in the Buck household—twenty-year-old Lucy, eighteen-year-old Nellie, and fifteen-year-old Laura—assumed responsibility for housework literally overnight when they awoke in 1863 to the news that all the family's house slaves had departed in the night. "We every one of us made a dash for our clothes, hauled them on, kindled a fire, brought water and Laura and I went to milk the cows while Ma, Grandma and Nellie cleaned the house, got the breakfast, and dressed the children," Lucy wrote. Over the next several days the Buck girls added cooking, ironing, and dairying to their repertoire.[63]

While girls of all ages reported learning to tend to "household duties" such as textile production, cooking and cleaning, gathering eggs, churning butter, and caring for livestock, one domestic task that nearly all elite girls managed to avoid was laundry. In the Old South laundry had been performed almost exclusively by black women, and even the most distressed elite families were eager to spare their daughters this task. Laundry was both physically demanding (requiring hauling and heating water, manufacturing soap from lye and ashes, and scrubbing clothes by hand) and a salient marker of class and racial difference. For Georgian Sarah Bull Barnwell, the prospect of "young girls . . . washing their clothes" was horrifying; "I hope y[ou]r daughters are not obliged to do that yet for themselves," she wrote to her cousin Mary Maxcy Leverett. Wherever possible, elite families assigned this task to the elderly female slaves who remained with them throughout the war; when no such loyal (or simply disabled) slave was available, older sons took on the job. Virginia teenagers Harry and Allan McDonald washed the family's "soiled clothes"; their mother merely "inspected the work."[64] Thus, even though work became a necessity of life for even the most privileged Southern children during the war years, some markers of social difference remained.

Because elite observers were more interested in recording their own experiences, and less-privileged children had always worked, changes in the work patterns of nonslaveholding and small-slaveholding white children, free black children, and slave children are more difficult to trace. Probably these children's labor also increased in quantity and intensity. In a Unionist enclave in Texas, far from the fighting, fourteen-year-old farmer's son Charles Nagel and his brothers nonetheless felt the effects of the war, for "all young men were gone, either to the front or in hiding. If crops were to be brought in at all, it was for us to help."[65]

In families that had previously relied on the male head of household rather than on slave labor to perform outdoor work, new chores fell to women and children. In Florida, farmwife Amanda Comerford recalled that her husband's departure for the front left her with six children, ranging from infancy to eleven years of age. "It is difficult to describe my struggles to provide food and clothing for this large family," she recounted. "I had to work on the farm during the day, go a long distance to milk, and a large part of the night was spent spinning and weaving to make cloth for wearing apparel." Had Mrs. Comerford's children been a bit older, no doubt they would have been pressed into service as well, either in the house or in the fields. In Tennessee, plain-folk farmwife Eliza Fain assigned "all the care of the house" to her daughters, enabling her to perform farm labor, while in Florida a Madison County farmer advised his wife: "Tell the Children to plow the best they can."[66]

With male adolescents and adults often away at war, girls in yeoman families often assumed primary responsibility for farm tasks. In South Carolina the nonslaveholding Pursley family relied on the labor of daughters Jane and Martha to plant and harvest crops. According to twenty-six-year-old Jane, she and her eleven-year-old younger sister Martha competed to see who could plant more rows of corn; Jane boasted that Martha was her equal in the field. When the time arrived to harvest the crop, neighbor girls helped to shuck corn. Very young children also engaged in heavy fieldwork, even in families with slaves. The Harris children, four boys and three girls, whose ages ranged from infancy to early adolescence, all worked in the field in 1863. The task was overly demanding for the youngest ones, who became ill from heat exhaustion.[67]

Slave children were accustomed to hard work, but their tasks increased in scope and intensity during the war as slaveholding families assigned new tasks both to replace store-bought goods and to fill in for absent adult males. Octavia Stephens sent the slave children on her

Florida plantation on hunting and fishing expeditions to supplement the white family's wartime diet. Another slaveholder required the children of a runaway slave to perform "the same work that he formerly had to do, such as chopping wood, splitting rails, &c." Tennessee slave Julius Jones, who was fourteen years old when the war began, recalled that "all the [slave] men on the place ran off and joined the northern army," which "left me behind with the work to do." Slave children and "half-grown" adolescents assumed an increased workload during the war years, often on reduced rations and sometimes to the detriment of their health. One teenage slave girl, Francesca Carrorra, who had been a relatively pampered house servant, was sent to her owners' Louisiana saltworks during the war, where she "died of pneumonia and neglect" in May 1863.[68]

*

For children in the slaveholding South, play and work were defining experiences. Before the war, work and play reinforced personal identity and prepared children for adult roles. During the war, play and work took on new importance. These activities served as daily reminders of the continued significance of social categories in the Southern Confederacy at the same time they allowed—and often required—children to cope with wartime poverty and danger. For all the adaptability that children displayed in their play and work, however, the fear of violence and the disruption of family life would become defining features of children's lives in the Civil War South.

CHAPTER FOUR

Refugees and Runaways

DISLOCATION AND OPPORTUNITY IN A WAR ZONE

Nineteen-year-old Lucy Buck of Virginia captured the meaning of war from children's perspective in an 1862 diary entry. Contrasting "our present situation" with a past in which she and her brothers and sisters were "so happy" in "an unbroken home circle," she ejaculated, "Oh, the change!" Two of Lucy's older brothers, Alvin and Irving, had left home to join the Confederate Army, and she described herself and her younger siblings as "separated from those dear members of our household by more than the mere distance of miles—by circumstances that might well preclude our ever hearing from them again." The Buck family plantation, Bel Air, was repeatedly caught in the crossfire as Union and Confederate armies vied for control of the neighboring town, Front Royal, during the three-month-long Shenandoah Valley campaign. As a result, the family witnessed "our country overrun by our remorseless foes" literally dozens of times during the war. At the time Lucy wrote this entry in her diary, the greatest of the battles, the Battle of Front Royal, was brewing, and she and her family were helpless in the face of impending doom. "There we sat," Lucy described her beleaguered family, "completely in the power of our implacable enemies whom we were hourly expecting—enemies who would pillage and destroy our homes . . . and leave us poor females and children defenseless, without the means of subsistence," and at the mercy of enemy troops. For Lucy Buck, as for other children in the Confederate South, the Civil War posed a serious threat to family security and personal safety.[1]

Unlike children living in the North, far from the battle lines, children in the South confronted the Civil War head-on. Living in a war zone, they experienced the constant threat of physical violence and family disruption. While not every Southern child lost a family member, witnessed a battle, experienced home invasion, or lived in occupied territory, the possibility was always there, and it was especially alarming for children. The terrifying experiences and fearful imaginings of the war years made an indelible impression on the children of the Confederacy. As Lucy Buck predicted, "We shall never *any* of us be the same as we *have* been."[2]

*

In later years, children who grew up during the Civil War offered unsparing and critical assessments of the conflict. Hammett Dell, a slave boy who lived near Murfreesboro, Tennessee, remembered the war as a time of constant anxiety and dangerous scarcity. "It was a continual roar," he described the din of battle. "The tin pans in the cubbard rattle all the time. . . . The house shakin' all time. . . . The earth quivered. It sound like the judgment." By the time both the Union and Confederate armies had passed through the contested area, it was a wasteland: "there couldn't be a chicken nor a goose nor a year of corn to be found." Decades later, when he was interviewed in the 1930s, Hammett solemnly pronounced, "War . . . ain't nuthin' but hell on dis earth."[3]

Southern children had ample opportunities to become familiar with the hell of war. The sights, sounds, and smells of battle reverberate throughout children's accounts. Margaret Hulm, an adolescent slave in Tennessee during the war, later described "what we called the black days" of the war years: "It would be so dark you couldn't see the sun even. That was from the smoke from the fighting. You could just hear the big guns going *b-o-o-m, boom,* all day." Arkansas slave Lizzie Dunn recalled the sight and sounds of battle: "The sound was like eternity had turned loose. Everything shook like terrible earthquakes day and night. The light was bright and red and smoke terrible." Planter's daughter Kate Stone and her siblings were startled awake on a daily basis by "the booming of cannon" near their Louisiana plantation. In Winchester, Virginia, Cornelia Peake McDonald and her nine children huddled together in their home and listened to the sounds of cannon, which she described as "one continued fearful roll." Later her sons found "the mutilated remains" of the dead on the battlefield—and "one foot was found in our garden." James Goings, a Missouri slave, observed decomposing bodies "all long de road" adjacent to the plantation where he lived and worked. He reflected, "In dem days it wuzn't nuthin' to fin' a dead man in de woods." Susie King, a fourteen-year-old slave in Charleston, South Carolina, near Fort Wagner, later recalled: "Outside of the fort were many skulls lying about; I have often moved them from one side out of the path. . . . They were a gruesome sight, those fleshless heads and grinning jaws." The sounds of battle, the smoke of gunpowder, and "the stench from the battlefield" all permeated Southern children's lives during the war years. One Virginia mother averred that "scenes of strife and confusion" had come to seem "the natural course of things" to children during the war years.[4]

Like adults, young Southerners suffered from wartime shortages of food and clothing and the need to hide at home or flee to safety. Eight-year-old Annie Marmion described wartime in Harpers Ferry, (West) Virginia: "The great objects in life were to procure something to eat and to keep yourself out of light by day and your lamps . . . hidden by night." Adeline Blakeley, a slave girl in Arkansas, recalled frantic retreats into the cellar and out of harm's way. She explained: "During the war even the little children were taught to listen for bugle calls and know what they meant. We had to know—and how to act when we heard them." Children were among the Southern civilians who met their death as a direct and indirect result of the war. In North Carolina, Confederates shot and killed Union sympathizers, including a thirteen-year-old boy; in Maryland, a small boy playing with a shell in the Antietam battlefield died when it exploded in his hands. Far from being spared the terrors and horrors of war, children proved to be especially vulnerable to them. Small wonder, then, that Louisiana slave La San Mire soberly observed, "During the war all the children had fear."[5]

Children who lived in areas near the battle lines were in a state of almost constant anxiety. As twenty-year-old Lucy Breckinridge, whose Virginia plantation was repeatedly invaded by Union troops, expressed it, "rumors of Yankees kept us in a state of excitement." At Green Mount, a tidewater Virginia plantation located just across the York River from the Peninsula campaign, a major Union offensive that featured some of the bloodiest battles of the eastern front and lasted from March through July 1862, members of the Fleet family—including fourteen-year-old Benjamin, eleven-year-old Maria Louisa, nine-year-old David, eight-year-old Florence, six-year-old Betsy, and four-year-old James—listened to "a dreadful roar of Cannon" from morning to night. The family's location between the York and Rappahannock rivers also made them vulnerable to federal troops who plied the waterway with gunboats and came ashore to loot and burn nearby homes and businesses. Thus the Fleets lived in fear of armed invasion throughout the war. Ben's wartime diary recorded "1001 reports that the Yankees are coming."[6]

On the western front, during the Vicksburg campaign in the spring of 1863, twenty-three-year-old Kate Stone and her younger brothers and sisters nervously awaited the arrival of Union troops at their Louisiana plantation. "We have been in a quiver of anxiety looking for the Yankees every minute," Kate recorded in her diary, "sitting on the front gallery with our eyes strained in the direction they will come, going to bed late and getting up early so they will not find us asleep." The situation was worst of all for children who lived on the borders between the Union and the Confederacy. Marylander Lizette Reese and her sisters were so frightened during the war that they did not want to go to bed at night: "Between the blue forces and the gray we were ground between two millstones of terror," she recalled.[7]

For many Southern children, the abstract concept of war was made real by the arrival of invading soldiers. Fourteen-year-old Sue Chancellor, whose Virginia plantation was occupied by Union forces in late 1862 and who was ultimately forced from her home by the Battle of Chancellorsville in May 1863, nonetheless described most Union soldiers as "kind and polite to us." Yet "the Yankees" were still "the enemy," and the teenager feared them accordingly. "I can never forget how they used to come in a sweeping gallop up the big road with swords and sabres clashing," she recalled years later. "I would run and hide and pray. I reckon I prayed more and harder than ever in my life, before or since."[8]

Confederate children frequently expressed fear of "Yankee" soldiers. During the war, tales of atrocities committed by invading Union soldiers were commonplace. Widely circulated and sometimes wildly exaggerated reports of Union invasion often highlighted the threats that military siege and occupation posed to children. As Edmund Drago remarks in his study of white children in Civil War South Carolina, Confederates "took every opportunity to highlight real or imagined Yankee atrocities against women and children." Fearful rumors of war crimes—wanton destruction, physical brutality, and sexual assault—convinced white Southerners that invading soldiers posed a particular threat to women and children. In Florida, as Confederate troops retreated from Pensacola in the face of a Union onslaught, a Confederate soldier cried, "Women and children, flee for your lives! The enemy is coming, burning homes and killing women and children."[9]

Southern children heard, believed, and repeated frightening and inflammatory reports about Yankee soldiers' attacks on defenseless women and children. In 1862 in Virginia, fourteen-year-old Benjamin Fleet heard that in a neighboring county invading Union soldiers took an eleven-year-old boy prisoner; according to local reports, "the child was taken sick and died there calling on his Mother with his last breath." Young Ben repeated this heartbreaking tale to his mother, who then passed it on to other family members and residents of the family's rural neighborhood. In August 1863 nineteen-year-old Pauline DeCaradeuc recorded reports of the siege of Charleston in her diary. The teenager's account highlighted the damage to homes and the danger to children. After giving the Confederate officials only four hours to evacuate, the Union Army attacked the town, "shelling the sleeping women and children." According to rumor, one shell struck a bed occupied by a sleeping child, who was miraculously unhurt. Nonetheless the shells destroyed homes and endangered their occupants, impressing the young Confederate with Yankees' disregard for the safety of civilians and their homes.[10]

White Southerners of all ages unquestioningly accepted and frequently repeated horrific stories like these. Centering as they did on the common themes of rape and pillage—violence directed toward family homes and defenseless women and children—such tales of Union soldiers' cruelty certainly aroused Confederate nationalism, but they also inspired terrible fear, particularly among children.[11]

Adolescent and young adult Confederates sometimes responded with outrage. Georgian Eliza Frances Andrews's expostulations were typical: "Yankee, Yankee, is the one detestable word always ringing in Southern ears. If all the words of hatred in every language under heaven were lumped together in one huge epithet of detestation, they could not tell how I hate Yankees. They thwart all my plans, murder my friends, and make my life miserable." Later the twenty-five-year-old wrote in her journal: "I used to have some Christian feeling towards Yankees, but now that they have invaded our country and killed so many of our men and desecrated so many homes, I can't believe that when Christ said 'Love your enemies,' he meant Yankees."[12]

Similarly, teenager Samuel Steel "hated the North with all the energy of [his] nature" from the very beginning of the war. "I breathed the very atmosphere of hatred toward the 'Yankees,'" he wrote years later; "the very name was to me a synonym of all that was odious and infamous." After his own plantation was ransacked by Union soldiers, his hatred deepened: "As I looked at the desolation of what had been a happy, lovely home, saw the wanton destruction of everything that makes a home sacred, I conceived a hatred toward the North that was simply unutterable! In my boy-heart I swore to an animosity as deep and holy as the oath young Hannibal took on the altar of his country's gods, and from that time on it was the one ambition of my life to kill a Yankee, then another, and another, and another!"[13]

Younger white children, however, almost universally responded with fear. Although Kate Stone described herself as "not frightened but . . . furiously angry" when Union soldiers plundered her Louisiana plantation in March 1863, even holding a gun to her head, she added, "the little girls were frightened." Fear, indeed, was most children's response to federal soldiers. Tennessee farmwife Eliza Fain and her twelve children were paralyzed with fear when Union troops were rumored to be approaching their home. Nine-year-old Nannie "drew up close" to her mother's side and whispered, "Mama they are coming" and "Is that them?" Eliza held the four-year-old, Lillie, and two of the girls began to cry. Her oldest daughter, Liz, age twenty-six, asked, "Mama if they shoot us will we go to heaven?" When Fain assured her that this would be so, Liz responded with relief, "They can't hurt us when we get there."[14]

Both by repeating stories of Yankee atrocities and by direct instruction, Confederate parents encouraged their children's distrust of Union troops. As one historian notes, "Southerners were committed to raising Yankee-hating children from birth." Eliza Frances Andrews related the tale of one Confederate mother who taught her children to precede every mention of the word "Yankee" with an "opprobrious epithet": "'a hateful Yankee,' 'an upstart of a Yankee,' 'a thieving Yankee,' and the like." Similarly, Georgia plantation mistress Gertrude Thomas remarked, "It is a part of the religion I have taught our children to dislike the Yankees." The lesson took; merely the sight of a Union soldier made eight-year-old Mary Bell Thomas "apt to produce" a quick warning in "frightened tones."[15]

Either in spite of their fear or because of it, children were often posted as lookouts. When the passing troops were friendly, children might enjoy this role. In May 1863 thirteen-year-old Amanda Stone and her siblings enjoyed watching Confederate soldiers march along-side their Louisiana plantation. Kate Stone wrote in her diary: "The children, headed by Sister, were in a great state of excitement and spent most of the day perched on the fence with buckets and gourds of water, offering it to the hot, tired soldiers, who every now and then hurrahed for the little girl in red. Sister was a blaze of scarlet in her Turkey-red calico." Likewise, in Virginia, the children in the Buck family carried buckets of water to the "weary, dusty, travel-worn" Confederate soldiers who passed the plantation.[16] The presence of Confederate troops in wartime offered white children an opportunity to act on the political beliefs they adopted during the secession crisis.

When the troops were hostile, children played an important—but also frightening—role by detecting the first signs of danger. It was little Channing, perhaps five or six years old at the time, who alerted the Ward family of Virginia that it was time to flee in the face of ap-proaching Union troops. While his mother said her morning prayers, the little boy had dressed himself and gone outdoors. He soon came running back. Tugging at his mother's skirts, Channing exclaimed, "Mamma, you'd better stop saying your prayers and get up. The Yan-kees are nearly here." Similarly, in Florida, the two young daughters of a woman drawing water from her well in the midst of a battle pleaded with her to go back in the house, saying, "come mama, you mustn't stay here, the Yankees will kill you."[17] Children's fear of soldiers made them exceptionally alert family lookouts.

Confederate children had good reason to fear Union soldiers, for Southern youngsters were especially vulnerable to invading troops. As Lisa Frank has pointed out in a recent analysis of Union military policy, federal officers made attacks on civilians "an integral aspect of the campaign," and "Union soldiers repeatedly and purposefully . . . wreaked havoc on Southern homes" as a way to destroy Confederate morale, demonstrate Union strength, and weaken Southern resistance.[18] Such tactics had devastating effects on Southern children. During home invasions the space that most children regarded as a refuge from hardship and harm suddenly became instead a site of destruction and danger. Because children derived their identities from their families, attacks on families demolished children's sense of self. By invading homes and assaulting families, Northern soldiers shattered the children's world and struck at their sense of identity.

Although some Union soldiers, homesick for their own families, made friendly overtures toward Confederate children, others singled them out for real and symbolic violence. Destroying families' food, furniture, and family heirlooms not only subjected children to material hardships but deprived them of their sense of security. A young girl in Winnsboro, South Carolina, recalled that Yankee soldiers maliciously destroyed her family's remaining stores of food. The Union troops spat into the family's jars of preserves and mixed soap into staples such as molasses, cornmeal, and coffee. According to Eliza Fludd, a Charleston refugee, invading soldiers broke her furniture, destroyed her family portraits, and stole her food, leaving the woman and her four grandchildren homeless and hungry. Similarly, in Columbia, South Carolina, Union soldiers not only despoiled a house of food and "carried off every piece of silver, every knife, jewel, & particle of possessions in the house" but also poured catsup on the family's paintings and "flung to the winds" all the family's written records. Teenager Maria Louisa Fleet suggested the symbolic importance of soldiers' actions when she wrote to her brother, "Just imagine their hateful hands dipping in the pickle we had just fixed,—taking the fruit, socks, in fact every thing. 'tis too dreadful to think of."[19]

Damage to children's belongings, such as toys, books, and clothing, highlighted children's vulnerability. In 1863 the motherless daughters of Virginia planter Thomas Smedes, ranging in age from twenty-three-year-old Susan to eleven-year-old Lelia, watched helplessly as invading soldiers took advantage of their father's absence to ransack their home. The soldiers "went into every room from the garret to the cellar, and through every closet, wardrobe, bureau, and trunk" in their search for weapons and other valuables, taking "everything that struck their fancy." When no key could be found for the youngest girl's doll trunk, the soldiers smashed the lid. Elsewhere in Virginia, according to Lucy Buck, "the Yankees went to the Academy and broke the school children's desks and tore up their books." Union soldiers subjected Confederate children to both psychic and physical hardships. In Columbia, South Carolina, in 1864, one soldier took blankets away from children, declaring, "[L]et the d___d little rebels suffer."[20]

Assaulting adults in children's presence suggested parents' inability to protect their children, subjecting them to the same sense of helplessness that slave children felt when they watched their caretakers being punished by slaveholders. A young woman in Anderson, South Carolina, recalled a particularly horrific encounter with enemy soldiers. While the soldiers threatened the adolescent girl's elderly aunt and uncle, she attempted to comfort the family's small children—including a newborn child—while the soldiers partially strangled her uncle, struck him in the head with a shovel, and slammed him against a wall to force him to give up the family's valuables.[21]

Physical attacks on children, while rare, were both painful and terrifying for youthful victims of wartime violence. Invading soldiers regularly brandished whips and pistols, threatening children with violence if they resisted—or even protested—the destruction of their homes and property. When eighteen-year-old Emma Smedes attempted to comfort her eleven-year-old sister during a home invasion by telling her, "Sister, do not be frightened. Only cowards try to scare women and children," one soldier shook a whip over her head, shouting, "You had better not exasperate me." Susan Smedes, who was twenty-three years old at the time, later recalled, "he was drunk enough to go to any lengths."[22]

The threat of sexual assault was omnipresent, especially when Northern soldiers encountered adolescent girls. Although some scholars have dismissed the significance of sexual assault in the Civil War South, characterizing the conflict as a "low-rape" or "no-rape"

Home invasions destroyed both children's material surroundings and their emotional security. In this etching, Union soldiers tear apart a bedroom during a search for weapons in a family's home. While the father struggles with soldiers at the door, the terrified mother and daughter cower in the curtains. The presence of soldiers in the bedroom and the fear of the mother and daughter suggest the potential for sexual violence; the father's inability to protect his family reveals the wartime disruption of family life. *(Library of Congress)*

war, recent research has indicated that "documented Civil War sexual crimes occurred against white and black women and girls of all social classes." A few victims, like thirteen-year-old Margaret Brooks, brought assault charges against Union soldiers. Brooks was attacked and raped by three soldiers outside Memphis, Tennessee, in 1863. In part due to the testimony of the sympathetic physician who examined her injuries, including swellings, bruises, and abrasions, all three assailants were executed for the crime.[23]

Both actual and symbolic rape enjoined feelings of horror, violation, and helplessness. Union soldiers and Confederate girls alike recognized the power of even the hint of potential sexual assault. Thus twenty-one-year-old South Carolinian Pauline DeCaradeuc was "almost frantic [and] sat up in a corner, without moving or closing my eyes once the whole night" and "trembled *unceasingly* till morning" when she learned that an invading soldier had "asked the servants if there were any young ladies in the house, how old they were & where they slept." Although the young woman was physically unharmed, she was profoundly disturbed by the soldiers' destruction of her underclothes, which she understood as an intimate, if imaginary, attack. Small wonder, then, that "none of us undressed or went to bed for six nights."[24]

Accounts of home invasion often suggested the all-too-real possibility of sexual assault on adolescent girls as well as the physical danger posed to women and children. Indeed, the vast majority of reported wartime rapes took place in the victim's home, often in the presence of family members.[25]

In Missouri, where guerrilla warfare continued into May 1865, Mary Hall was awakened from her sleep by a band of soldiers entering her home. They forced her to light a candle, then took it and set fire to her three young children's clothing and shoved the blazing garments under the bed where the little ones were sleeping. She hastily gathered the burning clothes and threw them in the fireplace, which angered the guerrillas. They went to the bed of her eighteen-year-old son and demanded his pistol. When he replied that he did not have one, they shot him in the head, killing him instantly. They then directed their violence toward the women in the house, including Hall's teenage niece. Hall described the terrible scene:

> I was screaming and entreating them all the time to spare his life. After they had killed him one of them says shut your God Damn mouth or I will blow a hole through your head. . . . All this time my niece, 16 years of age was lying in bed. One of the guerrillas stood by the bedside and as she made an effort to rise ordered her to lie still saying one woman was enough at a time. After they had killed my son and plundered the house one of the guerrillas ordered me out of the house and shut the door. The door had scarcely closed before I heard my niece scream and say

Lord Aunt Mary run here to me. I started and as I reached the door my niece who had succeeded in effecting her escape from the men came rushing out. . . . I do not think they effected their designs on the girl.[26]

In April 1863, after refugeeing to Trenton, Louisiana, with the Hardison family in an attempt to avoid soldiers near their plantation, twenty-two-year-old Kate Stone, her thirteen-year-old sister, Amanda, and Mrs. Hardison and her infant had a terrifying encounter with an all-black Union detachment. "Cursing and making the most awful threats," one soldier approached the bed where the Hardisons' baby was sleeping. Kate related the events in her journal: "Raising the bar, he started to take the child, saying as he waved the pistol, 'I ought to kill him. He may grow up to be a jarilla [i.e., guerrilla]. Kill him.' Mrs. Hardison sprang to his side, snatched the baby up, and shrieked, 'Don't kill my baby. Don't kill him.' The Negro turned away with a laugh and came over where I was sitting with Little Sister crouched close to me holding my hand. He came right up to us standing on the hem of my dress while he looked me slowly over, gesticulating and snapping his pistol. He stood there about a minute, I suppose. It seemed to me an age. I felt like I would die should he touch me. I did not look up or move, and Little Sister was as still as if petrified. In an instant more he turned away with a most diabolical laugh, gathered up his plunder, and went out. I was never so frightened in my life."[27]

Unforgettable encounters like these had lasting effects on Southern children. In 1864, after more than two years of rumored invasions, the Fleet family in Virginia confronted enemy soldiers for the first time. Mrs. Fleet counted her family's blessings that the soldiers "*left* the garden, the house, the farm and *all of us alive*," but not before her teenage daughter narrowly avoided gang rape. While soldiers searched the house for valuables and Mrs. Fleet and her oldest daughter hastened to hide food in the cellar, two of the men seized thirteen-year-old Florence in front of her younger siblings and took her into the bedchamber, locking the door behind them. After inquiring her age, one soldier reconsidered and released her, saying, "That's too young." Rather than sexually assaulting the girl, the soldiers subjected her to a sort of symbolic rape. One of the soldiers who held her captive demanded that she "hold his naked sword" while he ransacked the room. Although physically unharmed, the Fleet children were psychologically scarred by their encounter. Florence's older sister, fifteen-year-old Maria Louisa, later confessed, "I do think to hear the 'Yankees are coming' is the most awful sound I ever heard." Mrs. Fleet questioned if "there could be any union while these children lived."[28]

Union soldiers' presence not only posed physical danger to family members but also had important implications for family dynamics. As one historian of family life during the Civil War has noted, "families were caught up in the quagmire of a destructive and prolonged war that weakened the patriarchy." For children, challenges to parental—especially paternal—authority came as unfamiliar and unwelcome features of the domestic ramifications of military upheaval. In the Shenandoah Valley, Lucy Buck and her nine siblings—ranging in age from infancy to eighteen years old—were terrified when their plantation, Bel Air, was caught in the crossfire between Union and Confederate forces in 1862. Soldiers "poured in from every direction," shells screamed overhead, cannons boomed, and "all [was] confusion and uncertainty." Union officers occupied the family's home while Yankee soldiers set off repeated rounds of fire into the hill behind it. "No wonder the poor children run screaming to our sides and hide their heads in our dresses," Lucy wrote in her diary, sharply criticizing the enemy "for their inhumanity in shooting toward a house full of women and little children." While all the members of the family were "well nigh worn out with this constant excitement," the young children fared worst of all. "The little children are as nervous as they can be," Lucy wrote. "Crying and sobbing with fright" at the bullets whistling overhead, the little ones hid behind their mother's skirts and begged their father "to go out and make them quit." Of course neither parent could provide protection, a fact that must have been nearly as frightening as the gunfire to young children accustomed to looking to their parents for reassurance. "Poor children!" exclaimed

Lucy. "Little they knew how limited was Father's power." When a family's home was threatened, children's faith in parental protection was threatened as well.[29]

Four-year-old Jeff Davis discovered the limits of his father's authority when the Confederate president was taken captive at war's end. According to Virginia Tunstall Clay, after Jefferson Davis was led away, "the weeping of children and wailing of women announced the return of the stricken family." Little Jeff tried to be brave, telling Mrs. Clay, whose husband was incarcerated with President Davis, "My papa told me to keep care of you and my Mamma!" Burdened with his new responsibilities and saddened by his father's helplessness, however, the little boy could not hold back his tears. In her memoirs, Mrs. Clay wrote: "I heard a soldier say to Mr. Davis's little son, 'Don't cry, Jeff. They ain't going to hang your pa!' and the little fellow's reply, made through his sobs. 'When I get to be a man,' he cried, 'I'm going to kill every Yankee I see!'"[30]

Soldiers' actions disrupted family dynamics and reversed familial roles by rendering parents powerless and casting children as family protectors. Children in the Civil War South were both especially vulnerable to assault and uniquely positioned to demand protection. Susan Smedes and her sisters were alone in the house when Union troops arrived at their Virginia plantation, Burleigh, searching for the girls' father, Thomas Smedes, a notorious Rebel. Despite finding the house inhabited only by their intended victim's daughters, ranging in age from eleven to twenty-three, the soldiers insisted on searching the house. By turns they teased and tormented the girls. They broke open a doll trunk belonging to one of the younger girls, read aloud the love letters of one of the older girls, and threatened still another with a whip. One Union soldier importuned the three youngest girls for kisses. Already regarding federal troops "as little less than fiends," the girls fled, but the man "pursued" them, "puckering up his mouth with a smacking sound," and bestowed a "detested kiss" on the youngest girl. At the same time children were targets for mistreatment, they could also manipulate their youth and innocence to their advantage. Susan described another encounter in which two of the same "little girls" were called upon to deter federal troops' intentions to kill the family's overseer, Mr. Scarborough. "We had argued and entreated in vain," Susan explained, but "children might be listened to when grown people's prayers could avail nothing." Urged on by their elders, the girls "burst out crying, wailing, as we knew they would, and threw their arms around Mr. Scarborough. Their innocent, childish grief made a scene that was more than the men had bargained for," Susan explained, and the soldiers agreed to spare the overseer's life.[31]

Confederate children's encounters with Union soldiers ran the gamut from friendly to fearsome. George Robertson, who was eight years old when hostilities began, was initially frightened when Union soldiers entered his home in Asheville, North Carolina. "They rushed all over the house, their sabers rattling against the floors with noisy clanging, their spurs rasping, heavy boots thumping like the stamping of horses in a livery stable, all conspired to make a bedlam." Yet the soldiers did no damage, and one young soldier was even posted as a sentry to protect the family from further invasions. "We grew very fond of the man," George reminisced. "His name was Joe and he was almost like the other Joe [George's brother] in the house. He addressed my Mother as Mother. He churned for her, peeled apples and potatoes and swept the floors and made himself generally useful."[32]

Likewise the Buck children of Virginia, who were terrified by the fighting that took place literally in their backyard, responded favorably to the friendly overtures of the Union officers occupying their house. "The officers are all men with families and seem glad to be in the midst of little children again," explained Lucy, and the younger children, "although freely declaring their rebellious inclinations, have apparently made themselves great favorites with their new acquaintances," who offered them such rare treats as oranges and candy and even, on one occasion, silver coins. A staff attaché, Frank Crippen, "quite won the hearts of the children by his telling stories and treating them," while General Kimball, homesick for his own young son, took immediately to five-year-old Willie, explaining, "I've got a little Willie at home too!"[33]

In Winchester, Virginia, Cornelia Peake McDonald's nine children, ranging in age from infancy to fourteen years at the time of the town's occupation in 1862, had ample opportunity to interact with soldiers, especially after several Union officers commandeered the McDonald residence as headquarters. Once they had satisfied themselves that there were no military supplies hidden in the house, the officers were kindly enough, even supplying the family with food and fuel. Some of the men attempted to befriend the children. Initially the children rebuffed the soldiers' advances. When one "blue coat" passed by Donald, who was two and a half years old at the time, he laid a hand upon his head and greeted him with "'How d'ye do Bub.'" Donald "did not look up, but sullenly said, 'Take your hand off my head, you are a Yankee.'" Gradually the younger McDonald children warmed to the soldiers, especially one officer, Captain Pratt, who "did many little acts of courtesy and kindness." McDonald explained: "He often brought some delicacies for the sick children, which he knew we could not get, oranges, lemons, etc., and many a morning hour he spent walking up and down in the shade with my little Hunter [the second-youngest child] in his arms." But the older boys, who greatly regretted their mother's refusal to allow them to join the Confederate army, remained hostile to the occupying troops, so that when she retired for the evening, McDonald "took very good care to see Harry and Allan safe in their own room, lest, if left in contact with the soldiers they might talk themselves into trouble, as I was very sure they would not be able to hold their peace." Although the younger children accepted gifts and attention from the Union officers, they retained their Confederate loyalties and remained aloof and watchful. When McDonald accidentally left her diary out in the open, little Nelly, thinking "there might be something in it the Yankees ought not to see," hid the volume before admitting two Union officers into the house. "Great prudence on the part of a maiden of seven years," marveled her mother.[34]

Unexpectedly kindly Yankees sometimes confused white children who were thoroughly imbued with Confederate nationalism. Cornelia McDonald's story of an interaction between her young son, Donald, and Captain Pratt, a Union officer well known to the family after months of occupation, exemplified this childish uncertainty. McDonald's description of the scene, at once comfortably domestic and chillingly militaristic, went as follows:

> We were all around the fire, my children, Mary Green and her two, and myself; Capt. Pratt occupied a corner with his sofa. He was showing us a pistol, very finely mounted with gold, which he said a friend had sent him. I had taken it in my hand, and was turning it around to examine it, when my little urchin, Donald, three and a half years old, who was leaning on my lap, touched my hand and said, "Take care, Mama, you will shoot Captain Pratt." "Well" said I, "ought I not to shoot him, he is a Yankee?" Capt. Pratt had petted him, and seemed to like him, and his liking was reciprocated to such a degree that he had never thought of his being a Yankee. He turned his blue eyes on the Captain sadly and reproachfully, with a look that seemed to say, "My idol has been shattered"—gave a deep sigh and said, "Well, shoot him then."[35]

On Bladensfield plantation, also in Virginia, the twelve Ward children, ranging in age from one year to twenty-four at the start of the war, were similarly confused about their relationships with Union soldiers. When a party of Yankees arrived to take teenager Charley Ward, an infamous blockade-runner, prisoner, the younger children were terrified. "I . . . was trembling from head to foot," Evelyn recalled. "We knelt down all at one chair and prayed. For my part, I was crying my eyes out." One soldier made an effort to allay the children's fears: "The commanding officer of the Yankee force was standing opposite Charley's door," Evelyn explained. "He laid his hand on my head and said in a kind voice, 'Sissy, don't cry. We will bring him back again.'" Evelyn's reaction was immediate and visceral: "Oh! Dreadful!

Northern soldiers' efforts to befriend white children often confused youngsters who had learned to regard "Yankees" as ferocious enemies. In this engraving depicting "a scene in the Georgia campaign"—Union General William Tecumseh Sherman's tremendously destructive "March to the Sea"—a soldier reaches out to an infant while a small boy and girl look on. Behind them, another soldier gains the trust of the family's pet dog. *(Library of Congress)*

A Yankee soldier had patted me on the head!" she exclaimed. "I felt disgraced, disloyal to Will [another brother, a Confederate soldier], to Charley, to my whole world, especially so because in my heart I felt his kindness and felt drawn to him," she confessed. Her siblings reinforced her shame: "The children hanging over the garret stairway jeered me," Evelyn continued. "'Hum-m-mm-p! Let a Yankee pet you!' they called. Oh! I was disgraced!" Yet, apparently oblivious to the children's response, the officer then turned to the youngest Ward child, Randolph, who was only a toddler. "'What's your name, little fellow?' he asked. 'I'm a Rebel,' Ran answered. He had picked that up, and always said it when his name was asked. 'Poor little man!'

said Captain Wadworth. 'I hope it will all be over before you are old enough to have anything to do with it.'" Despite his youthful nationalism, the child was attracted to the kind Union soldier who treated his captive and the entire family with such respect and concern. Later "Baby Ran" asked his mother, "'Mamma, . . . if he should push and pull very hard don't you believe that tall, round-headed Yankee who lent Charley his overcoat could get to Heaven?' 'I believe he could, Ran,' answered Mamma, holding his baby hand pressed against her face."[36]

When Union officers took up residence in Confederate households, they developed familiar, even familial, relationships with the children. The sentry in George Robertson's home addressed Mrs. Robertson as "Mother"; General Kimball claimed "little Willie" Buck as his son; Captain Pratt cared as tenderly for Hunter McDonald as any parent. By "winning the confidence and affection of children," Union officers eased their own homesickness, but they also divided Confederate children's loyalties. By casting themselves as the protectors of those whose houses they occupied, Union officers and sentries undermined fatherly authority. Lucy Buck drew a sharp contrast between her ineffectual father and the commanding General Kimball. "Poor Father!" she cried. "He could only walk the pavement with folded arms and drooping head looking helplessly on the scene of desolation." By contrast, Kimball and his fellow officers established themselves as the Bucks' protectors, first reorienting the cannons to avoid striking the house and then promising to prevent looting after the family refugeed. When General Kimball bade the Buck girls "Farewell *daughters*," he called attention to the fact that he had displaced William Buck as family patriarch.[37] Thus Confederate children's relationships with Union troops, whether antagonistic or affectionate, called attention to their own and their parents' helplessness and upset the balance of power in Southern families.

Slave children's responses to Union soldiers were also complex. While adult slaves—and a few well-informed adolescents—may have viewed Union troops as an army of liberation, young slave children almost universally feared Union soldiers. As one ten-year-old put it, "Us was skeered of dem Yankees." In part this was because white Confederates, concerned that their slaves would leave the plantation and seek protection from Union troops, regaled slave youngsters with fearsome stories about Yankees, whom they depicted as cruel men, harsh taskmasters, or worse. Some white Southerners warned that Union soldiers were cannibals who were especially fond of the flesh of black children. Comparisons between Union soldiers and monsters, devils, and demons were commonplace. On one Arkansas plantation, the overseer told the black children, "A Yankee was somepin what had one great big horn on he haid and just one eye and dat right in the de middle of the breast." Elsewhere in the South, ten-year-old Mittie Freeman climbed a tree and refused to come down until the Union soldier who found her removed his hat to show her that he did not have horns.[38]

Slave children's actual encounters with Union soldiers often reinforced their fears. Many former slaves' accounts remark on the soldiers' weapons, suggesting the fear and awe the Yankees inspired, as well as on the frantic efforts of both slaveholders and slaves to conceal necessary supplies and valuable items. "I remember when Yankee soldiers came riding through the yard," Hannah Davidson recalled from the vantage point of the 1930s. "I was scared and ran away crying." The soldiers' imposing appearance made a lasting impression on young Hannah, who was only nine years old when the war began. She reminisced: "I can see them now. Their swords hung at their sides and their horses walked proud, as if they walked on their hind legs." Henry Cheatham, who was "jus' a chile, jus' big enough to tote water to de fiel's" during the war, vividly remembered the arrival of "de Yankees" on the Alabama plantation where he lived. Little Henry's reminiscences indicated that he saw Union soldiers as dangerous predators who deprived all members of the household, slave and free alike, of necessary supplies: horses, meat, and other valuables. "Dem Yankees tuk whatever dey wanted," he asserted, "an' you better not say nothin' neither 'caze dey had dem long swyords ahangin' at dere sides."[39]

For young Barney Laird, who lived in a comfortable home with his parents and grandparents on an Arkansas plantation belonging to a kindly master, Dr. Laird, the arrival of Union troops was devastating. Clad in blue uniforms and cursing terribly, the men methodically destroyed the plantation: "The soldiers tore down houses, burnt houses. They burnt up Dr. Laird's gin. I think it burned some cotton. They tore down fences and hauled em off to make fire at their camps. That let the stock out what they maybe did leave an old nag." Barney remembered Union soldiers as vengeful marauders. "They had cleaned us out," he declared.[40]

Union depredations on slaveholding households deprived slave children as well as white children of necessary supplies. Not surprisingly, then, former slaves' descriptions of soldiers' unwelcome visits are similar to those of white children. Cornelia Robinson testified, "De Yankees wuz a harricane." The soldiers who swept through the slave girl's plantation left a swath of destruction behind them. "Dem Yankees come through an' cleaned out de smokehouse; even lef' de lard bucket as clean as yo' hand," she recalled many decades later. In addition to stealing food, the invading troops engaged in vandalism: "Dey tore up everything dey couldn't take wid dem. Dey poured all de syrup out an' it run down de road lak water."[41]

Slave children, like white children, were subject to home invasion, partly because Union soldiers were aware of slaveholders' tactic of hiding food and valuables in slave cabins. Also like white children, slave children feared physical violence as well as material losses. Decades later, former slaves remembered their frantic efforts to avoid invading soldiers. Eda Harper, who was in her teens during the war, recalled multiple invasions at the Mississippi plantation where she and her siblings were enslaved. Usually, she explained, the slave children hid in the cistern when soldiers approached, but on one occasion, "when the Yankees come in a rush," there was no time to reach their accustomed shelter; instead, "my brother and me hide in the feather bed." On Cornelia Robinson's plantation, one small slave boy was so

The depredations of marauding soldiers from both armies left Southern families and children without food and other essentials. In some cases, invading troops targeted both black and white children for real and symbolic violence. Many children vividly recalled the arrival of armed men on horseback at their homes. In this drawing, foraging soldiers depart from a family farm with supplies (and perhaps stolen horses). A woman holds a small child in the doorway while a slightly older child stands at the gate watching the men leave. In the background, a line of covered wagons indicates that others in the vicinity have decided to refugee rather than confront armed invaders. *(Library of Congress)*

frightened that he hid inside a hollow stump overnight "an' nearly froze to death."[42]

Slave children had good reason to fear Union soldiers. Not all, or even most, Union soldiers saw themselves as agents of emancipation. In a particularly ironic encounter, a white officer sexually assaulted a young female contraband living in the camp under his supervision. Behavior like this revealed Union soldiers' disinterest in being cast as abolitionist liberators.[43]

In addition to laying waste to plantations and thus leaving all residents subject to hunger and cold, Northern soldiers were sometimes especially cruel to slave children. Lonely for their own children, many Union soldiers befriended Southern white children. Yet they treated Southern black children very differently, subjecting them to the same types of sadistic punishments and sexual assault so often rumored to be directed at white Southerners. On one plantation seized by Union troops, soldiers demanded that the slaves sing and dance, apparently in imitation of the blackface minstrel shows then common in the North. When one boy refused, another child recalled, "dey puts him barefooted on a hot piece of tin an' believe me he did dance." In Missouri three guerrilla soldiers gang-raped an eighteen-year-old slave girl; in Tennessee ten-year-old free black America Pearman was raped by a Union soldier who lured her into his tent by promising to give her clothing for her brothers.[44]

Both as individuals and as a group, Union soldiers posed a clear and present danger to slave children's welfare. Attacks on Confederate cities and camps endangered slave children as well as white civilians and soldiers. In Atlanta in the fall of 1864, a shell struck the Clayton family's servants' quarters, "went through the roof and fell into a bed where two little negro children were sleeping, burst and set the bed on fire." Amazingly, the children—a young girl and an eight-month-old baby—escaped unharmed.[45] A Virginia slave boy who accompanied a Confederate soldier to war was less fortunate; he lost an arm when a shell struck the company's camp.[46]

Even when Union soldiers did not directly threaten or harm slave children and adolescents, enslaved youngsters rightly regarded them as agents of sudden and perhaps catastrophic change. Sam Word of Arkansas, who was only two years old when the war began, remembered that the Union soldiers who came to his plantation "wanted to hang old master cause he wouldn't tell where the money was. They tied his hands behind him and had a rope around his neck. . . . I was just a boy and I was cryin' cause I didn't want em to hang old master." As Peter Bardaglio observes in his study of slave children in the Civil War era, "while many of the adult slaves viewed the coming of the Yankees as the visitation of God's wrath, the children perceived the sudden violence that accompanied their arrival as a collapse of all that was familiar and predictable."[47]

In some cases, Union soldiers attempted to allay slave children's fears. Hannah Davidson "was scared and ran away crying" when she first saw armed soldiers on the Kentucky farm where she lived. But while Hannah's master hastened "to hide his money and guns and things," the soldiers told the slave youngster, "We won't hurt you, child." Perhaps the sharp contrast between the evident threat posed to Hannah's owner—an adult white slaveholder—and the protection offered to Hannah herself—an enslaved black child—contributed to the girl's immediate change in attitude. "It made me feel wonderful," she concluded.[48]

Once news of the Emancipation Proclamation spread, slave children were more likely to welcome the arrival of Union soldiers. When General Sherman's troops arrived in Darlington, South Carolina, a young slave girl hollered out, "Bless the Lord the Yankees have come!" Yet the local whites' response to the youngster's voluble support for enemy troops served as a reminder that the presence of even sympathetic Union soldiers might represent danger to slave children: the girl was hanged for her seditious speech.[49]

Although most children—white or black, free or enslaved—initially feared Union soldiers, some came to admire them, and a few even felt genuine affection for them. Whether their response to soldiers' presence was positive, negative, or ambivalent, however, children's frequent comments on Union soldiers indicate that wartime encounters with "Yankees" had a significant effect on Southern children's lives.

*

Many white families chose to relocate farther south or west, away from the battle lines, rather than face the possibility of contact with Union troops. Refugees were motivated not only by their desire for personal safety but also by economic self-interest. By moving their slaves farther from the conflict, they hoped to stanch the flow of slaves who were running away to Union lines. Refugeeing disrupted both white and black families. In addition to the emotionally wrenching experience of leaving home behind and the physical challenges of the journey, refugeeing often separated both white and black family members. In white families, adolescent girls and young children might be sent to stay with relatives in safer regions; this practice ensured children's safety at the cost of considerable anxiety, loneliness, and homesickness. Meanwhile slaveholding families frequently sent their most valuable slaves—adult men and male adolescents—to isolated plantations, separating them from the enslaved family members who remained behind. Finally, refugees disrupted not only their own families but also those with whom they sought shelter. Elite plantation dwellers frequently took shelter in the homes of less-privileged farmers, creating additional work and stress for plain-folk children.

Evelyn Ward's memoirs offer one child's perspective on refugeeing. When the war broke out, eight-year-old Evelyn lived with her parents, eleven siblings, and several slaves at Bladensfield, a large farm in up-country Virginia. Ward and her siblings found the possibility of refugeeing more of an adventure than a hardship. Fearful that Union troops might invade their home and steal their belongings, Mrs. Ward "made up a little bundle for each one of us containing an entire change of clothes, and made us take our bundles out of doors and hide them for ourselves." Far from being frightened by these preparations, the Ward children made a game of them. "After the bundles were hidden," Evelyn explained, "everyone hunted for those of the others to test whether they were well hidden or not. All things considered," she concluded with satisfaction, "we got a good deal of fun out of the coming of the Yankees."[50]

When the approach of Union soldiers forced the family out of their home, Evelyn and her siblings each took their favorite possessions with them. "We made an odd-looking procession," she reflected afterward. "Everyone carried something. Harry had his cat and her kitten in a basket. I had some newly hatched chickens in my pretty black-and-white split basket. On top of the basket was the bamboo mat that went under the tea waiter at the table, and on the mat was my dear big doll, Lucy." Evelyn's description of the crossing of the river to safety read like an account of a family picnic: "It was a very bright, sunny morning in March, the Saturday before Easter. . . . The crossing was delightful. Not a sign of gunboats either up or down the beautiful river stretching out around us. . . . We were not anxious at all. We ran up and down the shore, picked up stones, and played in the sand." Even spending the night in a run-down, abandoned shack while awaiting rescuers did not daunt the younger Ward children. Evelyn simply marveled, "there were so many for one bed!" before falling off to sleep. The next morning a carriage arrived to take the Wards to the home of the Shacklefords, where they joined households with another family, the Joneses, to make up "a welter of children."[51]

The younger Ward children continued to treat refugeeing as a sort of holiday. Evelyn and her sister Fonnie, two years her junior, found much to enjoy in refugee life. "Much of the pleasure of Fonnie's young life and mine," Evelyn later recalled, "came from the Jones and the Shackleford households. The memory of them comes back to me with warm affection—the pranks and warm-hearted gaiety of the Shackleford young people, with the sympathetic background of their mother's cordiality. As for the Joneses, the many evenings we spent with them, the books we read and discussed together, the nights they took us in after dances in the neighborhood when perhaps the house was crowded are memories I can never part with."[52]

Evelyn Ward's account is a good reminder that children may experience events differently from adults, and that younger children may experience events differently from older ones. While Evelyn and her young siblings skipped rocks at the shore, slept many to a bed, and played pranks on each other, Mrs. Ward and the older children, "too anxious to sleep," prayed for protection and kept anxious watch over the youngsters. Evelyn's recollections also are an important reminder that free and enslaved children's experiences, while often similar, also were different in significant ways. Ward noted, without comment, that two slave children, Maria and Frank, accompanied the Wards to the Shacklefords; their mother stayed behind at the Wards' farm,

Bladensfield. How Maria and Frank occupied themselves—and how they felt about being separated from their mother—is not discussed in Evelyn Ward's memoir.[53]

Kate Stone's journal entries about her family's experience of refugeeing offer interesting parallels and striking contrasts to Evelyn Ward's recollections. At the outset of the Civil War, Kate was twenty years old; she lived with six brothers and sisters, ranging in age from eleven to twenty-one, her widowed mother, an aunt, and many slaves on a Louisiana plantation called Brokenburn. Midway through the conflict, when the nearby city of Vicksburg, Mississippi, was under siege, the Stones decided to refugee. Kate's oldest brother, twenty-three-year-old William, left home first, taking "the best and strongest of the Negroes" to the Stones' saltworks near Winfield, Louisiana; "only the old and sickly with the house servants are left here," Kate commented. Like other slaveholders, the Stones sought to protect their most valuable human property by moving slaves away from Union-occupied territory. As a result, slave families were torn apart as young, able-bodied men migrated with their masters, leaving behind women, children, and the elderly. According to one estimate, between 30,000 and 100,000 slaves involuntarily relocated to Texas during the Civil War, often leaving family members behind. When Rosa Green's master refugeed from Louisiana to Texas with a part of his slave workforce, for example, he "lef us little ones," she recalled, "say de Yankees could git us effen dey wan' to." Kate Stone's brief comment about the forced migration of the Stones' slaves—"The Negroes do so hate to go"—did not even begin to describe the despair and grief that the Brokenburn slaves must have felt at their involuntary separation.[54]

Kate Stone devoted significantly more space to her own family's journey, first to Monroe, Louisiana, and ultimately to Tyler, Texas. In April 1863, three months after William and most of the slaves had departed, the Stone women and children and their remaining slaves undertook a three-week journey to Monroe. In the final stage of the journey, "all seven of us, Mamma, Aunt Laura, Sister, Beverly, I, and the two boys, with an assorted cargo of corn, bacon, hams, Negroes, their baggage, dogs and cats, two or three men, and our scant baggage" floated downstream for six hours in "an immense dugout." "It was a dreadful trip," pronounced Kate, and what they found on their arrival was no better:

> We were very crowded, the hot sun beaming on us we were creeping down the bayou, hungry and tired. . . . We were glad enough to get out at the railroad bridge and walk the mile to reach Delhi. The scene there beggars description: such crowds of Negroes of all ages and sizes, wagons, mules, horses, dogs, baggage, and furniture of every description . . . thrown in promiscuous heaps. . . . While thronging everywhere were refugees— men, women, and children—everybody and everything trying to get in the [railroad] cars, all fleeing from the Yankees or worse still, the Negroes.[55]

In addition to describing the general confusion of the refugee experience, Kate Stone's diary sheds light on poor whites' lives and attitudes. The Stones and their entourage joined the throngs of refugees seeking shelter in the homes of local poor whites. In doing so they created additional work for plain-folk children, who were the primary source of labor in nonslaveholding households. Attributing what she saw to place rather than to class or circumstance, Kate observed: "Texas seems a hard land for women and children. They fly around and work like troopers while the men loll on the galleries and seemingly have nothing to do." Like other Southern women of her class, Kate Stone was contemptuous of her plain-folk hosts, describing the men as habitual drunks, the women as overworked drudges, and the children as dirty "tow-heads." She noted with some surprise the rather different reaction of her younger sister, thirteen-year-old Amanda, who befriended the local whites: "Little Sister is the only one who adapts herself readily to circumstances. She is cheerful and happy and quite at home."[56]

Plain folk—both adults and children—were often hostile toward haughty refugees. Kate Stone and her family were denied hospitality frequently en route to Texas. "At house after house," she lamented, "would come the response, 'Naw, we don't take in travelers,' in a tone of contempt, as though the very name of traveler was a disgrace." Once the Stones reached Tyler, Texas, Kate again noted, with some bewilderment, the "great prejudice existing here against the unfortunate refugees." Poor white children took an active part in this class warfare. At school, Kate's brothers were "very unpopular" with their less-privileged classmates, who took offense at the "refugee upstarts" in their broadcloth suits and gold watch chains. Kate was just as baffled by the actions of both sets of boys—who went around armed with pistols and ready to do battle at all times—as she was by the class antagonisms. "How little we can know what is in the heart of a boy," she marveled. "Here we were, so pleased with their innocent sports, thinking them absorbed in their marbles and horses and marching around, when every boy was expecting a deadly encounter and burning with hatred for his enemies."[57]

Kate Stone and her family certainly experienced hardships; they left behind the comforts of home to enter unfamiliar—and often hostile—territory. But their wealth was sufficient to provide them all with safe transportation to a new home and to maintain their status as wealthy slaveholders once they arrived there. Less-privileged refugees faced greater difficulties, with children bearing the brunt of hunger and disease. In Augusta, Georgia, for instance, Arabella Nash died in a boxcar surrounded by strangers; when her relatives tried to adopt her orphaned children, they could find only four of the five. In 1864 a Union soldier in Tennessee stumbled across a house crowded with women and children, refugees from Georgia and South Carolina, all infected with measles. In one room he found the corpse of a woman and her young son, and in the next another woman who had just given birth to a child. From Nashville, an 1864 appeal on behalf of refugee women and children commented, "last spring the mortality among children was fearful" and predicted a "decrease in the population of women and children" as a result of hunger and disease. In Winchester, Virginia, Cornelia Peake McDonald heard

Refugeeing took its greatest toll on children. In this engraving of Missouri refugees arriving in St. Louis, which appeared in *Harper's Pictorial History of the Civil War* in 1894, ragged children cling to their haggard parents while a dog begs for scraps. The girl in the center clings to a doll, perhaps the last remnant of her prewar existence. *(Library of Congress)*

"fearful stories of suffering" in mid-December 1862, when Union soldiers bombarded the town: "Families flying in the midnight darkness and bitter cold, after being all day in their cellars to avoid the shells. Women, and many children were killed in their flight through the streets," she reported, "and thousands houseless, shelterless and starving are wandering in the woods, there to abide the frost and cold of the winter days and nights. The old, the sick and the young children, all alike, driven out of their homes."[58] Clearly, just as children were especially vulnerable to violence at the hands of invading soldiers, they also were the greatest sufferers when their families fled their homes to avoid approaching troops.

Even comparatively fortunate families found refugeeing difficult in both practical and emotional ways. When Lucy Buck and her family fled the family plantation, Bel Air, in November 1862 they "hastily threw a few garments and necessaries for the children into a sheet" and "hurried through town with the cannon booming loudly" all around them. The twenty-year-old was more sorrowful about leaving home than she was frightened of being struck by a shell, however. "It would almost break my heart to lose the old place of mine nativity," she reflected. "The dearest ties of our lives have been formed there," she mused, wondering if she would ever return. The family home was a symbol of family unity; leaving home seemed to augur the dissolution of family ties.[59]

Teenage girls who had been sent away from home to presumably safer locations sometimes had to refugee without their parents. Fifteen-year-old Sallie Bird, who had been sent to a cousin's home in Savannah for safekeeping during the war, had only a few hours' notice of approaching troops when she fled to the home of relatives in Augusta during Sherman's destructive March to the Sea in late 1864. With an assortment of other refugees, including three children under the age of six, Sallie traveled through the night "in the roughest old ambulance imaginable," arriving in Pocataligo, South Carolina, at 3 A.M. "very much fatigued." The following day the party again traveled by wagon through the night to Charleston, which they reached at 5 A.M. They then promptly boarded a train to Augusta, where Sallie and her cousin finally found safe lodgings with another relative, though, she wrote to her mother, "no one thinks we will be here very long without Yankees." For all "the horrors and discomforts" of her journey, Sallie counted herself lucky in having acquired a seat on the train from Charleston to Augusta and arrived at her destination safely. "The poor women and children" on the road had to huddle in the ditches for protection from the shells that "fell thick and fast all around."[60]

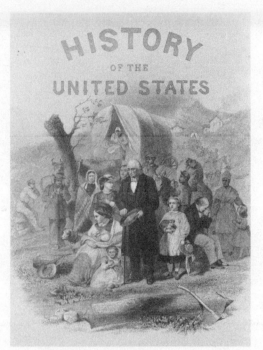

Refugeeing disrupted both black and white families in the Civil War South. In this image from a nineteenth-century U.S. history textbook, white parents and their children take center stage while black families appear in the background. Smoke in the distance indicates that all are fleeing from the destruction of war. *(Library of Congress)*

By separating family members, forcing them out of their homes, and leaving children alone and vulnerable, the refugee experience in some sense universalized the experience of slave families in the Civil War South. In September 1863 Kate Stone commented on the plight of another slaveholding family: "It looks like the whole family is to be ruined, root and branch. Every member of it is broken up and all the women and children fleeing from the Yankees, while all the men and half-grown boys are in the army."[61] As Michael Johnson observes, "the war exposed one generation of white Southerners to four years of a notably mild version of the family separations experienced by ten generations of black Southerners for almost 250 years." During the Civil War, family disruption became a common experience for all Southern children.[62]

*

Like refugeeing, military siege and Union occupation subjected Southern children to similar difficulties—with the added stress of constant danger. During the six-week siege of Vicksburg in the early summer of 1863, residents took refuge from the shelling in cellars, basements, and caves dug in the hillsides surrounding the city. Four-year-old Lida Lord, the daughter of an Episcopalian minister, found that even her father's church was not safe. One night when the family was sitting down to dinner in the rectory, "a bombshell burst into the very center of the dining room, blowing out the roof and one side, crushing the well-spread table like an eggshell, and making a great yawning hole in the floor, into which disappeared supper, china, [and] furniture." Lida, her four siblings, her parents, and the family's house-hold slaves hastily retreated to the basement, where they moaned, cried, and prayed for protection while shells shook the ground around them. Attempting to comfort Lida, Mrs. Lord assured her, "Don't cry, my darling, God will protect us." Through her tears, Lida responded, "But mamma, I's so 'fraid God's killed too!"[63]

Later the Lords joined eight other households—sixty-five people in all, "packed in, black and white, like sardines in a box"—in a cave on the outskirts of town. Mrs. Lord proudly boasted, "the children bear themselves like little heroes. At night when the balls begin to fly . . . and I call them to run to the cave, they spring up . . . like soldiers, slip on their shoes without a word and run up the hill to the cave." But the children's brave actions did not reduce their mortal peril. Little Lucy McRae, who narrowly avoided being buried alive when a blast triggered a landslide in the cave she shared with the Lord fam-ily, later watched the tent where she had been staying demolished by mortar shell. "I sat, stunned with fear," she recalled. "The shots fell thick and fast . . . the booming cannons sounded terrible. . . . When we finally could look out upon the daylight, it was with thankful hearts that we had been spared."[64]

Not all children were so fortunate. Adults reported horrific tales of danger and damage: a three-year-old boy's arm shattered by an exploding shell; a young slave girl mangled by shrapnel; a shell that narrowly missed a boy's head when he stooped to pick something up; another that struck and killed a girl running for shelter. "There is no safety," one Vicksburg resident soberly reported. "Several accidents have occurred. In one cave nearly a whole family were killed or crippled." In addition to mortal fear and mortar fire, children dealt with prolonged confinement and persistent hunger. Unwilling to brave the "circle of fire," families went without food for long periods of time. One diarist wrote: "People do nothing but eat what they can get, sleep when they can, and dodge the shells." Near the end of the siege, a soldier observed "delicate women and children, with pale, care-worn and hunger-pinched features" who "peered at the passer-by with wistful eyes from the caves in the hillsides." Years later Lucy McRae reflected, "I do not think a child could have passed through what I did and have forgotten it."[65]

When Sherman's army arrived in Atlanta a year later, another city's children were exposed to the unforgettable experience of daily bombardment. As in Vicksburg, the city's residents took shelter underground, either in the basements of houses or in "bombproofs," which one young boy described as "holes dug in the earth eight or ten feet deep . . . covered overhead with heavy beams which contained a covering of boards or tin to keep out the rain and then covered with earth from three to five feet deep."[66]

Life underground was both monotonous and terrifying. Ten-year-old Carrie Berry's diary, a matter-of-fact record of her daily activities, conveys the stress of living under siege:

Aug. 4. The shells have been flying all day and we have stayed in the cellar. . . .

Aug. 5. . . . In the evening we had to run to Auntie's to get in
the cellar. We did not feel safe in our cellar, they fell so thick
and fast.

Aug. 6. We have been in the cellar all day. . . .

Aug. 9. We have had to stay in the cellar all day the shells have
been falling so thick around the house. Two have fallen in
the garden, but none of us were hurt. . . .

Aug. 11. We had to go to the cellar often out of the shells. How
I wish the federals would quit shelling us so we could get
out and get some fresh air.

Aug. 14. We had shells in abundance last night. We expected
every one would come through and hurt some of us but to
our joy nothing on the lot was hurt. . . . I dislike to stay in
the cellar so close but our soldiers have to stay in ditches.[67]

Even after Union forces withdrew, children's hardships were not
over, in part because of the enemy's common practice of burning cities
before departure in order to destroy anything of use to the Confederates. When Sherman's soldiers moved through Winnsboro, South Carolina, they destroyed more than thirty buildings, plundered homes
for provisions, and dug up yards and gardens in a search for valuables.
According to one young observer, all that was left were "vacant lots
. . . filled with homeless families."[68]

In Atlanta, Union officers ordered the families of Confederate
soldiers to evacuate the city and prepared to burn it to the ground.
Again, Carrie Berry's diary became a daily record of anxious watchfulness:

Nov. 12. We were fritened [sic] almost to death last night. Some
mean soldiers set several houses on fire in different parts of
the town. I could not go to sleep for fear that they would set
our house on fire. We all dred [sic] the next few days to come
for they said that they would set the last house on fire if they
had to leave this place.

Nov. 13. The federal soldiers have been coming to day and burning houses and I have been looking at them come in nearly all day.

Nov. 14. They came burning Atlanta to day. We all dread it because they say they will burn the last house before they stop. We will dread it.

Nov. 15. This has been a dreadful day. Things have been burning all around us. We dread to night because we do not know what moment they will set our house on fire.

Nov. 16. Oh what a night we had. They came burning the store house and about night it looked like the whole town was on fire. We set up all night. If we had not sat up our house would have been burnt up for the fire was very near and the soldiers were going around setting houses on fire where they were not watched. They behaved very badly. They all left town about one o'clock this evening and we were glad when they left for no body knows what we have suffered since they came in.[69]

The diary entries of this young girl capture the atmosphere of dread that surrounded Southern children during the Civil War. Not all children suffered home invasion, experienced occupation, or lived in besieged cities, of course, but all understood that disaster could occur at any moment. Small wonder that for many Southern children, the dominant emotion of the war years was fear.

*

While Atlanta's white residents arranged to evacuate or stayed to protect their homes, the city's enslaved African Americans, including the Berrys' slave girl, Mary, followed the Union Army's wagons out of town and toward freedom.[70] Difficult as the disruptions of wartime were, they also offered possibilities to enslaved African Americans, who seized the opportunity to escape slavery and seek freedom. Running away, like refugeeing, was fraught with danger and uncertainty.

But unlike refugeeing, which often separated the members of slave families, running away offered the prospect of reuniting family members. For slave children, then, the war years represented both new hardships and new opportunities.

The Civil War offered slaves both new possibilities to claim freedom and new motivations for escaping slavery. From the beginning of the war, Union troops offered the possibility of protection for runaway slaves by seizing them as "contraband" and refusing to return them to their legal owners. This possibility became a probability after the Emancipation Proclamation of 1863, under which slaves in Union-occupied Confederate territory were declared free. In March 1863, shortly after Union forces took Vicksburg, one Louisiana master watched "six of the men with their children and their clothes" leave the plantation "in broad daylight." Indeed, more than fifty thousand runaway slaves camped out along the Mississippi River near the occupied city, seeking protection for their newfound freedom from Union troops.[71]

Runaways were motivated by family as well as by freedom. Slaveowners' wartime actions, including refugeeing with their slaves and sending slaves away to prevent them from escaping to Union lines, strained slave relationships and separated slave families. Some slaves were motivated to escape by the prospect of forced migration and family separation. This was the case for Missouri slave child George Johnson. George's father, Joe, a slave wagoner who hauled grain to the mills across the state line to Iowa for his master, heard rumors "that they [the slaveholders] was going to send as many of the slaves as they could further south . . . cause they thought 'twould be too easy for most of 'em to get away, if they staid too near the boarder [sic] of the free state line." To avoid being forcibly separated from their families, Joe Johnson and a fellow slave wagoner "dumped all of us in the wagon"— "my father and mother, and brothers and sisters, an' the other man an' his wife an' family"—and crossed the border to freedom, evading detection from "a bunch of rebels" guarding the state line by pretending to be transporting a load of grain for their master.[72]

Many enslaved African-American families seized the opportunity for escape offered by the presence of Union troops. In this 1863 photograph captioned "Arrival of Negro Family in the Lines," an extended family, including several children, arrives at a Union camp seeking shelter and protection. *(Library of Congress)*

Other slaves were not as fortunate. In April 1863 Virginian Cornelia Peake McDonald recorded the sad situation of a hired slave woman, Lethea, in her journal. Lethea, who was hired out from her master to McDonald, had been reclaimed by her legal owner, who "wants to sell her to prevent her leaving with the Yankees," McDonald explained. Lethea "wept and wrung her hands" as she explained that while she would be accompanied by one of her children, her other child was to remain behind. "Poor Lethea," McDonald wrote sympathetically. "It is dreadful to see her tears and distress."[73]

Confronted by a similar situation, several slaves in McDonald's own household determined to run away rather than be torn apart. Manuel, Catherine, and their two children attempted an escape upon learning that Manuel was to be impressed into the Confederate Army. Manuel had become separated from Catherine and the children, however, when she "fled to save her children" from "the cruelty of [Union General T. J. "Stonewall"] Jackson's men." McDonald found Manuel taking shelter in an abandoned house, "emaciated almost to a skeleton" and frantic with worry for his wife and children. According to his mistress, the slave was "very repentant." He "said he never would have left me if he had been permitted to stay at home, but that he knew if he went into our lines he would never see Catherine again." An acquaintance of McDonald's found Catherine "making her way painfully along the road from Harpers Ferry, with her baby in her arms and little Manuel following her, the picture of famine and grief," and returned her to McDonald. McDonald's detailed description of Catherine's plight, while intended as validation of her own care for her slaves, indicated the hardships that slave children and their parents endured for the sake of freedom and family:

> When I saw her gaunt figure approaching the house with her poor baby and her arm and the other little one clinging to her ragged skirt, I could not believe the starved, forlorn creature could be my trim-looking, neat nurse, who looked so prosperous when she left me. She said she had had only three hard crackers in the three days past, and that she had turned back because she saw women drop by the roadside with their babies to die.[74]

Fellow Virginian Lucy Buck related a similar tale in her diary in 1863. After her family's slave men had been impressed into service to fortify the capital city, at least two slave women fled with their children. "Nothing was known of Harriet and her clique," but "Mahala and her children had been captured" in Pennsylvania. According to the report that Lucy recorded in her diary, Mahala told one of the men guarding her, a neighbor of the Bucks, that "she wished she was back in her home . . . that now she had spent all her money and was without food and had no one to provide for her. The children next she said—crying and in great distress. Poor things!" exclaimed Lucy.

"I feel sorry for them because they are the innocent sufferers by their mother's folly and I'm afraid this will be only the commencement of their suffering."[75]

Escaping slaves—including children—braved difficult and dangerous situations to achieve freedom and reunite families. Near the occupied city of Vicksburg there were "crowds waiting all the time" to be ferried across the river to a Union camp. The Stone family's slave cook, Jane, and her two "half-grown" children departed from Brokenburn plantation to join the runaway slaves seeking shelter at a nearby Union camp, only to be drowned while crossing a river in an unsteady dugout. "A short space of freedom for them," Kate commented in her journal. Undeterred by the danger, slave families seized every opportunity to gain their freedom. In Virginia, Lucy Breckinridge noted that the women and children who followed Union troops were "just dropped, so tired and dirty, and yet 8 more of ours joined them," including a slave woman, Lydia, with her two children.[76]

Some slave families escaped together; one Union soldier complained that "whole families of them" came to Union-occupied areas seeking freedom. More often women, children, and teenagers set out alone or together in search of other family members. In 1863 Martha Forrest, enslaved in Tennessee, escaped to the occupied city of Nashville after Union soldiers took her father to work on the fortifications there and her mother followed him. She was "determined to follow my parents" and walked two days to get to the city. Following male family members who joined the Union Army was a common pattern, in part because slaveholders often mistreated the family members of African-American men who joined the Union Army. From Fulton, Missouri, one Union captain wrote to his senior officer to ask for advice when a black soldier's enslaved wife arrived in camp with her two-year-old child after being "severely beaten and drive from home by her master and owner." Her departure had been so hasty that she had been forced to leave two older children behind. With no official policy regarding runaway slaves in the Union state of Missouri (where the Emancipation Proclamation did not apply), the officer demanded,

"What is proper for me to do in such cases? *What are we to do with the women and children?*"[77]

Teenage boys also attempted escape, not always successfully. In 1863, shortly after the Emancipation Proclamation went into effect, Henry, a sixteen-year-old Tennessee slave, ran away from his owner. He made it across the border to Kentucky before he was captured and jailed by local whites. When his original owner failed to claim him, Henry was sold at auction. Later that same year a Tennessean "about 14 or 15 years of age" also found himself on the auction block after an unsuccessful escape attempt.[78]

Slave runaways of all ages faced not only difficult journeys but also the possibility of recapture. The costs of recapture, especially for children, were considerable. In 1864 a Missouri slaveholder recaptured a slave woman in the process of running away to join her soldier-husband. Having anticipated his approach, the woman had carefully concealed her three children. When she refused to tell her master where they were hidden, he beat her so severely that she died. What happened to the children is not recorded. In Kentucky another soldier's wife walked to the city of Lexington, seven miles distant, to secure housing for herself and her three children. When she returned to her master's plantation to reclaim her children, she found one too ill to travel. Setting off with the two healthy children, she was captured and returned to the plantation with them. The woman finally escaped—without her children—to Camp Nelson.[79]

Escapes undertaken with the intent of reuniting families, then, could end in family tragedy. In 1864 Emilie Riley McKinley, governess to the Batchelor family near the occupied city of Vicksburg, recorded in her diary:

> A negro man from Mrs. Batchelor's on his way from town yesterday picked up a little negro boy about four years old. He says his mammy lost him. She had a barrel of meat and no room for him in the wagon and pushed him out. He said he belonged to Mr. Wiggins of Livingston. Some Yankees told us yesterday that

negro women were actually wrapping their children in cotton and burning them up to get rid of them. This is a terrible fact. The poor negro is a great sufferer by this war.[80]

Even taking into account McKinley's Confederate loyalty and racial bias, it is clear that slave mothers and children often did become separated in the process of running away to freedom, sometimes with disastrous results. Thousands of runaway slaves, including "vast numbers" of women and children, followed victorious Union soldiers on their marches. Some women and children were accidentally separated; some mothers sent their children ahead without them, determined that they should become free. A soldier in Sherman's army watched one weary mother, unable to walk any farther, secrete her two young sons, no more than five years old, in an army wagon, "intending that they should see the land of freedom if she couldn't." So common was it for slaves attempting escape to be separated from family members that after the war African-American newspapers ran free advertisements for individuals seeking lost family members.[81]

It is also an indisputable fact that black children were "great sufferer[s]" during wartime escapes. Just as slaveholders abused the families of slave men who ran away to join the Union Army, they also mistreated the children of adult slave runaways. In a particularly heartbreaking case in Nashville, a nine-year-old boy died as a result of the severe beatings his mistress administered because of her "anger that his mother had run away in search of freedom."[82]

Because runaways' freedom depended on the presence of Union troops, Yankee retreats could spell disaster for black families and children. In Winchester, Virginia, when Union soldiers left the town in May 1862, diarist Laura Lee commented on the hardships of both runaway slaves and free blacks. "A great many of the colored fugitives have been brought back," she wrote, "the slaves to be returned to their owners, and the free people to be held as prisoners of war." Fearful of enslavement and imprisonment, "numbers of the free people fled in terror," leaving all their belongings behind. In the frantic scramble, children were separated from their parents. Alone and disoriented, "many children have died from exposure and from being accidentally killed in the terror and confusion of the flight."[83]

Even if they successfully escaped their owners and somehow avoided recapture, runaway slaves confronted an unenviable situation. With no food but what they could carry, no clothes except those they wore, and no home but the one they left behind, escaped slaves depended on Union troops for both physical protection and basic necessities—and not all Union soldiers welcomed their role as liberators and defenders of African Americans. Lucy Breckinridge remarked that the Union soldiers who came to her Virginia plantation in 1864 "talked dreadfully about the negroes and said they took no care of them whatever." Union soldiers' willingness and ability to offer aid to escaped slaves were indeed limited, lending credence to Cornelia Peake McDonald's charge that "the Federals had induced them to fly, but could not succor them in their distress."[84]

Willing or not, however, Union soldiers were runaway slaves' best hope for protection and freedom. Declared contrabands of war, escaped slaves formed enclaves everywhere Union troops gained even temporary control. By November 1863 an estimated 50,000 slaves had fled to refugee camps. Children made up a significant portion of camp populations. Nearly half of the 2,000 contrabands living in a camp near Murfreesboro, Tennessee, were children, for example, while out of fewer than 2,000 African Americans in a camp near Helena, Arkansas, approximately 800 were children. In some cases children outnumbered adults. At one camp in Missouri, an Iowa soldier reported: "We have now here some two dozen women and not less than a hundred children—more or les [sic] varying in age from two weeks to 15 years."[85]

Conditions in refugee camps varied widely, depending on Union soldiers' interest in succoring fugitive slaves as well as available supplies. (Andrew Johnson, military governor of Tennessee, refused to issue tents to contrabands during the winter of 1863, arguing that to do so would make them overly dependent on government assis-

Wherever Union soldiers went, runaway slaves followed in search of family and freedom. In this sketch of a contraband camp in Newport News, Virginia, in 1861, a large family with several children seeks refuge with the Union Army. Conditions in contraband camps were spartan at best; in many camps, hunger and disease took their greatest toll on children. *(Library of Congress)*

tance.) Most camps, however, were dismal if not dangerous places. One observer characterized refugee camps as places of "extreme destitution and suffering." Many camps inhabited by runaway slaves were crowded and filthy, fostering epidemic diseases and resulting in mortality rates of nearly 50 percent. At one camp near Nashville, one-quarter of the residents died in a three-month period in 1864. Near Vicksburg, one observer called the contraband camp there "a vast charnel house" with "thousands of people dying without well ones enough to inter the dead."[86]

Disease, exposure, and hunger took their greatest toll on children. In the shadow of the national capital, one group of a dozen or so runaways living in a stable in Washington, D.C., included a young girl with tuberculosis, an infant dying of malnutrition, and an orphaned boy with pneumonia. Another group of six children, all under the age of twelve and dressed in rags, took shelter in a shed in the capital. At a Mississippi plantation, a government agent found thirty-five "poor wretched helpless negros" living in a cattle shed; the group included a disabled man, five women, and twenty-nine children under the age of twelve. And in New Orleans a newspaper carried the bleak notice: "A negro child has been lying dead at No. 81 Perdido Street . . . three days. Warm weather is coming on and it ought to be removed."[87]

Risking danger, disease, and death, enslaved African Americans nonetheless found new opportunities for freedom and family togetherness in the Civil War South. Mary Barbour's earliest memory was of "my pappy wakin' me up in de middle o' de night" to leave the North Carolina plantation where Mary lived with her mother and three other children, all under the age of four. Mary's father, who lived on a different plantation, had taken advantage of the confusion resulting from the arrival of Union troops to steal a wagon and mules, escape the plantation, and go in search of his wife and children. "Half asleep an' skeered stiff," Mary hastily dressed in the dark and set out with the rest of her reunited family for the stolen wagon, which was hidden in a nearby thicket. Only Mary was old enough to walk even a short distance; her father held one child in one arm and held Mary's hand with the other while her mother carried the other two children. "I reckons dat I will always 'member dat walk, wid de bushes slappin' my laigs, de win' sighin' in de trees, and' de hoot owls and whippoorwhills hollerin' at each other frum de big trees," Mary reminisced. Traveling by night and hiding by day "fer a long time," the family eventually made their way to the town of New Bern. There they joined "a pretty good crowd" of refugees seeking shelter with Union soldiers, and Mary's father, a skilled artisan, managed to support the reunited family by making boots for the federal troops.[88]

The Civil War offered African-American children unprecedented opportunities to achieve personal freedom and family security. In the spring of 1864, watching runaway slaves make their way into the Union-occupied city of Vicksburg, Union soldier Isaac Shoemaker compared the weary but hopeful travelers to the Israelites being led out of slavery in Egypt. Like their biblical counterparts, Southern blacks in search of freedom may well have seen a divine power at work in their lives. Certainly they recognized the importance of the Civil War and the end of slavery for the younger generation. Praising the "spirit of freedom," an elderly slave man declared, "I'se berry ol massa, but de little one—dey'l see it; dey'l see it yit."[89]

*

The Civil War had profound and personal effects on Southern children. Children's homes were invaded by soldiers and destroyed by mortars; family members were separated and family loyalties challenged; fear, hunger, and danger became a part of children's daily lives. All children in the Civil War South feared physical violence and family disruption. Despite the differences among them, Southern children experienced the war in similar ways. As the war drew to a close, however, children's differences became more apparent. As slavery ended and the social order foundered, race emerged as the most salient category of social identity and political loyalty. Despite the many similarities in their wartime experiences, white and black children exhibited very different responses to Confederate defeat and African-American emancipation.

CHAPTER FIVE

Defeat and Freedom

THE RECONSTRUCTION OF SOUTHERN CHILDHOOD

In April 1865 physician's daughter Anna Maria Green of Georgia wondered "how long it will be before the dark horrors of war shall cease." Rumors of both imminent defeat and likely victory flooded twenty-one-year-old Anna Maria's hometown of Milledgeville, and she alternated between "dark and gloomy" news of Robert E. Lee's surrender at Appomattox and optimistic reports that the Confederacy had gained powerful European allies. "What is to be the sequel of our struggle God only knows," she mused. On May 1 she wrote:

> This beautiful May-day while the gentle breezes of our Southern clime blow fresh and fair, and the sunny skies bend o'er us, our hearts no longer beat lightly in joy and pride for our armies have surrendered and our state is under yankee dominion. Great God! Must a happy people a mighty nation be bowed to the dust in slavery. O Liberty, Liberty—how sweet thou art. We would give up Luxury, if even in homespun garments and with coarse fare we might be free—Our people might be free. . . . O God grant us freedom![1]

Katie Rowe was at work in the cotton field with the rest of the slaves on her Arkansas plantation when news of freedom came. When they heard the blast of the overseer's horn, she recalled, "we all stop and listen, 'cause it de wrong time of day for de horn." Only after a second blast and a hurried consultation between the slave supervisors did the workers leave the field to investigate the reason for the summons. "When we git to de quarters," Katie recalled, "we see all de old ones and de chillun up in de overseer's yard, so we go on up dar." They found an unexpected scene. "De overseer setting on de end of de gallery wid a paper in his hand, and when we all come up he say come and stand close to de gallery. Den he call off everybody's name and see we all dar. Setting on de gallery in a hide-bottom chair was a man we never see before." Katie, who was probably under fifteen years of age at the time, did not know what was happening, though some of the older slaves guessed. "I think we all been sold off in a bunch," she remembered, but "I notice some kind of smiling, and I think they sho' glad of it." In the next few minutes, young Katie's life changed profoundly:

> De man say, "You darkies know what day dis is?" He talk kind, and smile.
>
> We all don't know of course, and we jest stand dar and grin. Pretty soon he ask again and de head man say, "No, we don't know."
>
> "Well dis de fourth day of June, and dis is 1865, and I want you all to 'member de date, 'cause you allus going 'member de day. Today you is free, jest lak I is, and Mr. Saunders and your Mistress and all us white people,' de man say.
>
> "I come to tell you," he say, "and I wants to be sho' you all understand, 'cause you don't have to git up and go by de horn no more. . . . I wants to bless you and hope you is always is happy, and tell you got all de right and leif dat any white people got," de man say, and den he git on his hoss and ride off.

Although Katie was still not sure what freedom would bring, the news of emancipation made a lasting impact. Interviewed in the 1930s, she exclaimed, "I never forget de day we was set free!"[2]

These two accounts highlight the differences between black and white Southern children's responses to news of the war's end. Whereas African-American children regarded the end of the Civil War with jubilation and looked forward to the future with hope, the children of slaveholders responded to Confederate defeat and the emancipation of slaves with despondency and regarded the future with dread. These accounts also indicate the equal importance—if different meanings— that Southern children attached to freedom in the postwar era. White youngsters regarded themselves as enslaved by the Union troops who occupied the former Confederacy and oppressed by Republican politicians who required Southern states to grant freedom to slaves and civil rights to blacks. Black youngsters, by contrast, viewed Union soldiers as liberators and looked to the Republican government to protect their liberties and advance their rights. During Reconstruction, as during the secession crisis, black and white children evinced divergent political views that reflected their competing understandings of freedom.

*

Regardless of race, children often learned of Confederate defeat and African-American emancipation in a halting and incomplete manner. In part this was a function of disrupted communication systems, which resulted in lengthy delays and consequent confusion. In addition, white Southerners often simply refused to believe reports of Confederate defeat, preferring to follow news of continued fighting on the western front or cling to the hope of outside assistance. Twenty-three-year-old Floride Clemson, who was in Pendleton, South Carolina, in the final months of the war, confessed that "the spirit seems to be getting very despondent every where" but clung to "the only ray of hope" left: "an unfixable report" that France and England intended to recognize the Confederacy as an independent nation. Over the next several weeks Floride complained that although "we hear all kinds of reports," reliable information was hard to come by: "We scarcely ever see a news paper, & are bewildered groping in impenetrable darkness,

& mystery." Unaware that the war had already officially ended, as late as May 1865 Floride feared fresh fighting at any moment. Not until August 1865 was she sure that the war was over.[3]

A further reason for delayed news was that slaveholders attempted to forestall the coming of freedom as long as possible, withholding information from enslaved blacks until the actual arrival of Union troops. In Texas, Susan Merritt and her fellow slaves remained uninformed and enslaved until September 1865, when "a Government man" came to the plantation to inquire "why Master Watt hadn't turned his negroes loose" and "read a paper to the slaves telling them they was free. That's the first we knowed anything about it," Susan pronounced.[4] The end result of these barriers to communication was that in the final weeks of the war Southern children gathered fragments of information (and misinformation) from gossip and newspapers. Many of them nonetheless vividly recorded or recalled the moment they realized the end of the war and its consequences.

Just as children's lessons were disrupted by the secession crisis and the first shots of the Civil War in 1861, they were again halted by Confederate defeat and Union occupation in 1865. A week after Confederate General Joseph E. Johnston's surrender to Union General W. T. Sherman in North Carolina, on May 4, 1865, students at the Lucy Cobb Institute in Athens, Georgia, were granted an unexpected—and unwanted—holiday when their town was occupied by victorious federal troops. "They came without a word of warning," recalled one schoolgirl, "We were at school; Miss Lipscomb was called hurriedly from the room about ten o'clock. Of course we suspected something wrong, and rushed to the windows, although this was forbidden, and to our utter horror saw the streets in front of the Lucy Cobb Institute full of bluecoats." The teacher quickly arranged the students in groups "for our mutual protection and sent us home," but they found no pleasure in the excuse to leave their lessons. "I will never forget my terror," one student pronounced.[5]

Slave children had a different response. From the vantage point of the 1930s, former North Carolina slave Mary Anderson offered an

especially detailed account of the coming of freedom from the perspective of an African-American child. "One day I heard something
that sounded like thunder and missus and marster began to walk
around and act queer," she recalled. Nor were the white adults the
only ones to behave strangely. "The grown slaves were whispering to
each other," Mary remembered. "Sometimes they gathered in little
groups in the grove." The tense atmosphere on the plantation and
the adults' secretiveness must have reminded the young girl of the
months leading up to the beginning of the war. Certainly she was
just as eager to gather information as slave children had been during
the secession crisis. But although she asked her mistress to tell her
what was happening, her mistress sidestepped the question, directing
Mary to "run along and play." Finally, after three days of suspense,
"Marster ordered all the slaves to come to the great house at nine
o'clock." When the time arrived, Mary testified, "you could hear a
pin drap everything was so quiet." Trying desperately to project their
authority over the plantation household, the master and mistress bade
the slaves a good morning, but neither of them could refrain from
crying. "Then marster said, 'Men, women, and children, you are free.
You are no longer my slaves. The Yankees will soon be here.'" Sure
enough, within an hour Mary saw Union soldiers approaching the
house. These Yankees embraced their role as liberators, introducing
themselves to the slaves, sharing their rations, inviting them to leave
the plantation with them, and telling them 'You are free.'" If Mary
had not known how to react to the earlier suspenseful silence, she now
took her cue from the adult slaves, who "were whooping and laughing
and acting like they were crazy."[6]

Like Mary Anderson, many former slaves recounted spontaneous celebrations, complete with singing and dancing, when news of
freedom came. "The end of the war, it come jus' like that—like you
snap your fingers," Felix Haywood declared. "Hallelujah broke out"
as the slaves on his Texas plantation composed songs in celebration.
"Everyone was a'-singin'," he described the joyous occasion. "We was
all walkin' on golden clouds. Hallelujah!"[7]

Slaves who had used song to lighten their labors, express their desire for freedom, and support the Union cause now turned to music to celebrate emancipation. Charlie Moses recalled that when news of freedom came to his plantation, the emancipated blacks there sang:

Free at las',
Free at las',
Thank God Almighty
I's free at las'[8]

On Charlotte Miller's Virginia plantation, the slaves also responded to the news of freedom with spontaneous song. One elderly slave woman, "Sister Carrie," began to chant:

Tain't no mo' sellin' today,
Tain't no mo' hirin' today,
Tain't no pullin' off shirts today,
Its stomp down freedom today.
Stomp it down!

"Fust thing you know," Charlotte recounted the events of that day, the rest of the slaves on the plantation joined in. "Dey done made up music to Sister Carrie's stomp song an' sang an' shouted dat song all de res' de day," she reminisced. "Dat was one glorious time!" she exclaimed.[9] Freedom was indeed a glorious prospect for black children. The celebrations they remembered highlighted issues of particular importance to children who had grown up in slavery, promising a future in which family bonds would be respected and family members would be protected from harm.

The children of slaveholders also recorded the war's end in detail, though their accounts are characterized by desolation and despair. The news of Confederate General Robert E. Lee's surrender at Appomattox on April 9, 1865, "flashed over Richmond like a funeral pall." Richmonder Benjamin Wilkins and his brothers soberly watched Confederate soldiers retreating from the capital city, setting bridges and warehouses ablaze as they departed. The city was in "turmoil" as African Americans and poor whites looted downtown stores and warehouses and Confederate slaveholders hid in their homes awaiting the arrival of federal troops. A stockpile of ammunition only six blocks from the Wilkins's home caught fire, exploding "like a roaring volcano that rocked the foundation of every house in a mile radius." Nine-year-old Benjamin "thought the end of all time had come."[10]

Other white youngsters likewise described Confederate defeat in apocalyptic terms. When Susan Bradford heard the news of Lee's surrender, the nineteen-year-old penned a dramatic entry in her diary: "Oh, I wish we were all dead!" she exclaimed. "It is as if the very earth had crumbled beneath our feet." Twenty-one-year-old refugee Eliza Frances Andrews, who arrived in Macon, Georgia, in mid-April 1865 to find the town "in wildest confusion," wrote in her diary: "The demoralization is complete. We are whipped, there is no doubt about it. Everybody feels it, and there is no use for the men to try to fight any longer, though none of us like to say so. . . . There was an immense crowd at the depot on our return, and when I saw what a wild commotion the approach of the Yankees created, I lost all hope and gave up our cause as doomed." A few days later, when confirmation of Lee's surrender at Appomattox and the armistice between Johnston and Sherman arrived, any lingering hopes were dashed. "It is all over with us now," Eliza lamented, "and there is nothing to do but bow our heads in the dust and let the hateful conquerors trample us under their feet."[11]

"*Conquered, Submission, Subjugation* are words that burn into my heart," twenty-four-year-old Kate Stone wrote in her diary in May 1865. She continued:

> The war is rushing rapidly to a disastrous close. Another month and our Confederacy will be a Nation no longer, but we will be slaves, yes slaves, of the Yankee Government. The degradation seems more than we can bear. How can we bend our necks to the tyrants' yoke? Our glorious struggle of the last four years, our hardships, our sacrifices, and worst of all, the torrents of noble blood that have been shed for our loved Country—all, all in vain.

... There is a gloom over all like the shadow of Death. We have
given up hope for our beloved Country and all are humiliated,
crushed to the earth.[12]

White children's accounts of Confederate defeat acknowledged and
lamented the fact that the social order they had known from infancy
was in jeopardy. When white children described themselves as slaves,
they indicated that the end of slavery, which had undergirded the
South's rigid hierarchies, signaled a profound reordering of society.
Emancipation turned enthusiastic Confederate sympathizers into
downcast conquered slaves.

Southern children's reactions to the end of the war thus divided
sharply by race. White children regarded the war's end with sorrow
and dread. In accord with Confederate nationalism, they equated the
end of the Civil War with the beginning of Union occupation and
described their situation in terms of subjugation, submission, and
slavery. Black children, by contrast, responded to the war's end with
joy and hope. They saw the end of the Confederacy as the beginning of
African-American liberation and rejoiced in their newfound freedom.
While white Southerners described themselves as enslaved, black
Southerners found themselves emancipated.

*

Children of all ages and both races wondered what exactly Confederate defeat and African-American emancipation would bring. "We did
not know what would happen next," Richmonder Benjamin Wilkins
succinctly summed up the situation in the defeated capital city. In
the aftermath of surrender, Macon resident Eliza Frances Andrews
witnessed mobs of "Negroes and children" plundering the military's
supplies of food and ammunition. She lamented: "The props that held
society up are broken. Everything is in a state of disorganization and
tumult. We have no currency, no law save the primitive code that
might makes right. We are in a transition state from war to subjugation, and it is far worse than was the transition from peace to war. The
suspense and anxiety in which we live are terrible." Floride Clemson's

sympathies also were with the defeated Confederacy. "We are crushed indeed, & humiliated," she mourned. Yet she wondered what the future would bring for newly freed slaves as well as for her own family. "The negroes being freed, almost everyone is turning them away by hundreds to starve, plunder, & do worse," she commented, while planters' fields lay fallow, producing neither food for human consumption nor seed for future growing seasons. "The times ahead a[re] fearful," she worried.[13]

Freed slave children did not share elite whites' sense of humiliation, but they also expressed concern about the future. Emancipated adolescent Katie Rowe rejoiced at the coming of freedom yet was unsure what liberation would mean. After the government official who informed the slaves on her plantation of their emancipation departed, she recalled, the newly freed people turned to their former master for direction. "He jest grunt and say do lak we dam please, he reckon, but git off dat place to do it, les'n any of us wants to stay and make de crop for half of what we make." Unsure what else to do, and unwilling to leave the only home they had ever known, the former slaves elected to remain on the plantation as wage laborers. "None of us know whar to go, so we all stay," Katie recollected.[14]

Although at times no less confusing than the disorder of the war's end, the interventions of Northern whites, as well as the demands of former slaveholders, quickly established some parameters for the meaning of emancipation for African-American children. When fourteen-year-old Susie King and her extended family left the Georgia mainland for the Union-occupied islands just off the coastline in the first year of the Civil War, they joined approximately ten thousand other blacks who achieved an early and experimental freedom in the contraband camps of the Sea Islands. On the barrier islands off the coasts of Georgia, South Carolina, and Virginia, slaves who fled to freedom joined those who had been left behind when their masters and mistresses refugeed to the mainland. Declared contrabands of war, the old and new residents of the coastal islands participated in what the historian Willie Lee Rose has termed a "rehearsal for reconstruc-

Education was a priority for African-American families in the postwar South. Adults made considerable sacrifices—and children sometimes confronted violent opposition—to ensure that the next generation would become free educated citizens of the reunited nation. Even before the Civil War ended, schools for freedmen were established by Northern missionaries. African-American communities also set up their own schools, like the Zion School for Colored Children in Charleston, South Carolina, pictured in *Harper's Weekly* in 1866. Neatly dressed schoolchildren hold open books, the emblems of literacy, on their laps in this schoolroom, probably a church sanctuary. *(Library of Congress)*

tion." While the war raged on the mainland, the Sea Islands became a test site for the transition from slavery to freedom. With the Union Army, the federal government, and the self-proclaimed "Gideon's Band" of Northern evangelical abolitionists all vying for authority and influence over both the confiscated lands and the contraband slaves, the islands' residents were subjected to a series of conflicting policies and ideologies regarding work requirements and land redistribution.[15]

The one constant in a welter of contradictory policies and competing priorities was educational opportunity. Northern white abolitionists, seizing the opportunity to promote the free labor values of self-improvement and hard work, sent schoolteachers—mostly single white women—south to teach both literacy and morality to the contrabands. Although Yankee schoolmarms taught adults in evening classes and in Sunday schools, the majority of their efforts were directed at contraband children. As Maine native Sarah Jane Foster expressed it: "With the children lies the hope of the race. . . ."[16]

Newly freed African Americans, previously denied formal education, were enthusiastic students. Susie King, who had secretly acquired an education first from a free black woman and then from a white schoolgirl, was one of the few black teachers in the Georgia Sea Islands. She found that African-American adults and children were anxious to achieve literacy, describing them as "so eager to learn to read, to read above anything else." Sister schoolteachers Lucy and Sarah Chase, who taught contrabands at Craney Island, off the coast of Virginia, in 1863, likewise found their pupils enthusiastic. "Our school children delight us," Sarah Chase wrote. The Chase sisters discovered that their students were eager to learn the mysteries of reading and writing: "I wonder if white children pore over books as my colored little ones do!" exclaimed Sarah Chase. "And I wonder, also, if any white child ever leaped into the mastery of the penmanship of his own name with the agility which characterizes my little children." Even lackluster abolitionists like Sarah Jane Foster concluded that their students' dedication to learning and their ability to progress in their studies was indisputable proof of African Americans' intellectual equality and potential for citizenship. Foster, who taught first in West Virginia and later in South Carolina, proudly reported that a partially blind boy under her tutelage had "plodded on to the Third Reader," even though he could see only half a line at a time, and studied both arithmetic and Geography "with the book at the end of his nose." "Is not that equal to any white person's application?" she demanded.[17]

Both during and immediately after the Civil War, African American children became a focus of public attention and the targets of Northern reformers' efforts to demonstrate that emancipated African Americans could become educated and responsible citizens. As the historian Mary Niall Mitchell and others have pointed out, an important part of this vision for the future included wage labor. To Northern reformers and federal officials alike, the "educable, employable black freechild" represented "the tidy, disciplined future of freed black labor." Edward Pierce, one of the leaders of the "Port Royal experiment," engaged students in a "dialogue" that emphasized the importance of work:

> "Children, what are you going to do when you grow up?"
> "Going to work, Sir."

Thus, long before the cessation of hostilities—even before the Emancipation Proclamation of 1863 transformed "contrabands" into "freedmen"—black children represented not only the future of the race but the future of free labor.[18]

Education and labor were thus linked both in the transition from slavery to freedom and in African-American children's lives in the postwar era. At first the members of "Gideon's Band" and then the officials of the Freedmen's Bureau, the federal agency set up to aid the transition from slavery to freedom, preferred to minimize the authority of parents and ignore the priorities of freedmen. But the conflict between African Americans' preference for self-sufficient family farming and their former owners' desire for wage labor in cash crops would come to define many black children's lives in the aftermath of emancipation.

This conflict was evident even during the war on the Georgia Sea Islands, where contrabands insisted on cultivating food crops rather than devoting all their attention to cotton. This forced the Northern missionaries to accept a task system in which workers were paid by the job and could use their free time to tend their own gardens and livestock, rather than a gang system in which workers, like slaves, worked "from sunup to sundown," with minimal time to devote to their own priorities. Edward Philbrick, a missionary turned planter, complained that without constant supervision the workers on his plantation, "mostly women and children," simply abandoned the cotton fields for other pursuits, ranging from family farming to crab catching, preferring "work for ourselves" to "working for our driver or massa."[19] Philbrick's account, written in 1862, demonstrates both African Americans' preference for diversified farming over monocrop agriculture and the importance of children's labor to black families' strategies for survival. Both of these would be challenged by former slaveowners' demands and Freedmen's Bureau policies in the years to come.

Ultimately African Americans would achieve limited autonomy and family togetherness under the "sharecropping compromise," in which black families cultivated cotton or tobacco on small plots of land in exchange for a "share" of the crop. In the immediate aftermath of the war, however, many engaged in wage labor, either for their former owners under the share-wage system (also earning a share of the crop, but working in large gangs rather than in family groups) or for other Southern whites as contract laborers (with the contracts supervised by the Freedmen's Bureau). Both of these options posed unique difficulties for black children.

Children living in female-headed families encountered the greatest challenges. In the countryside, former owners, no longer anticipating the future labor of African-American youngsters, often refused to employ the mothers of young children, arguing that the children's "keep" would cost more than their mothers' labor was worth. A Freedmen's Bureau agent from Virginia noted: "There is little call for female help, and women with children are not desired." Because labor and lodging were connected, being denied work also meant being denied a home. After emancipation, many planters summarily evicted mothers of small children from the premises. Northern schoolteachers Lucy and Sarah Chase, working in Columbus, Georgia, were horrified to encounter "a worn, weary woman with 11 children, and another, with three," who "came in one night from ten days in the woods; coming away from the plantation." The women explained: "'We was driv off, Misses, kase wese no account with our childer.'"[20]

Forced to leave their old homes, female-headed families roamed the countryside in search of employment. Charlie Moses's matter-of-fact account illustrates this pattern. "When the mistis tol' us we was free (my pappy was already dead, then) my mammy packed us chillun up to move," he explained. A series of short-term jobs, each linked to a move, followed: "We jus' traveled all over from one place to another." Similarly, Samuel Watson's former owner "asked the mother to take her little ones and go away" as soon as freedom was declared. She then "worked from place to place until her [three] children became half starved and without clothing." In both instances, the older children "hired out" as day laborers to earn extra money while the younger children were indentured "for a long number of years." Both practices resulted in long-term or even permanent separation from other family members. Charlie Moses, who took a job transporting lumber along the Gulf Coast, "lost track o' my family then an' never seen 'em no more."[21]

Indenture or apprenticeship—in which individuals entered long-term contracts exchanging labor for food, clothing, shelter, and occasionally some education—had long been used in the South as a way to provide care for orphaned or indigent children without public expense. In the post–Civil War South, however, the laws functioned to help former slaveowners regain control of African-American labor and, in particular, of freed children. South Carolina, Georgia, Mississippi, Arkansas, and Texas all enacted special apprenticeship provisions under the notorious Black Codes. While theoretically race and gender blind, in practice, apprenticeship provisions were used to indenture the children of black female-headed families until adulthood—most frequently defined as age eighteen for females and twenty-one for males. In many cases, newly freed children were bound to their former owners, who received preferential treatment in several states. Within a month of the war's end, more than 2,500 African-American children were apprenticed to their former masters.[22]

Apprenticeship had a devastating effect on these children and on black family life. While some apprentices were orphans, apprenticeship also forcibly removed children from their families without regard for either the adults' or the children's wishes, taking advantage of vague language that permitted indenture in cases of indigence, vagrancy, or immorality. In Harford County, Maryland, during the first two weeks of November 1865, the marshal apprenticed 25 children against their parents' wishes; ten of them were under ten years old. By the end of the month, in Kent County, Maryland, there were 130 indentured black children; 102 of them had parents who protested the court's action. Although some agents criticized the practice of forcible apprenticeship "without respect to the wish of parents or conditions of the children," on balance the Freedmen's Bureau supported indentures as part of its commitment to contractual labor—and indeed, bureau agents sometimes initiated apprenticeships themselves.[23]

Black parents and other kin vigorously protested the apprenticeship of African-American children. As Karin Zipf points out in her study of children's forced labor in North Carolina, "the threat of southern whites' kidnapping their children revived [black adults'] most terrible fears of slavery." At a freedmen's conference in 1866, the attendees described apprenticeship as a ruthless practice that destroyed family life: "Our children, the dearest ties of which bind us to domestic life, and which makes the time of home endearing, are ruthlessly taken from us, and bound out without our consent," they lamented. In addition to the emotional costs of separation, freedpeople also called attention to the financial costs of losing their children. As both planters and parents in the postwar South recognized, children's labor was a valuable commodity. By allocating that labor to whites rather than to blacks, apprenticeship bolstered white supremacy at the cost of black self-sufficiency. Zipf observes, "In an age when children provided essential labor to maintain households, apprenticeship threatened the very independence these families hoped to achieve."[24]

For former slaves, freedom was defined in large part by family—both family togetherness and family self-sufficiency—and apprenticeship thus rendered emancipation meaningless. As one Maryland freedwoman put it in an appeal to the Freedmen's Bureau: "We were delighted when we heard that the Constitution set us all free, but God help us, our condition is bettered but little; free ourselves, but deprived of our children. . . . It was on their account we desired to be free."[25]

Freedmen's Bureau records and local court cases reveal countless contests between black parents and white masters for control of African-American children. An agent for the Freedmen's Bureau in Annapolis, Maryland, testified: "Not a day passes but my office is visited by some poor woman who has walked perhaps ten or twenty miles to . . . try to procure the release of her children taken forcibly away from her and held to all intents and purposes in slavery." Most of these cases involved children above the age of ten, the age at which the value of children's labor surpassed the expense of their keep, and female-headed families, which proved most vulnerable to charges that they were incapable of supporting their families. While children's voices are often lost in these legal proceedings, it is clear that many black youngsters suffered from hunger, exposure, overwork, and abuse at the hands of their white masters. It is certainly true that many, if not all, of these circumstances might characterize the lives of black children living with their parents or other relatives as well. But the case of teenager Lilly Pryor, who in 1865 was taken to a remote county in North Carolina with fifteen other emancipated children while their parents remained in Virginia, suggests that African-American children preferred to take their chances with their own kin. Over the next five years, all the children except Pryor escaped. In 1870 Pryor, by then eighteen years old and bound as a domestic servant until age twenty-one, wrote to her father to beg him to rescue her. "I shall go crazy if I don't get to go home soon," she wrote, adding, "I will kill myself soon if I have to Stay here."[26]

The extent as well as the strength of African-American family ties is revealed in appeals to recover apprenticed children. One Freedmen's Bureau agent noted with some acerbity, "In every case where I have bound out children thus far Some Grandmother or fortieth cousin has come to have them released." In Louisville, another agent received an appeal from Adam Woods, a Kansas resident who hoped to secure custody of his three nephews, who had been left with their owner when their father enlisted in the Union Army in 1864 and later orphaned. In 1867, at the time of the appeal, the boys, ages fourteen, ten, and eight, were apprentices to their former owner. Woods revealed extensive family ties in Kentucky: two sisters and one brother in the city limits, and two additional sisters and a second brother in the countryside. Woods testified that "all of them are able and willing to assist in raising and educating these children." In addition to relying on networks of extended kin in order to care for orphaned children rather than allowing them to be apprenticed to Southern whites, former slaves continued the tradition of "fictive kin" in freedom. As one Freedmen's Bureau agent observed: "I find the colored people themselves taking into their families the orphaned children of their former friends and neighbors thus saving us the necessity of bearing large expenses in caring for them."[27]

As parents' and other relatives' insistence on caring for African-American children suggest, newly freed slaves did everything in their power to reunite families that had been torn apart under slavery. A South Carolina observer noted that "they had a passion, not for wandering, as for getting together, and every mother's son among them seemed to be in search of his mother; every mother in search of her children. In their eyes the work of emancipation was incomplete until the families which had been dispersed by slavery were reunited."[28]

At times such reunions were made difficult by the lengthy separations that had occurred in slavery. Some children had been apart from their mothers from such a young age that they did not even recognize them. Lou Turner of Texas, who had no memories of her mother and called her mistress "mama," recalled: "Old missy have seven li'l nigger chillen what belong to her slaves, but dey mammies and daddys come git 'em. I didn't own my own mammy. I own my old missy and call her 'mama.' Us cry and cry when us have to go with mammy." Similarly, South Carolina slave Mingo White, who was sold away from his parents when he was "jes' a li'l thang," had been cared for by his father's friend, John White, and a slave woman "what ever'body called mammy, Selina White." Unaware that he had "anudder mammy,"

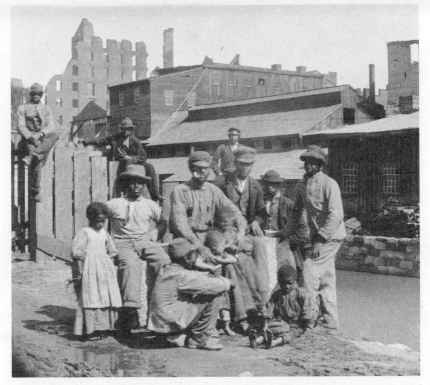

At the close of the Civil War, many former slaves migrated to cities in search of family members and paid employment. Here, a family group poses in front of Haxall's Mill in Richmond, Virginia, in 1865. The family reunion takes place against a backdrop of wartime destruction. *(Library of Congress)*

Mingo gave his biological mother a cold reception when she came to collect him. Decades later he narrated this heartbreaking scene:

> One day I was settin' down at de barn when a wagon come up de lane. I stood 'roun' lack a chile will. When de wagon got to de house, my mammy got out an' broke and run to me an' th'owed her arms 'roun' my neck an' hug an' kiss me. I never even put my arms 'roun' her or nothin' of de sort. I jes' stood dar lookin' at her.[29]

Despite such difficulties, most former slave children rejoiced at family reunions and regarded family togetherness as a defining feature

of freedom. Indeed, African Americans' ability to realize the norma-
tive Southern family—a household headed by a married couple—
increased substantially after the Civil War. In one South Carolina
county, for example, the historian Orville Vernon Burton found that
by 1870 more blacks than whites resided in households containing
both parents and their children (59.5 percent for blacks; 57.7 percent
for whites). While adults celebrated family freedom by legalizing
long-standing unions, children affirmed their family ties by emphasizing the important place of fathers in the family unit. Ellis Bennett
reveled in the right to bear his father's name rather than his master's.
Interviewed in the 1930s, he introduced himself: "Mah name is Ellis Bennett." Regarding his surname as a statement about his family
ties, the former slave insisted that the interviewer record his name
correctly. "Put dat down," he directed, explaining: "Ah tell da man
to change mah name to mah father's name. Da man whut owned me
was name Frierson. Ah took mah father's name. His name is Bennett;
mah name is Bennett."[30] By changing his surname from his master's
to his father's, Ellis Bennett rejected slaveholders' patriarchal notion
of "our family, white and black" and insisted on the primacy of the
black family unit and the authority of African-American fatherhood.
Family togetherness and fatherly authority alike were defining aspects
of the free black family.

*

The black family in freedom was a work unit, and African-American
children were important contributors to the household economy. For
freed children, the difference between slavery and freedom was not
that slavery meant work and freedom meant leisure, but rather that
under freedom they worked as part of the family unit rather than for
white masters. Most black children continued to live in the countryside and do farm labor. Under freedom, however, they took their
orders from their own family members rather than from white owners
or overseers. Children's testimony suggests that they both understood
and appreciated this distinction. William Holtzclaw, for instance, had

For former slaves, creating stable families was an essential aspect of freedom. This "Family Record," designed by a Tennessee printer "for the colored people of America," highlights the difference that emancipation made for African-American families and children, including the opportunity to live and work in family units and to reinstate fatherly authority. *(Library of Congress)*

been apprenticed to a white man when he was ten years old. He remembered how happy he and his brothers and sisters were when their father decided to rent a farm for the family: "We were so happy at the prospects of owning a wagon and a pair of mules and having only our father for boss that we shouted and leaped for joy."[31]

In the countryside, black children worked under their fathers' direction. As Sylvia Watkins succinctly put it: "We wuked in de fiel' wid mah daddy." As in slavery, both boys and girls did all kinds of work. Lucy Gallman remembered: "When freedom come, all slaves went to some place to get work. My father give me six cuts a day to work in the house to spin the yarn. . . . I helped at the corn mill, too, always went there and tote a half bushel corn many days. . . . I worked hard, plowed, cut wheat, split cord wood, and other work just like a man." Although children's work assignments were similar to those in slavery, their attitudes toward work were quite different. Whereas slave children had collaborated in work slowdowns, freed black children exhibited a strong work ethic. Betty Powers was only eight years old when freedom came, but she spoke proudly of her work on the land her father bought in Texas: "De land ain't clear, so we 'uns all pitches in and clears it and builds de cabin. Was we 'uns proud? There 'twas, our place to do as we pleases, after bein' slaves. Dat sho' am de good feelin'. We works like beavers puttin' de crop in."[32] Clearly the significance of black children's work, if not the actual tasks performed, was much different in freedom than it had been in slavery.

While most African-American children in the postwar South belonged to two-parent households, lived in the countryside, and farmed under their fathers' direction, a significant minority did not. As under slavery, many black children in the postwar South grew up in female-headed families. In postwar Southern cities, nearly one-third of black families were headed by women. Driven to the cities in search of work by discrimination against female-headed families in the countryside, single and widowed mothers engaged in wage labor—usually as domestic servants, cooks, washerwomen, or seamstresses—to support their families. Much like free black families before the war, female-headed families in the postwar South often pooled their resources in order to care for the very young and the very old. In Alabama the Hammond household consisted of an elderly woman, Esther, who was ill and no longer able to work. Esther had two unmarried daughters, thirty-three-year-old Nettie and twenty-nine-year-old Ata, who had a total of six children between them. Presumably Esther cared for the children at home while Nettie and Ata found paid work to support the family. Another survival strategy was to put older children to work. Teenage boys found employment in seasonal and extractive industries as cotton-pickers, railroad workers, and lumberjacks while adolescent girls performed domestic labor in white households. In the countryside or in the city, emancipated African-American children worked to support their families.[33]

Work responsibilities notwithstanding, black children in the postwar South had the benefits of more adult attention and greater educational opportunities than they had experienced in bondage. In large part, black women's postwar withdrawal from full-time field labor—and their important contributions to the household economy through domestic work—account for this change. Some examples from a survey of blacks in Alabama in 1865 are suggestive. When Caroline and William Jones, formerly a house servant and a railroad worker, were reunited after slavery, she reported no paid occupation but said she was "caring for her family," which included a daughter and the family's first freeborn child, a son. Presumably William Jones earned enough as a skilled laborer to support the family single-handedly. When that was not feasible, freed black women often engaged in income-producing activity from home, which allowed them both to contribute to the household economy and to care for their children. Nelson and Phoebe Humphrey, who were reunited with their five children after freedom, demonstrate this pattern. Both the Humphreys were formerly field hands, and their teenage daughters had been house servants and field workers. Now, however, Nelson did miscellaneous manual labor while Phoebe took in laundry. Joanna, the fifteen-year-old-daughter who used to be a house servant, now went to school, and Elizabeth, thirteen, no longer worked in the fields but helped her mother with the washing. The younger children evidently either remained at home or attended school.[34]

*

Enabling their children to attend school was a priority for African-American parents in the postwar South. As one freedman expressed it, "leaving learning to your children was better than leaving them a fortune; because if you left them even five hundred dollars, some man having more education than they had would come along and cheat them out of it all." Black Southerners regarded education as an essential aspect of freedom: a route to economic success, a guarantee of citizenship, and a badge of equality. At the Colored People's Convention in South Carolina in 1865 (one of many such conventions in the immediate aftermath of emancipation), those in attendance resolved: "Whereas, Knowledge is power, and an educated and intelligent people can neither be held in, nor reduced to slavery . . . we will insist upon the establishment of good schools for the thorough education of our children."[35] Denied education in slavery, African Americans were determined to have it in freedom.

Immediately following the war, Southern blacks and their Northern allies established private schools for black children and attempted to create a public school system for all Southern children. At every step, however, they found their efforts frustrated by the opposition of local whites, who resisted blacks' attempts to elevate their social status and resented the decline of their own. The education of black children thus became a topic of debate and a point of conflict in the postbellum era. One of the places where the conflict was most acute was Louisiana, where a large population of prosperous African Americans—those who before the war had been classified as *gens de coleur*, or free people of color—allied with former slaves to demand educational opportunities. The port city of New Orleans was one of the few places in the South where public schools had been established. Under Radical Reconstruction, a short-lived political regime that guaranteed the civil rights of freedmen while limiting those of former Confederates, pro-education forces managed to adopt a state constitution that ordered public schools open to all children regardless of their race, color, or former legal status. The possibility of an integrated educational system—what supporters called "common" schools and opponents referred to as "mixed" schools—aroused both fervent support and rabid opposition. The Republican *New Orleans Tribune* touted common schools as the basis of an equal and united society: "In order to have only one nation and one people, we must educate all children in the same public schools." But even those white Democrats who supported public education were opposed to mixed-race schools, since their goal in providing free schooling was, as school superintendent Robert Lusher put it, to "vindicate the *honor and supremacy of the Caucasian race*."[36]

Similar debates swirled around schools for former slaves in rural areas throughout the South. Even before the war's end, some white children attended the freedmen's schools established by Northern missionaries. Because the South as a whole lacked a public school system, and elite whites sent their children to private schools, white children who attended freedmen's schools were "poor whites," or plain folk. Freedmen's schools thus offered new educational opportunities to nonelite white children as well as to former slave children. Freedmen's schoolteacher Sarah Jane Foster, who had one white child in attendance in 1866, sagely remarked that the boy "very wisely discards prejudice that he may have the benefits of a free school." But many white parents were unwilling to send their children to what one father disparagingly called "a 'nigger school.'" As a result, the existence of free schools for blacks in the absence of a parallel system for whites created resentment on the part of Southern whites who were excluded from—or refused to attend—newly established schools for black children. "For many working-class whites," explains the historian Mary Niall Mitchell, "freedchildren's schools raised the possibility that black children might achieve a status equal to that of white children—or, worse, still, in their view, a generation of black children better educated than white children." Such attitudes were evident in Savannah, where freedmen's schoolteachers Sarah and Lucy Chase reported in December 1865 that local whites told the teacher they wanted their children to have "the advantages the Niggers were enjoying" in free school but also asserted that they "would rather they'd die than go to school with the Niggers" or declared, "I will never get so low as to have my children learnin with nigs [sic]." Nor were plain folk the only whites to object to education for black children. While Louisiana resident Tryphena Blanche Holder Fox, like some other planter-class women, established a school for the children of freed slaves on her plantation in order to earn extra money, she resentfully noted, "Only *negroes* are worth being taught now-a-days & the little white children must get their education as best they may."[37]

While politicians and educators debated the issues of public education and mixed-race schools, black and white children fought the same battles in classrooms and on playgrounds. Both integrated public schools in the cities and freedmen's schools in the countryside were plagued by vandalism and arson. In many communities the Ku Klux Klan targeted freedmen's schools for harassment and violence. In 1871 a congressional committee reported that the Mississippi Klan was "marked by the development of most decided hostility to all free schools, and especially to free schools for colored children." Freedmen's schoolteacher Sarah Jane Foster complained repeatedly of catcalls from local whites at her school in Harpers Ferry, West Virginia; Edmonia Highgate, her black counterpart in Vermillionville, Louisiana, narrowly avoided being shot. Children bore witness to such threats and attacks. Elizabeth Hite, born a slave in Louisiana, recalled that when "religious people" tried to establish freedmen's schools in her community, "some kind of riders came along an tol dem dey must not teach niggers."[38]

Children—black and white—also took part in the violence. In Maryland in 1866, a group of white children threw rocks at a freedmen's schoolteacher. From Harpers Ferry, Sarah Jane Foster reported that attendance had fallen off at her school because the younger children were afraid to come to school; "the white boys will molest them when they find an opportunity," she explained. Black children were perpetrators of violence as well as victims; indeed, Foster noted, "the boys of both races seem rather pugilistic about here. They have had several battles for the possession of this hill as a playground. The weapons were stones, and both parties were in earnest." Fistfights between white and black boys were commonplace. In New Orleans one African-American mother declared: "I don't want my children to be pounded by dem white boys. . . . I don't send them to school to fight, I send them to learn."[39]

While girls do not seem to have engaged in physical combat, they did participate in verbal warfare that reveals the pervasiveness of racial tension in postbellum schools. When a fair-skinned girl enrolled in Foster's school for freedmen's children, she became the target of mockery from students with darker complexions. She "indignantly denied being white when the children called her so at recess," Foster wrote in her journal. White schoolgirl Martha Moore related an encounter with a group of black schoolchildren in New Orleans in which one of the black students, spying the white child's geography book, inquired, "Sissy, is dat a jogafry?' Of course," Martha haughtily explained, "I took no notice of the impudent little monkey."[40]

While the issue of educational opportunity clearly divided whites and blacks, the actual content of children's learning also likely promoted racial antagonisms. During the Civil War, Southern authors published textbooks tailored for Confederate children. Marinda Branson Moore was especially prolific, publishing *The Dixie Primer, for the Little Folks*; *The First Dixie Reader: Designed to Follow the Dixie Primer*; and *The Geographical Reader, for the Dixie Children*. Confederate textbooks defended slavery, celebrated the Confederacy, and promoted racism.

The *Dixie Reader* taught pro-slavery beliefs along with sentences and syllables. One selection, "The Cane Mill," described the process of making syrup and celebrated its nutritional value, especially for slaves. Asserting that "many poor white people would be glad of what they leave for the hogs," Moore depicted enslaved African Americans as well-fed "darkies." Other pieces included in the *Reader* likewise suggested that blacks were better off under slavery than they would be in freedom. "Old Aunt Ann" assured young readers that although old, sick, and unable to work, "Aunt Ann knows that her young Miss, as she calls her, will take care of her as long as she lives." As in "The Cane Mill," this piece compared slaves' situation favorably to that of poor whites, concluding, "Ma-ny poor white folks would be glad to live in her [Ann's] house and eat what Miss Kate sends out for her din-ner." Another entry, "Uncle Ned," told the story of "a good old dar-key" who "lov-ed his mas-ter well," but was lured away with his wife and children by the cunning "Yan-kee" who deceived the old man with promises of high living. "He did not fare so well" in freedom, however, "so one dark night he slip-ped away, and kept go-ing till he got back to his kind mas-ter." Having run away from his liberators and abandoned his wife and children in favor of his master, Ned be-came both a loyal servant and a loyal Confederate. The tale concludes: "Ned says 'he wants eb-ry nig-ger to stay at home and mind his work, and let dem Yan-kees do der own work."[41]

The Geographical Reader, for the Dixie Children, contained even more overtly racist messages. This text—perhaps like the "jogafry" Martha Moore read in the New Orleans school district?—divided the earth into "Torrid," "Frigid," and "Temperate" zones. According to the book, while the inhabitants of the "Torrid Zone" were "dark complected, indolent and warlike," and "very ignorant," those from the temperate regions were "white" and "generally industrious and intelligent." After acquainting young readers with the different zones and their inhabitants, the text proceeds to discuss the "Races of Men." Predictably, it depicts Caucasians as "far above the others": civilized, educated, and possessed of a "regular form of government." By con-trast, Africans are described as "slothful and vicious" and ignorant of Christianity. The author editorializes: "The slaves who are found in America are in much better condition. They are better fed, better clothed, and better instructed than in their native country."[42]

The Geographical Reader contains lessons in history and politics as well as in geography. The chapter on the United States consists entirely of a defense of slavery, secession, and the Civil War, explaining that it was the English who first brought "poor heathen negroes" to America; that Northerners practiced slavery until it proved unprofitable, and then sold the slaves south; that power-hungry abolitionists sought to deprive Southerners of their slaves, thus giving the Southern states no option but to secede; and that Abraham Lincoln was "a weak man" who "declared war, and has exhausted nearly all the strength of the nation, in a vain attempt to whip the South back into the Union." The chapter on the Southern Confederacy praises Jefferson Davis as "a good and wise man," describes the new nation as a Christian one with "many good praying people," and reassures young readers that although slaves are "sometimes mistreated," for the most part, slaves are "contented and happy." *The Geographical Reader* even delves into religion and philosophy, explaining that Africans were foreordained for servitude by God's curse on Ham, the son of Noah, and along the way reminding young readers that it is exceedingly "wicked" to disrespect one's parents![43]

White children learned their lessons in racism—whether from schoolbooks or from family members—well. White parents' vociferous objections to interracial schools and white teachers' use of Confederate texts reinforced white children's early socialization rather than encouraging them to rethink hierarchies in the postwar South. Although a handful of white children attended freedmen's schools in the 1860s, and several hundred students attended common schools in Southern cities during their brief experiments with racially integrated schools in the 1870s, the ultimate outcome of the Reconstruction debate over education was the creation of an underfunded and overextended public school system that provided separate—and woefully inadequate—schools for both white and black children. White children in the postwar South thus had extremely limited contact with black children—probably much less than they had had under slavery. Together with the sharp decline in whites' standards of living after the Civil War, this may help explain what some historians regard as a hardening of racial divisions after the war, ultimately leading to the "nadir" of Southern race relations at the turn of the century.

*

While the children of freedmen seized new educational opportunities, the children of former slaveholders confronted new economic difficulties. In some cases these children drew an explicit connection between their own postwar difficulties and black children's new opportunities. "Our circumstances are so reduced that it is necessary to reduce our establishment and retrench our expensive manner of living," Eliza Frances Andrews noted in August 1865. "We have not even an errand boy now, for George, the only [black] child left on the place . . . is going to school!"[44]

In truth, former slaveholders experienced a drastic decline in wealth and status as a consequence of the Civil War. In addition to the loss of human property resulting from emancipation, white Southerners found that their wartime investments and Confederate currency were worthless. Many formerly wealthy families found themselves heavily indebted, and their creditors proved far less sympathetic and patient after the war than they had been earlier. Planters found it difficult to recoup their wealth and pay their debts. Those whose plantations had been in the path of invading soldiers had lost livestock, fences, and tools as well as slave labor; those who had refugeed often returned home to find their houses ransacked by soldiers and their fields ruined by neglect. Small wonder, then, that many elite whites regarded the postwar South as a world turned upside down. As once-wealthy Charlestonian Eliza Mason Smith wrote to her daughters, "Our whole world is demoralized—turned topsy turvy."[45]

Not surprisingly, then, white children's accounts of the immediate postwar period almost universally emphasize their financial difficulties and material losses. In October 1865 Louisiana plantation daughter turned Texas refugee Kate Stone declared: "Our future is appalling." With "no money, no credit, [and] heavily in debt," the

Stone family also confronted the unappealing prospect of returning home to a residence destroyed by flood and a plantation with no workers. "We all had the blues and look forward with dread to our return to Louisiana," twenty-four-year-old Kate remarked, adding, "But there is nothing else to do." The Stone family seemed doomed to "a past of grief and hardship, a present of darkness and despair, and a future without hope." Nor were the Stones alone in their hopelessness. Former Confederates seemed weighed down by an unbearable burden of despondency and dread. As planter's daughter Frances Butler expressed it, "The white population was conquered, ruined, and disheartened, unable for the moment to see anything but ruin before as well as behind."[46]

The physical desolation of plantations and the psychic damage to parents affected planter-class children in profound ways. Even the smallest children felt the melancholy and hopelessness of their parents, who agonized over their difficulties and worried about how to provide for their children. In her reminiscences, planter's daughter Susan Dabney Smedes praised her father's determination to repay his debts and educate his children, yet she also revealed that he was deeply depressed by his dire financial straits after the war. "His heart was well-nigh broken," she recalled, and "he lay in bed, not eating and scarcely sleeping." She recorded a speech her father gave that must have been terrifying to children accustomed to seeing their father confident and in control:

"My children," he said, "I shall have nothing to leave you but a fair name. But you may depend that I shall leave you that. I shall, if I live, pay every dollar that I owe. If I die, I leave these debts to you to discharge. Do not let my name be dishonored. Some men would kill themselves for this. I shall not do that. But I shall die."[47]

While Thomas Smedes managed to pull himself out of the depths of despair, other fathers did not. Benjamin Wilkins described his father, defeated in battle and a failure at farming, as "bitter and broken in health and spirit and estate." Susan Bradford observed that her father was "heartbroken and miserable" and unable to sleep.[48]

Both military and economic failure were difficult for planter-class men, who had been socialized to measure their self-worth in terms of their ability to protect and provide for their dependents. In addition, former soldiers probably suffered from posttraumatic stress disorder, making their adjustment to a changed world even more difficult. Many elite men sank deep into depression and alcoholism, never to recover. Finally, despite their efforts to maintain relationships with their children via correspondence, soldier-fathers necessarily had attenuated relationships with their children. Edgeworth Bird, an affectionate and expressive father who often reminded his wife to "kiss our dear children" on his behalf while he was away at war, nonetheless realized that since his two adolescent children "see very little of him as they verge with maturity," they might "grow into forgetfulness of Papa."[49]

All these factors combined to make it difficult for planter-class fathers to enjoy intimate relationships with their children in the postwar era. Ella Gertrude Thomas, whose journal entries reverberate with her anxiety about her children's futures, nonetheless found joy in their company, writing that they were "a great comfort" to her in her trials. But this was "an unshared joy" with her alcoholic husband, who had "so morbid a dread of our having more mouths to feed" that he grew distant from the couple's ten children. Thomas no doubt spoke truly when she remarked that her husband's "extreme depression of spirits, joined to unusual irritability reacts upon us all."[50]

Mothers too were demoralized by financial difficulties. Virginian Maria Louisa Wacker Fleet was "saddened" to learn that a widowed friend had become "deranged" to the point that she was committed to an asylum. "They say the care of her large estate, debt and other troubles were the cause," she explained. The disturbed mother's children were sent to live with their grandfather. Even much milder forms of depression in parents no doubt caused children considerable distress. Ella Thomas tried not to be "morbid" in her son Turner's presence; "I do not wish to cloud his young life," she confided in her journal.

Yet it hardly seems possible that Thomas—who wrote in her diary that she would die gladly if it would better her children's lives, and who did not regret the death of a newborn because of the difficulties she foresaw for him—could have concealed her melancholy from her children entirely.[51]

Other mothers found that their relationships with their children had been permanently damaged by wartime stress. Texas plantation mistress Lizzie Neblett, for instance, vented her frustration at her increased responsibilities in her soldier-husband's absence toward her children. She whipped all five children (ranging in age from ten months to six years) often, and she frequently expressed her wish to be childless. Not surprisingly, her behavior fed a cycle of abuse and led to emotional distance: six-year-old Billy responded by striking and scratching his siblings until he left scars, and Lizzie accurately predicted that all her children would desert her once they reached adulthood. "I fear my conduct . . . will cause my children to love and respect me less than I deserve," the unhappy mother wrote in 1863, "and yet I fear it is beyond my power to reform."[52]

Most mothers, however, had developed especially close relationships with their children in wartime. Planter-class children took seriously the advice that fathers and other adults gave them to assist and comfort their mothers. "You both owe her *double* duty and love during life," Edgeworth Bird sternly admonished his children, Sallie and Bud, who were thirteen and eleven years old, respectively, when the war began. Even very young children seem to have assigned themselves the task of relieving their mothers' anxiety and lightening their burdens during the difficult war years. Virginian Cornelia Peake McDonald commented frequently on her children's ability to cheer her during the military occupation of her town and her home. "One satisfaction I have through all this distress," she confided to her wartime diary, "and that is, that the children are comparatively well and enjoy life." The nine McDonald children, ranging in age from infancy to fourteen years during the occupation of 1862, were "good children, all of them," McDonald pronounced. "When I look at the happy faces of the children I can almost forget grief and care, for they do not grieve long and though they feel, sorrow sits lightly on them. . . ." McDonald's diary entries make it clear that the children tried to lift their mother's spirits with their affection, even when they had to pretend to happiness. "Nelly, little thing as she is, is companionable, and almost too sympathizing," McDonald wrote about her seven-year-old daughter, adding, "her feeling for me makes her poor little face often look sad and dejected." Six-year-old Roy and four-year-old Donald also comforted and cheered their mother: "Roy with his unceasing busy energy, and Donald quite melts me when he comes in with a lilac, or a tulip or snowdrop, and his blue eyes look so confiding as he offers them."[53]

Planter-class children's affection for their parents and their awareness of their parents' difficulties and distress imbued many of them with a strong sense of responsibility. Elite white children's duties increased significantly after the war. Parents evinced a desire to protect their children from hardship, making material sacrifices, increasing their own labor, and pooling family resources in order to provide their children with a good education, leisure time, and small luxuries. In spite of—or perhaps in recognition of—parents' heroic efforts to shelter them from difficulties, many white children voluntarily took on new responsibilities in the household. In addition, planter-class children and their parents increasingly regarded education as a route to financial recovery for both children and their parents. Thus, in unforeseen ways, the lives of the children of former slaveholders came increasingly to mirror those of the children of former slaves: children from both extremes of Southern society contributed to the household economy, sought education as a route to self-support, and engaged in (or planned to engage in) paid work.

Planter-class parents did everything in their power to minimize disruption to their children's lives in the postwar era. Rather than allow his teenage daughters to launder clothing (a task that had been performed by slave women), Thomas Smedes did the family's laundry himself, proudly declaring, "General Sherman has not brought my daughters to the wash-tub. I could not stand that." Concerned that her children were "mortifie[d]" by appearing in worn-out clothing, Tryphena Fox spent countless hours outfitting them in elaborately designed garments, painstakingly sewn by hand in the evening hours after the day's housework had been completed. Ella Thomas sought financial assistance from her mother to give her daughter dancing lessons. Such actions were intended at least in part to protect planters' claims to elite social status, but they also enabled children to forget their families' difficulties at least for a time. As seventeen-year-old Emma LeConte put it in her diary, "young people cannot be depressed and gloomy *all* the time."[54]

Yet the children of formerly wealthy Confederates never really forgot their families' troubles. Indeed, the financial and familial strategy that most white Southern parents adopted—educating their children for professional work that would enable them to support themselves and help their families—was a constant reminder of how much had changed for elite Southern children. Like their antebellum forebears, white children in the postwar era usually received their primary education at home from their parents and pursued a secondary education at boarding schools or academies. But unlike their predecessors, white children in the postbellum South expected to use their education to earn a living.

No matter how dire their immediate circumstances, planter-class parents made the education of their children a priority. Virginia plantation widow Maria Fleet, like many other financially strapped planters, turned her home into a school in the postwar era. She expected it to succeed, she explained, because "Virginians will educate their children if they possibly can even if they have money for little else." Fleet's observation held true throughout the postbellum South. As Charlestonian Louise North, a member of the enormous (and once enormously wealthy) Petigru clan, aptly remarked, "every one is poor but everyone strives also to be educated." In the post–Civil War era, North's vast extended family sold belongings, pooled family resources, and mortgaged property in order to educate the next generation. Ella

Thomas, who taught school herself in order to educate her children, spoke for an entire generation of white Southerners when she wrote, "Our children, the children of the country should be educated."[55]

The younger generation fully appreciated the sacrifices made for their benefit and eagerly anticipated being able to repay their families for the investment in education. Emma LeConte, who studied at home and taught her younger sister as preparation for a career as a teacher, was anxious to translate her training into earnings: "I wish I could get some employment *now*," she agonized in 1866. "If only I could make a little money—ever so little—just to help Father a little bit." In many families the work of older siblings helped subsidize the education of younger siblings. Just as children expected to repay their parents for investing in their education, they anticipated lightening their siblings' burdens as soon as they were able to do so. Virginia planter's son David Fleet, whose education at Virginia Military Institute was financed in large part by the teaching income of his sisters, praised them for "bearing their part *nobly* and *bravely*" and promised that after graduation, "I shall do all in my power to help."[56]

Elite black children also were eager to help their families financially and frequently turned to teaching to do so. Catharine Geraldine Johnson, the academy-educated daughter of wealthy free blacks in the antebellum South, confronted financial difficulties when her family's slaves achieved freedom in the postwar era. Twenty-year-old Catharine was "so unhappy" at the prospect of poverty in the new social order that she sank into a deep depression following the war. "I feel so useless and so helpless," she wrote in 1866. "I know not what I shall do." Like her white counterparts, the former slaveholder's daughter took up teaching to support herself and contribute to her family's welfare. The desire to help her family pulled her out of her depression. Several years later she wrote in her diary: "I must study hard . . . so that I will be ready should they call upon me to teach again. I do hope sincerely that I may be selected for then I could help them at home. . . ."[57]

The postwar obsession with educating the young created new career opportunities for elite children. Planter-class girls universally

expected to teach, either at the primary level in private homes (occasionally their own, when parents combined the education of their own
children with the income derived from teaching other people's) or at
the secondary level in girls' boarding schools. Boys from the planter
class also prepared themselves to teach, but generally at a secondary
or even college level. But boys had other options as well, including
engineering, business, medicine, law, and the military. Regardless of
gender, planter-class children in the postwar era expected to pursue
professional careers off the plantation. As seventeen-year-old Emma
LeConte reflected shortly before the war's end, "perhaps we will all
have to work for a living before long."[58]

Bidding "farewell" to her "old life" in September 1865, South
Carolina planter's daughter Grace Elmore declared: "Now our voca-
tion is work, and we all recognize it to be so, for young and old, men
and women are pushed by a necessity, before unknown, the need of
bread." Unlike their parents, the younger generation of elite whites
anticipated that they would have to "make a living" rather than relying on either marriage or inheritance to acquire wealth in the form of
land and slaves. Louise Fleet of Green Mount plantation in Virginia,
who taught first at a school in a neighboring town and then at the
boarding school established at her family's home, reinforced this point
with a verse that she required all her students to memorize: "Work is
the weapon of honor."[59]

While planter-class children expected to initiate careers in their
late teens or early twenties, they began to contribute to the household
economy much earlier. White children living in the postwar South
built on their wartime work experience and continued to perform
valuable labor in the home and on the farm. Benjamin Wilkins, whose
family moved from Richmond to the Virginia countryside after the
war, explained that he and his siblings, ranging in age from two to
seventeen years, shared responsibility for farm work. "We had no servants so [mother] divided work among the children, old and strong
enough to carry a pail of water." Younger children—those who had
not yet entered their teens—assumed responsibility for household

chores, including caring for younger siblings, tending livestock, and assisting in housework. Older children took on greater—and more gendered—responsibilities, such as sewing for girls and farm work for boys. Children were keenly aware of their responsibilities to their families. Georgia plantation mistress Ella Thomas marveled that her sixteen-year-old son, Turner, uncomplainingly shouldered the burden of farm work in 1869, when his father declared bankruptcy. "He never murmurs—never complains that he has little spending money— that he has been taken from school and is assisting in ploughing— driving wagons and other farm work." Similarly, Tryphena Fox's oldest daughter, Fanny, was "a great comfort & help" to her mother. "Thoughtful, far beyond her years, & extremely conscientious," as her mother described her, in the months immediately following the war, eight-year-old Fanny displayed a "*natural* watchfulness" for her younger brother and voluntarily took over his care. By the time she was twelve years old, again without prompting from her mother, she was regularly taking care of poultry and helping her mother with housework.[60]

In part because of their increased responsibilities, planter-class children in the postwar era rarely kept diaries commenting on their work or their feelings about it. But in their postwar memoirs the children of former slaveholders revealed that they sometimes found it difficult to adjust to their new circumstances. Benjamin Wilkins, whose family took up farming after the war, wrote extensively about his work responsibilities, which included plowing fields, harvesting wheat, milking cows, chopping wood, and trapping game. In his memoirs the self-styled "farm boy" exhibited weariness rather than pride when he recalled ten-hour workdays. His back ached from long days in the fields, his stomach rebelled at a constant diet of rabbit stew, and he missed the days when he could hunt for sport rather than out of necessity. As an adult, recalling the five years of hard labor and constant hunger he experienced as an adolescent after the war, Benjamin "wondered why fate had dealt so harshly with his boyhood."[61]

*

Planter-class youth lost not only their leisure but also their status in the postwar era. An anecdote about a neighbor child that Susan Bradford recorded in her diary suggested the connection between elite whites' leisure and their socioeconomic status. Having never before seen a white person performing manual labor, the four-year-old boy was thunderstruck to see a white man plowing a field. "Look, look," he cried, "See de marster working in de field." Of course the loss of leisure was directly connected to the departure of slaves, another postwar development that white children found difficult to comprehend. Virginian Evelyn Ward, who was twelve years old at the war's end, recalled: "It was strange to look at [former slaves] Jack and Lewis, Amy and Maria, and know they were no longer our little maids and men."[62] "Strange" indeed. Given the importance of social status in the antebellum South, elite children must have been keenly aware of their loss of white superiority and class privilege.

While daily distinctions between white and black, privileged and poor, diminished in the postwar South, at least some privileged white children clung fiercely to status symbols they remembered from the prewar years. In 1871 Georgia plantation mistress Ella Thomas recorded an altercation between her teenaged son, Turner, and the free black workers on the plantation, who, "very tenacious of their honor," refused to grant him the title "Master Turner." While Turner grudgingly accepted the "compromise" of his childhood nickname, "Buddy," when a worker named Henry responded "Yes" to the white boy's query (rather than "Yes, Sir"), Mrs. Turner intervened, ordering Henry to "be more respectful" or leave the plantation.[63] Clearly, names and titles remained important markers of social status in the postwar South.

Elite children and adolescents in the years after the war, as in the antebellum era, also marked social distinctions in dress (recall that Tryphena Fox's daughter was "mortified" by her shabby garments), in employment (by assigning certain difficult and dirty tasks, such as laundry, to servants, for example), and in education (during Reconstruction there were rumors that white children stole schoolbooks from black children). The continuing importance of such markers of social standing—and elite parents' determination to maintain them—suggests that neither elite white children nor their parents regarded their loss of status with equanimity. As one Georgia plantation mistress firmly stated in a letter to her teenage daughter in 1866, "*caste* is absolutely necessary in society."[64]

Less-privileged white children also both recognized and resented their loss of status vis-à-vis former slaves. George Robertson, the adolescent son of a small farmer and newspaper editor, recalled an incident at Christmas 1865 in which he and his white companions engaged in a violent skirmish with some recently freed black teenagers. George and his friends had pooled their funds to purchase firecrackers, which they used as weapons in an ongoing battle between two gangs of white youth. A group of black boys attempted to join the fray, with disastrous results. "Of course we resented it, for reasons I need not give here," George wrote in his memoirs, "and we turned our guns upon them with all our might." Both white groups hurled incendiary devices at the black interlopers; George himself used a rock to bash in one youth's head and cracked a heavy wooden pole over another's.[65] Whether with physical violence, as in this case, or with verbal warfare, as in the case of the "jogafry" incident related earlier, children of both races and sexes tested and reinforced social distinctions in the postwar South.

*

Different as their attitudes may have been, the everyday experiences of white and black children were strikingly similar in the post–Civil War South. If one imagines antebellum Southern society as a spectrum, with slaveholding children at one end, slave children at the other, and the children of plain folk and free people of color in the middle, one might say that in the postwar era, those at the extremes moved toward the center. Distinctions of class, race, and gender certainly remained, but the common experiences of education and employment came to characterize the lives of all Southern children, regardless of their social standing. As is clear in Southern children's memories of the Civil War, however, shared experiences did not necessarily lead to similar perspectives.

CHAPTER SIX

Memory and Meaning

REMEMBERING SLAVERY AND THE CIVIL WAR

In his postwar memoirs, planter's son Samuel Steel recalled his first encounter with freed slaves in the occupied town of Memphis, Tennessee. Accompanied by his mother and his aunt, the teenager was taking a wagonload of farm produce to town to exchange for necessary supplies when he drove past a regiment of Union soldiers and a group of African-American contrabands. As he passed by, a black girl mockingly called out, "Bottom rail on top now!" Infuriated, Samuel leaped out of the wagon to do battle. "I jumped out of the rockaway and picked up a brick-bat, and the next minute I would have knocked her flat," he recalled, but for his female relatives' pleas and the federal soldiers' presence. Restraining himself with difficulty, Samuel rode on with the girl's final insult ringing in his ears: "Go 'long there, don't look at me that way, you low-down poor white trash, you!" Unable to contain his "impotent rage," as soon as young Samuel was out of earshot he turned to his mother and expressed his desire to "shoot every nigger in the land and every Yankee, too!"[1] The unnamed black girl left no record of this event, but presumably Samuel Steel's intense humiliation was matched, if not surpassed, by this freed slave's sense of victory.

This wartime interracial encounter presaged the very different meanings that children of different backgrounds would attach to the

Civil War in their memories of the tumultuous events of the mid-1860s. Children's converging experiences during and after the Civil War coexisted with their divergent interpretations in postwar memoirs. Telling their stories allowed Southern children-turned-adults to assert control over their wartime experiences after the fact. Narration also enabled authors to advance differing interpretations of the conflict.

Southern children's recollections of the Civil War were shaped by their social position. Race, class, and gender affected both the form and content of children's memories. As adults, well-to-do white children of the Civil War period wrote extensively about their experiences before, during, and after the war. Often dedicating their accounts to their own children and grandchildren, elite white memoirists joined a regional effort to glorify the Old South and defend slavery. Former slave children, by contrast, maintained a public silence about their experiences until the 1930s, when many elderly poor blacks were interviewed under the auspices of the Works Progress Administration (WPA) as part of the New Deal's economic relief program. Although WPA interviewees often echoed whites in their accounts of material comfort under slavery, they also emphasized the psychic costs of the institution, particularly the separation of family members. And where white memoirists exhibited an enduring hatred for Yankee conquerors, black interviewees expressed sincere gratitude to Northern liberators.

Just as race was the most salient factor determining children's responses to Confederate defeat and African-American emancipation, it was the most significant determinant of Southern children's evaluation of the Old South. White memoirists—including diarist-memoirists, who combined their wartime diaries with their adult recollections—universally included defenses of slavery in their accounts. According to white children's recollections, slavery had been a humane institution, one that benefited slaves materially, spiritually, and intellectually. Although such defenses often began or ended with a pro forma statement that the author would not wish for slavery to be reinstated, and sometimes acknowledged isolated instances of cruelty, overall whites' memoirs depicted slavery as a beneficent institution, slaveowners as kind masters, and slaves as loyal servants. As the literary scholar Sarah E. Gardner comments about white women's postwar narratives of the Civil War, they "glorified the antebellum southern civlization," including slavery, "while acknowledging the impossibility of its return." White children, as adult memoirists, demonstrated slaveholders' benevolence and slaves' gratitude by relating anecdotes of loyal retainers and faithful playmates as well as by direct statements or impassioned arguments.[2]

John G. Clinkscales published his memoirs, *On the Old Plantation: Reminiscences of His Childhood*, in 1916 with the express purpose of defending slavery. Dedicating the book to his children and grandchildren, he expressed his concern that "too many of our young people know of the institution of slavery only what they've learned from 'Uncle Tom's Cabin.'" He contended that "Slavery was not all bad," and announced his intention to expose "our children" to the "many bright spots" of the institution. Detailing his personal relationships with slaves as a child, including the slave driver on his plantation, "Unc' Essick," and his slave playmates, Jack and Peter, the memoirist asserted: "The attachment between master and slave was, in some cases, very strong and very beautiful."[3]

Samuel Arnold Steel's 1925 account, *The Sunny Road: Home Life in Dixie During the Civil War*, was still more direct. To counter "the reports put in circulation by the Abolitionists about the cruelty of the Southern slave-holders," he, like Clinkscales, turned to his own childhood experiences: "I was born and brought up among slaves, nursed by them when a baby, and they were my playmates as a boy; but I had never seen any of them treated cruelly." In addition to relating his own positive experiences with slavery, this memoirist also used standard "positive good" pro-slavery arguments to bolster his position. "I am not writing a defense of slavery," he prefaced his extended discussion of the topic. Beginning with the disclaimer that "we are all glad that African slavery . . . is forever ended," he proceeded to give a defense of slavery based on "a great deal" of study on the subject—the study apparently consisting of antebellum proslavery texts that described slavery as a school of civilization and found biblical justifications for human bondage. The Bible did not condemn slavery, the grown-up S. A. Steel observed, and history validated it. "History, which is a great interpreter of truth, shows that slavery was the agency by which some primitive and untutored races have been advanced in civilization," he confidently asserted, concluding, "African slavery in the South converted the ignorant savages from the Dark Continent into civilized men and women."[4]

Sallie Clayton's postwar memoirs (probably written around 1920 but not published in her lifetime) likewise described African Americans as "a poor depraved race" saved from "barbarism" only by "the white man's influence." She also emphasized the physical comforts blacks enjoyed under slavery: "They were as a whole fat, cheerful, [and] jolly," she asserted, "all of which could only be from a life free from care; they didn't have to trouble about food, clothing, house rent, fire, old age or medical attention." Similarly, Benjamin Wilkins related a tale in which a former slave gratefully accepted an offer of employment with her former owners and averred, "The negro race never had a better friend than their old Masters."[5]

White accounts both implicitly and explicitly compared the "ole-time slav'ry nigger" with the emancipated African American, depicting the former as loyal and trustworthy and the latter as lazy and dangerous. Samuel Steel, for instance, asserted: "The Negro is a docile and kind being in his nature, especially the Negro in slavery, for then he was under the educative influence of a humane system, which, while denying him freedom, taught him virtue." The inference, of course, was that in the post–Civil War South, African Americans had freedom but not virtue. Many white memoirists defended slavery by comparing freedom unfavorably with bondage. In *A Small Boy's Recollections of the Civil War*, George F. Robertson indicated that former slaves were unprepared for freedom. African Americans, he suggested, had thoughtlessly welcomed an independence for which they were not equipped. "It took time to realize that care had been forfeited, the care of kind masters, and that responsibilities were facing them to which they had always been strangers," he wrote. Describing former slaves as "improvident," incapable "children," he asserted that disease and crime increased in the absence of white guidance and care. Although he professed that "no sane person would turn his hand to reproduce slavery," the memoirist's portrayal of the former slaves of kind masters now needing to "look out for themselves"—and not doing it very well—was intended to demonstrate that slavery was a better system than free labor. Similarly, Sallie Clayton's memoirs alleged that African Americans' "childlike disposition" did not fit them for freedom. While it was "far better to have them free" for former owners, who were thus relieved of responsibility for slaves' care, she asserted, Southern blacks themselves had been "better off" under slavery. In freedom their "inborn immorality" manifested itself in "criminal tendencies" and domestic violence.[6]

While whites' evaluations of African Americans ranged from positive descriptions of loyal childlike slaves to negative statements about violent free blacks, their discussions of "Yankees" were overwhelmingly negative. As Sarah Gardner observes in her study of Southern white women's narratives of the Civil War, "although a 'conciliatory culture' might have dominated the late-nineteenth-century North, such an attitude merely brushed the South." White female authors in the postbellum South "lionized the actions of the Confederates while casting moral aspersions against the Federals. Both tactics underscored the superiority of antebellum southern civilization."[7]

Instead of emphasizing national reunification, white Southerners who published accounts of the Civil War in the following decades featured anti-Northern vitriol. Emma LeConte, who was seventeen years old at war's end, anticipated the theme of many postwar memoirs in a wartime diary entry. "Oh, my country!" she exclaimed on New Year's Eve 1864. "Will I live to see thee subjugated and enslaved by those Yankees[?]" she demanded. Despite almost certain defeat, the teenager refused to even consider the possibility that the Southern

The Civil War brought the death of family members and the destruction of family homes. Here, a war widow embraces her daughter in front of a boarded-up building. Many Confederate children were embittered by the hardships brought to their families first by the war and then by African-American emancipation. *(Library of Congress)*

Confederacy would rejoin the Union. "Is this a time of submission?" she demanded. "Now when the Yankees have deepened and widened the breach by a thousand new atrocities? A sea rolls between them and us—a sea of blood. Smoking houses, outraged women, murdered fathers, brothers and husbands forbid such a union. Reunion! Great Heavens! How we hate them with the whole strength and depth of our souls!"[8]

Many white memoirists revealed a lasting animosity toward Northerners. Samuel Steel, who as a teenager during the war had vowed "to kill a hundred Yankees" to avenge his family's wartime losses, unapologetically described himself in his 1925 memoirs as "bitter and intolerant to the last degree." Eliza Frances Andrews, who had the opportunity to edit her wartime diary before its publication in 1908, did not expunge the many harsh statements it contained about "Yankees," including a remarkable passage from May 1865 in which she predicted a second Civil War (or perhaps a Second Coming) in which the South would emerge victorious: "Ah, we'll bide our time," she promised. "Though the whole world has deserted us and left us to perish without even a pitying sigh at our miserable doom, and we hate the whole world for its cruelty, yet we hate the Yankees more, and they will find the South a volcano ready to burst beneath their feet whenever the justice of heaven hurls a thunderbolt at their heads." In her introduction to the journal, she offered a blanket justification for her expressions of hatred, explaining, "the author's lot was cast amid the tempest and fury of war, and if her utterances are sometimes out of accord with the spirit of our own happier time, it is because she belonged to an era which, though but of yesterday, as men count the ages of history, is separated from our own by a social and intellectual chasm as broad almost as the lapse of a thousand years."[9]

On balance, girls evinced greater bitterness than boys. Perhaps white women felt the loss of social status more than their male counterparts. After all, both African Americans and white women had been politically powerless and economically disadvantaged in the slaveholding South; with the end of slavery, the dividing line between white women and former slaves was a thin one indeed. White men, on the other hand, retained their economic dominance and, after the disfranchisement of blacks in the late nineteenth century, their political power as well. Perhaps Civil War boys grown into powerful men had less need to hold on to wartime resentments than Civil War girls grown into powerless women, who saw emancipation as stripping them of the racial privileges that had at least partially compensated elite white women for their inferior social status in the antebellum South.

When evaluating the war overall, Southern white girls found less to praise and more to lament than their male counterparts.[10] The reflections of two elite white children, both thirteen years old when the war broke out, serve to demonstrate this gender divide. Shortly before the end of the war, in January 1865, South Carolinian Emma LeConte recorded an extended lament in her diary: "Truly we girls, whose lot it is to grow up in these times, are unfortunate!" she declared. "No pleasure, no enjoyment—nothing but rigid economy and hard work—nothing but the stern realities of life." For Emma, the war years represented a loss of girlhood and the pleasures she associated with both youth and femininity. "These [cares] which should come later are made familiar to us at an age when only gladness should surround us," she mused. "We have only the saddest anticipations and the dread of hardships and cares, when bright dreams of the future ought to shine on us. I have seen little of the light-heartedness and exuberant joy that people talk about as the natural heritage of youth," she concluded. "It is a hard school to be bred up in and I often wonder if I will ever have my share of fun and happiness."[11]

Samuel Steel, by contrast, despite his family's wartime losses, celebrated the drama of the Civil War in his postwar memoirs. "The spirit of the time was heroic," he declared. "The very atmosphere one breathed was charged with the electricity of passion, and each day brought its new occasions of rejoicing or alarm, and every day was full to the brim with anxiety and hope." Samuel's reflections, unintentionally but repeatedly, called attention to the ways in which his outlook was shaped by his gender as well as his age. Despite the hardships, he explained, "there was a certain pleasure in it all, too, for a boy. The excitement, the adventure, the wild freedom of it all, was full of subtle intoxication for a young mind." Like Emma, Samuel described the Civil War as "a hard school," but he found the lessons in hard work and self-reliance worthwhile. "It was a severe school," he acknowledged, "but it taught useful lessons in a way that you never could forget them." He concluded: "It was a splendid training school for a boy."[12]

The Civil War may have been a "school" for black children as well as for white children, but it taught different lessons to children of different races. Where white children described slavery as a beneficent institution, criticized the effects of emancipation, and expressed enduring hatred for Yankee conquerors, black children depicted slavery in harsh terms, celebrated freedom, and lavishly praised Union liberators.

Elderly African Americans interviewed in the 1930s evaluated slavery based on their childhood experiences. In some cases they waxed nostalgic about their early years, contrasting them favorably with the hard times of the Great Depression. Many former slaves, like former slaveholders, characterized the material circumstances of slavery in favorable terms and credited masters and mistresses with providing solid housing, ample food, and medical care. Henry Cheatam told his interviewer, "Dem was good ol' days, Mistis, . . . an' I don't know iffen it warn't better'n it is now." He elaborated: "I has to almos' go hungry, an' I can't git no he'p from de government. . . . Fact is, I believe I druther be alivin' back dere dan today 'case us at least had plenty som'n t'eat an' nothin' to worry about." As Belinda Hurmence points out in the introduction to one collection of ex-slave narratives: "To an aging, destitute black person, bondage may well have seemed less onerous in retrospect, particularly if coupled with memories of an easygoing master, a full stomach, [and] the energy of childhood."[13]

Childhood experiences could also imbue African Americans with an enduring hatred of slavery. Harsh punishments and family separation loomed large in adult blacks' memories of childhood in slavery. John Fields, eighty-nine years old at the time of his interview, admitted that "my innerds turn yet" at the memory of a time that he and all the other slaves on his Kentucky plantation were forced to witness a vicious whipping. Despite his positive statement about "good ol' days" in slavery, Henry Cheatam also recalled seeing "turrible things" on his Mississippi plantation. In addition to watching the overseer whip his mother on numerous occasions, "one day I seen him beat my Auntie who was big wid a chile." He explained: "Dat man dug a roun' hole in de groun' an' put her stummick in it, an' beat an' beat her for a half hour straight till de baby come out right dere in de hole." Although he recalled living in a comfortable house and having "plenty of good, plain food," Cheatam criticized slaveholders for separating slave families: "Sometimes de chilluns would be seprated [sic] from dere maws an' paws," he noted somberly. Delia Garlic remembered overhearing "awful whippings" as a child. "It's bad to belong to folks dat own you soul an' body," she observed, "dat can tie you up to a tree, wid yo' face to de tree an' yo' arms fastened tight aroun' it; who take a long curlin' whip an' cut de blood ever' lick." Owning slaves "soul an' body" also meant that slaveholders could separate slave families with impunity. "Babies was snatched from dere mother's breas' an' sold to speculators," the former slave girl recalled. "Chilluns was separated from sisters an' brothers an' never saw each other ag'in. . . . I could tell you 'bout it all day, but even den you couldn't guess de awfulness of it."[14]

Whereas white children evinced unmitigated hatred for "Yankees," black children directed their bitterness at individual slaveholders and the institution of slavery. Charlie Moses, for instance, forthrightly denounced both slavery and slaveholders. "Slavery days was bitter an' I can't forgit the sufferin'. Oh, God! I hates 'em, hates 'em," he said of his former owners. Many former slaves bitterly recalled childhood injuries—physical and psychological—that had never healed. "Dere am one thing Massa Hawkins does to me what I can't shunt from my mind," Rose Williams told her interviewer. At age sixteen, Rose had been forced to marry against her will in order to produce "portly children" and increase her master's labor force. "I allus holds it 'gainst him," she admitted. Henrietta King, who was permanently disfigured as a result of her mistress's punishment for a childish infraction, stated that when she learned that her former mistress had died, the news "didn't make me drap no tears." As a child, Delia Garlic had been separated from her mother; she also had been burned with a hot iron when she was judged too lax in her care for her owner's child. As an adult, she was unsparing in her critical assessment of slavery: "Dem Days was Hell." And Jenny Proctor, who as an elderly woman still bore scars from a beating incurred when she was ten years old for the offense of stealing and eating a biscuit, stated firmly: "I's hear tell of dem good slave days but I ain't nev'r seen no good times den."[15]

Just as they evaluated slavery based on their childhood experiences, African-American interviewees assessed freedom in terms of its effect on their lives as children. Henry Cheatam, who at age fifteen was about to be sent away from his mother to go to Texas with his mistress's grown daughter, recalled: "I come pretty near to bein' tuk away from my maw. . . . I was goin' to have to go when somebody hollered 'Freedom', an' I sho' was glad 'caze I could stay wid my mammy now." William Curtis, whose father had been sold away from the family under slavery, recalled, "that was the best thing about the war setting us free, he could come back to us." And Charlie Barbour, who was fourteen years old at war's end, explained: "Yes 'um, I reckon I wuz glad ter git free, case I knows den dat I won't wake up some mornin' ter fin' dat my mammy or some ob de rest of my family am done sold." As the historian Peter Bardaglio has pointed out, "black youth . . . perceived the coming of freedom primarily in terms of its impact on their family life."[16]

Where white memoirists denigrated Northerners, black interviewees praised one of them in particular: President Abraham Lincoln. On Felix Haywood's Texas plantation, freed slaves celebrated Lincoln in song:

> Abe Lincoln freed the nigger
> With the gun and the trigger;
> And I ain't goin' to get whipped any more.
> I got my ticket,
> Leavin' the thicket,
> And I'm a-headin' for the Golden Shore![17]

Although the lack of detail in their accounts indicates limited (and sometimes inaccurate) knowledge of the wartime president's politics and policies, African-American interviewees who mentioned Lincoln generally characterized him as the single person responsible for bringing about their freedom. Hannah Davidson's statement about Lincoln was typical. "I thought Abe Lincoln was a great man," she told her interviewer in 1937. "What little I know about him, I

Former slave children learned to regard the Civil War as a war to end slavery and to revere President Abraham Lincoln as the Great Emancipator. In this 1865 print, the central scene focuses on a freed family gathered in a cozy parlor where a portrait of Lincoln hangs on the wall. Below is another portrait of Lincoln, and above, Thomas Crawford's statue of "Freedom." To either side are scenes contrasting slavery and freedom. At left, fugitive slaves flee pursuers, a family is separated at an auction, and slaveholders whip and brand slaves. At right, a black mother in front of a small but comfortable cottage holds an infant and ushers her older children off to public school while a free black man receives a paycheck. This engraving, based on a drawing by Thomas Nast, highlights the importance of family unity and security to African-American emancipation. (*Library of Congress*)

always thought he was a great man. He did a lot of good." Charlie Moses replied to questions about the Civil War: "I don't 'member nothin' 'bout Jefferson Davis. Lincoln was the man that set us free. He was a big general in the war."[18]

Black interviewees' enthusiasm for Lincoln was so great that some related surely fictional tales of wartime encounters with the Great Emancipator. Margaret Hulm, who was twenty years old when the war began, claimed to have met Abraham Lincoln in disguise before the war. "He stayed the night," she reminisced, adding, "we heard after he was gone that he was Abraham Lincoln and he was a spy."

Wade Owens, who was not born until 1863, claimed to have heard Lincoln speak on the theme "for people, by people, and through people." "I always 'membered dat," he stated. According to North Carolinian Frank Patterson, who was fifteen years old when the war began, the president came to his plantation and sat down to breakfast with his master. "They had for breakfast ham with cream gravy made out of sweet milk and they had biscuits, poached eggs on toast, coffee and tea, and grits. They had waffles and honey and maple syrup. That was what they had for breakfast," Frank detailed the encounter. According to Frank's account, Lincoln expressed his distaste for slavery at the breakfast table. "He told my old boss that our sons are 'ceivin' [conceiving] children by slaves and buyin' and sellin' our own blood and it will have to be stopped," Frank asserted. "And that is what I know about that."[19]

For all the differences in black and white Southerners' recollections of the Civil War and its aftermath, they evinced one basic similarity: the war made a lasting impact on Southern children's perceptions of themselves and the world around them, inspiring them to leave a lasting record of their experiences. "That the Civil War still consumed the consciousnesses of southern women to such a degree that they felt compelled to write about it forty years after Appomattox," Sarah Gardner writes of white women writers, "suggests the war's transformative role in southern women's lives." Gardner's observation also applies to wartime children turned postwar authors, who continued to record their memories of the war into the 1930s.[20]

The Civil War profoundly and permanently changed Southern children's daily lives and future prospects. Asked about his memories of the war, former slave Felix Haywood replied: "It's a funny thing how folks always want to know about the War. The war weren't so great as folks suppose." From his vantage point in Texas, far from the fighting, Felix attached little importance to the war itself: "Sometimes you didn't knowed it was goin' on," he recalled. But he conferred tremendous significance on the war's results, declaring: "It was the endin' of it that made the difference." The war—and its aftermath—did indeed make a difference. In the introduction to her wartime diary, Eliza Frances Andrews asserted: "In the lifetime of a single generation the people of the South have been called upon to pass through changes that the rest of the world has taken centuries to accomplish."[21]

These two assessments of the war—one from a former slave, the other from a former slaveholder—suggest that while the Civil War era was a time of upheaval for all Southern children, it certainly did not affect all children the same way. The war's outcome elevated black children's status at the same time it depressed white children's. As Samuel Steel's unnamed antagonist so aptly expressed it, the bottom rail was on top now. Not surprisingly, then, black and white children's recollections of the Civil War era diverged. These children may have lived through many of the same experiences, but they remembered them very differently. Still, a generation of Southern children would have been compelled to agree with thirteen-year-old Jane Friend's final summation: "War is transforming."[22] For generations afterward, Southern children would live with the Civil War's transformative effects.

Notes

Introduction

1. Frank Towers, ed., "Military Waif: A Sidelight on the Baltimore Riot of 19 April 1861," *Maryland Historical Magazine*, 89 (Winter 1994), 429.
2. Ibid.
3. Susie King Taylor, *A Black Woman's Civil War Memoirs*, ed. by Patricia W. Romero and Willie Lee Rose (1902; reprinted Princeton, N.J.: Markus Wiener Publishers, 1988), 31–33.
4. Sue Chancellor, "Personal Recollections of the Battle of Chancellorsville," *Register of the Kentucky Historical Society*, 66 (April 1968), 138–142.
5. William Rose Interview, South Carolina Narratives, Vol. 14, Part 4, pp. 48–50.
6. Earl Schenck Miers, ed., *When the World Ended: The Diary of Emma LeConte* (New York: Oxford University Press, 1957), 41, 90–91.
7. Ibid., 113–115.
8. Drew Gilpin Faust, *This Republic of Suffering: Death and the American Civil War* (New York: Alfred A. Knopf, 2008), xi–xii, 82, 149.
9. Cynthia Monahon, *Children and Trauma: A Guide for Parents and Professionals* (San Francisco: Jossey-Bass Publishers, 1993), 8–10.
10. Chancellor, "Personal Recollections," 146.
11. James Marten, *The Children's Civil War* (Chapel Hill: University of North Carolina Press, 1998).

Chapter One. Family and Identity

1. Harriet A. Jacobs, *Incidents in the Life of a Slave Girl, Written by Herself*, ed. by Jean Fagan Yellin (Cambridge, Mass.: Harvard University Press, 1987), 29.
2. Annie L. Burton, *Memories of Childhood's Slavery Days* (Boston: Ross Publishing Co., 1909), 3, 36–37.
3. Wilma King, ed., *A Northern Woman in the Plantation South: Letters of Tryphena Blanche Holder Fox, 1856–1876* (Columbia: University of South Carolina

Press, 1993), 36–37. See also Adele Logan Alexander, *Ambiguous Lives: Free Women of Color in Rural Georgia, 1789–1879* (Fayetteville: University of Arkansas Press, 1991); Ira Berlin, *Slaves Without Masters: The Free Negro in the Antebellum South* (New York: Vintage Books, 1974); and Michael P. Johnson and James L. Roark, *Black Masters: A Free Family of Color in the Old South* (New York: W. W. Norton, 1984).

4. Ibid.; Wilma King, *The Essence of Liberty: Free Black Women During the Slave Era* (Columbia: University of Missouri Press, 2006), 92; and Virginia Meacham Gould, ed., *Chained to the Rock of Adversity: To Be Free, Black, and Female in the Old South* (Athens: University of Georgia Press, 1998), ln15, liin63.

5. Melton A. McLaurin, *Celia, a Slave: A True Story* (Athens: University of Georgia Press, 1991).

6. Frederick Douglass, *Narrative of the Life of Frederick Douglass, an American Slave, Written by Himself* (1845; reprinted New York: Signet Books, 1968), 23.

7. Frank Lawrence Owsley, *Plain Folk of the Old South* (Baton Rouge: Louisiana State University Press, 1949).

8. Evelyn D. Ward, *The Children of Bladensfield* (New York: Viking Press, 1978), 12, 14, 66.

9. Charles East, ed., *Sarah Morgan: The Civil War Diary of a Northern Woman* (Athens: University of Georgia Press, 1991), 65, 77, 123–124.

10. See especially Elizabeth Fox-Genovese, *Within the Plantation Household: Black and White Women of the Old South* (Chapel Hill: University of North Carolina Press, 1989); Eugene Genovese, "'Our Family, White and Black': Family and Household in the Southern Slaveholders' World View," in Carol Bleser, ed., *In Joy and in Sorrow: Women, Family, and Marriage in the Victorian South, 1830–1900* (New York: Oxford University Press, 1991), 69–87; and John Michael Vlach, *Back of the Big House: The Architecture of Plantation Slavery* (Chapel Hill: The University of North Carolina Press, 1993). In her memoirs, Susan Dabney Smedes said of her mother, "her motherliness extended over the whole plantation." See *Memorials of a Southern Planter* (1887; reprinted Jackson: University Press of Mississippi, 1981), 95.

11. Case studies of slave households, based on both slaveowner records and slave recollections, suggest that roughly half of all slave families lived in "complete" nuclear families (consisting of mother, father, and child or children), with another one-fourth living in "simple" nuclear families (consisting of two of the three elements of a complete nuclear family), and the remainder living with extended family or unrelated individuals. The half of slaves not sharing quarters as complete nuclear families, then, may have been cross-plantation families, families broken by sale, or simply groups of individuals who chose, for either practical or cultural reasons, to define family more broadly than the nuclear unit. See especially Herbert G. Gutman, *The Black Family in Slavery and Freedom, 1750–1925* (New York: Pantheon Books, 1976); Ann Patton Malone, *Sweet Chariot: Slave Family and*

Household Structure in Nineteenth-Century Louisiana (Chapel Hill: University of North Carolina Press, 1992); Emily West, *Chains of Love: Slave Couples in Antebellum South Carolina* (Urbana: University of Illinois Press, 2004). See also Orville Vernon Burton, *In My Father's House Are Many Mansions: Family and Community in Edgefield, South Carolina* (Chapel Hill: University of North Carolina Press, 1985); and Brenda E. Stevenson, *Life in Black and White: Family and Community in the Slave South* (New York: Oxford University Press, 1996).

12. On tri-generational African-American families, see Jacqueline Jones, *Labor of Love, Labor of Sorrow: Black Women, Work, and the Family, from Slavery to the Present* (1985; rev. ed., New York: Vintage Books, 1995).

13. On planter kin networks, see especially Joan E. Cashin, "The Structure of Antebellum Planter Families: 'The Ties that Bound us Was Strong,'" *Journal of Southern History*, 56 (February 1990), 55–70.

14. Historians estimate that approximately one-third of slave couples who separated did so because of slaveholder demands. One study indicates that nearly three-fourths of Virginia slaves sold farther south left family members behind. See Stevenson, "Distress and Discord," in Bleser, ed., *In Joy and in Sorrow*, 103–109.

15. On Southern white families, see especially the essays in Bleser, ed., *In Joy and in Sorrow*; Joan E. Cashin, *A Family Venture: Men and Women on the Southern Frontier* (New York: Oxford University Press, 1991); Jane Turner Censer, *North Carolina Planters and Their Chidlren, 1800–1860* (Baton Rouge: Louisiana State University Press, 1984); Anya Jabour, *Marriage in the Early Republic: Elizabeth and William Wirt and the Companionate Ideal* (Baltimore: Johns Hopkins University Press, 1998); Jan Lewis, *The Pursuit of Happiness: Family and Values in Jefferson's Virginia* (New York: Cambridge University Press, 1983); and Daniel Blake Smith, *Inside the Great House: Planter Family Life in Eighteenth-Century Chesapeake Society* (Ithaca: Cornell University Press, 1980). On slave families, see Eugene Genovese, *Roll, Jordan, Roll: The World the Slaves Made* (New York: Pantheon Books, 1976); Gutman, *Black Family*; Deborah Gray White, *Ar'n't I a Woman? Female Slaves in the Plantation South* (New York: W. W. Norton, 1985).

16. King, ed., *A Northern Woman*, 87.

17. Douglass, *Narrative*, 42.

18. Frances Anne Kemble, *Journal of a Residence on a Georgian Plantation in 1838–1839*, ed. by John A. Scott (New York: New American Library, 1961), 93.

19. Anya Jabour, *Scarlett's Sisters: Young Women in the Old South* (Chapel Hill: University of North Carolina Press, 2007), 25; see also Drew Gilpin Faust, *Mothers of Invention: Women of the Slaveholding South in the American Civil War* (Chapel Hill: University of North Carolina Press, 1996), Introduction.

20. King, ed., *A Northern Woman*, 70, 78, 86, 89. See also 81, 87.

21. Ibid., 90, 102, 120. See also 69, 85, 87, 105, 129, 135.

22. Douglass, *Narrative*, 43, 46.

23. Peter Bardaglio, "The Children of Jubilee: African American Childhood in Wartime," in Catherine Clinton and Nina Silber, eds., *Divided Houses: Gender and the Civil War* (New York: Oxford University Press, 1992), 218.

24. Stevenson, *Life in Black and White*, 113; Hannah Davidson Interview, Ohio Narratives, Vol. 12, 27.

25. John Hammond Moore, ed., *Plantation Mistress on the Eve of the Civil War: The Diary of Keziah Goodwyn Hopkins Brevard, 1860–1861* (Columbia: University of South Carolina Press, 1993), 110–111.

26. Jacobs, *Incidents*, 11; A. C. Pruitt Interview, Rawick, ed., *American Slave*, Louisiana, Vol. 5, Part 3, 218–219 (thanks to Katie Knowles for this reference); Morris Sheppard Interview, Oklahoma Narratives, Vol. 13, p. 287.

27. J. G. Clinkscales, *On the Old Plantation; Reminiscences of His Childhood* (Spartanburg, S.C.: Band & White Publishers, 1916), 98; Douglass, *Narrative*, 33, 44; see also 28, 43.

28. James M. Denham and Canter Brown Jr., eds., *Cracker Times and Pioneer Lives: The Florida Reminiscences of George Gillett Keen and Sarah Pamela Williams* (Columbia: University of South Carolina Press, 2000), 115–116.

29. For more examples of white girls' adoption of adult attire, see Eleanor P. Cross and Charles B. Cross, Jr., eds., *Child of Glencoe: Civil War Journal of Katie Darling Wallace* (Chesapeake, Va.: Norfolk County Historical Society, 1983), 62; and Jabour, *Scarlett's Sisters*, 31–35.

30. Dr. John W. Fields Interview, Indiana Narratives, Vol. 5, p. 78.

31. For boys, see Robert F. Pace, *Halls of Honor: College Men in the Old South* (Baton Rouge: Louisiana State University Press, 2004); for girls, see Christie Anne Farnham, *The Education of the Southern Belle: Higher Education and Student Socialization in the Antebellum South* (New York: New York University Press, 1994).

32. Gould, ed., *Chained to the Rock of Adversity*, xlviii, liin63, 13, 15.

33. Charles Nagel, *A Boy's Civil War Story* (St. Louis: [Eden Publishing House], 1934), 104; Towers, ed., "Military Waif," 428.

34. Douglass, *Narrative*, 43, 53–54; Smedes, *Memorials*, 65; Taylor, *Black Woman's Civil War Memoirs*, 30.

35. Heather Andrea Williams, *Self-Taught: African American Education in Slavery and Freedom* (Chapel Hill: University of North Carolina Press, 2005), 41.

36. Gerda Lerner, ed., *Black Women in White America: A Documentary History* (New York: Pantheon Books, 1972), 34–35.

37. Jacobs, *Incidents*, 9.

38. Stevenson, *Life in Black and White*, 111, 112, 249.

39. Douglass, *Narrative*, 25.

40. Ira Berlin, Marc Favreau, and Steven F. Miller, eds., *Remembering Slavery: African Americans Talk About Their Personal Experiences of Slavery and Emancipation* (New York: New Press, 1998), 19–21.

41. Kathryn Kish Sklar, "Women's Rights Emerges Within the Antislavery Movement: Angelina and Sarah Grimke in 1837," in Kathryn Kish Sklar and Thomas Dublin, eds., *Women and Power in American History: Volume I to 1880*, 2d ed. (Upper Saddle River, N.J.: Prentice-Hall, 2002), 169.

42. For quotation, see James M. Denham, "Cracker Women and Their Families in Nineteenth-Century Florida," in Mark I. Greenberg, William Warren Rogers, and Canter Brown, Jr., eds., *Florida's Heritage of Diversity: Essays in Honor of Samuel Proctor* (Tallahassee, Fla.: Sentry Press, 2007), 18. For more on patriarchy in plain-folk households, see Stephanie McCurry, *Masters of Small Worlds: Yeoman Households, Gender Relations, and the Political Culture of the Antebellum South Carolina Low Country* (New York: Oxford University Press, 1995).

43. James Marten, "Fatherhood in the Confederacy: Southern Soldiers and Their Children," *Journal of Southern History*, 63 (May 1997), 276.

44. Dr. John W. Fields Interview, Indiana Narratives, Vol. 5, 77–78.

Chapter Two. Taking Sides

1. Lucy Paxton Scarborough, "So It Was When Her Life Began: Reminiscences of a Louisiana Girlhood," *Louisiana Historical Quarterly*, 13 (July 1930), 428.

2. Wylie Nealy Interview, Arkansas Narratives, Vol. 2, Part 5, 188.

3. Lily Logan Morrill, ed., *My Confederate Girlhood: The Memoirs of Kate Virginia Cox Logan* (Richmond, 1932), 1.

4. Joan Cashin, ed., *Our Common Affairs: Texts from Women in the Old South* (Baltimore: Johns Hopkins University Press, 1996), 275, 288.

5. Susan Bradford Eppes, *Through Some Eventful Years* (1926; reprinted Gainesville: University of Florida Press, 1968), 30, 32, 41–42, 57, 62, 64.

6. Ibid., 47–48.

7. Ibid., 87.

8. Ibid., 44–45; Ward, *Children of Bladensfield*, 15.

9. Eppes, *Eventful Years*, 32, 38–39, 44–45, 54.

10. Berlin, et al., eds., *Remembering Slavery*, 211, 231.

11. Adeline Blakeley, Arkansas Narratives, Vol. 2, Part 1, 183; Wade Owens, Alabama Narratives, Vol. 1, 308.

12. Berlin, et al., eds., *Remembering Slavery*, 275–276.

13. Donald E. Reynolds, *Texas Terror: The Slave Insurrection Panic of 1860 and the Secession of the Lower South* (Baton Rouge: Louisiana State University Press, 2007), 20.

14. Ibid., 20.

15. Sarah Lois Wadley Diary, October 24, 1860, Southern Historical Collection.

16. Betsy Fleet and John D. P. Fuller, eds., *Green Mount: A Virginia Plantation Family During the Civil War: Being the Journal of Benjamin Robert Fleet and Letters of His Family* (Charlottesville: University Press of Virginia, 1962), 56, 64.

17. Berlin, et al., eds., *Remembering Slavery*, 216; Wilkins, *"War Boy,"* 39; see also Robertson, *Small Boy's Recollections*, 36, 101.

18. Reynolds, *Texas Terror*, 34–38, 110, 125.

19. Edmund L. Drago, *Confederate Phoenix: Rebel Children and Their Families in South Carolina* (New York: Fordham University Press, 2008), 5; Reynolds, *Texas Terror*, 47; see also 58, 67, 97, 176, 183, 185, 192, 193.

20. Eppes, *Eventful Years*, 119.

21. [Constance Cary Harrison], "A Virginia Girl in the First Year of the War," *Century Magazine* 30 (1885), 606; George F. Robertson, *A Small Boy's Recollections of the Civil War* (Clover, S.C.: George F. Robertson, 1932), 16.

22. Nagel, *A Boy's Civil War Story*, 206, 212.

23. James Miller and John Thompson, *Almanac of American History* (Washington, D.C.: National Geographic Society, 2006), 156–157.

24. Sarah Lois Wadley Diary, October 24, 1860; Elizabeth R. Baer, ed., *Shadows on My Heart: The Civil War Diary of Lucy Rebecca Buck of Virginia* (Athens: University of Georgia Press, 1997), 31.

25. Berlin, et al., eds., *Remembering Slavery*, 271.

26. Frank A. Patterson Interview, Arkansas Narratives, Vol. 2, Part 5, 278. Patterson's mistress's response, if any, is not included in his account.

27. Berlin, et al., eds., *Remembering Slavery*, 216–217.

28. Fannie Page Hume Diary, November 6, 1860, Southern Historical Collection.

29. Ward, *Children of Bladensfield*, 18.

30. "A Virginia Girl in the First Year of the War," 606.

31. Robertson, *Small Boy's Recollections*, 15.

32. Fannie Page Hume Diary, November 26, 1860; and Sarah Lois Wadley Diary, December 4, 1860.

33. Berlin, et al., eds., *Remembering Slavery*, 213–214. For another account of slaves' secret prayers for freedom while maintaining a façade of politeness before their owners, see ibid., 233.

34. Adeline Blakeley, Arkansas Narratives, Vol. 2, Part 1, 183–184.

35. Daniel W. Crofts, *Reluctant Confederates: Upper South Unionists in the Secession Crisis* (Chapel Hill: University of North Carolina Press, 1989).

36. Peter W. Bardaglio, "On the Border: White Children and the Politics of War in Maryland," in Joan E. Cashin, ed., *The War Was You and Me: Civilians in the American Civil War* (Princeton, N.J.: Princeton University Press, 2002), 325.

37. Fleet and Fuller, eds., *Green Mount*, 14, 17; *New York Times*, Oct. 2, 1860; *Harper's Weekly*, May 14, 1864; John Minor Botts, *The Great Rebellion: Its Secret History, Rise, Progress, and Disastrous Failure* (New York: Harper and Brothers, 1866).

38. Fleet and Fuller, eds., *Green Mount*, 9, 16, 18, 27

39. Ibid., 33–35.

40. Ibid., 38–40.

41. Ibid., 40, 42, 48, 50.

42. Ibid., 51–52, 57.

43. Bardaglio, "On the Border," 320, 323–325.

44. Joan Cashin, ed., *Our Common Affairs: Texts from Women in the Old South* (Baltimore: Johns Hopkins University Press, 1996), 288; Nagel, *A Boy's Civil War Story*, 206.

45. Eliza Frances Andrews, *The War-Time Journal of a Georgia Girl, 1864–1865*, ed. by Spencer Bidwell King, Jr. (Macon, Ga.: Ardivan Press, 1960), 312–313.

46. Berlin, et al., eds., *Remembering Slavery*, 211.

47. Ibid., 214–215. Katie's age is unknown, but since she also mentioned believing in Santa Claus and did not mention her work responsibilities, she was probably around six years old.

48. Moore, ed., *Plantation Mistress*, 110–111.

49. Ward, *Children of Bladensfield*, 26.

50. Drago, *Confederate Phoenix*, 7.

51. Sophia Haskell Cheves, "A Schoolgirl's Recollection of Fort Sumter," Sophia Lovell Haskell Cheves Papers, South Carolina Historical Society.

52. John Q. Anderson, *Brokenburn: The Journal of Kate Stone, 1861–1868* (Baton Rouge: Louisiana State University Press, 1995), 33; Emmy E. Werner, *Reluctant Witnesses: Children's Voices from the Civil War* (Boulder, Colo.: Westview Press, 1998), 8; [Benjamin Harrison Wilkins,] *"War Boy": A True Story of the Civil War and Re-Construction Days* (Tullahoma, Tenn.: Wilson Brothers, 1938), 21–22.

53. Werner, *Reluctant Witnesses*, 39, 444.

54. Ward, *Children of Bladensfield*, 32, 52.

55. C. Alice Ready Diary, July 15, 1861.

56. John Rozier, ed., *The Granite Farm Letters: The Civil War Correspondence of Edgeworth and Sallie Bird* (Athens: University of Georgia Press, 1988), 48, 50, 76, 80, 95.

57. Fleet and Fuller, eds., *Green Mount*, 60–61, 86, 111, 119, 123–124, 166–168, 193, 223, 271.

58. Sarah Lois Wadley Diary, August 21 and 28, 1861. See also July 22 and 28, October 19, 1861. The accuracy of Sarah's information depends on what battles she was referring to. She probably referred to the August 10 battle of Wilson's Creek in Missouri, in which U.S. Colonel Franz Sigel attacked Confederates southwest of Springfield; the battle ended in Confederate victory and resulted in U.S. Brigadier General Nathaniel Lyon's death, which is consistent with Sarah's diary. The remainder of her entry is inaccurate, however. The West Virginia battle she mentioned may have been a July 2 encounter at Martinsburg or a July 11 engagement at Rich Mountain, in both of which the Union, not the Confederacy, prevailed. The reports of engagements in Texas and at Leesburg, Virginia, were entirely erroneous,

though it is possible that Sarah meant the July 25 Battle of Mesilla, Arizona, in which Texas forces won a victory and lost only seven men.

59. Sarah Lois Wadley Diary, July 22 and 28, November 15, 1861; February 2, April 13, 1862; January 1, 1863.

60. Ward, *Children of Bladensfield*, 18, 26, 76–77.

61. Berlin, et al., eds., *Remembering Slavery*, 245, 262, 272; Kym S. Rice and Edward D. C. Campbell, Jr., "Voices from the Tempest: Southern Women's Wartime Experiences," in *A Woman's War: Southern Women, Civil War, and the Confederate Legacy*, ed. by Edward D. C. Campbell, Jr., and Kym S. Rice (Charlottesville: University Press of Virginia, 1996), 106.

62. Werner, *Reluctant Witnesses*, 45; James Johnson Interview, Florida Narratives, Vol. 3.

63. Anderson, ed., *Brokenburn*, 33; Bardaglio, "Children of Jubilee," 219. Williams, *Self-Taught*, suggests that parents encouraged such eavesdropping. See pp. 9–10.

64. Faust, *This Republic of Suffering*, 141; Erika L. Murr, ed., *A Rebel Wife in Texas: The Diary and Letters of Elizabeth Scott Neblett, 1852–1864* (Baton Rouge: Louisiana State University Press, 2001), 348, 390, 437.

65. Berlin, et al., eds., *Remembering Slavery*, 233.

66. Anderson, ed., *Brokenburn*, 37.

67. Berlin, et al., eds., *Remembering Slavery*, 245.

68. Sarah Lois Wadley Diary, December 26, 1862. Although New Orleans and thirteen parishes were exempt, Wadley's Amite County was included in the Emancipation Proclamation.

69. Drago, *Confederate Phoenix*, 6, 9, 13; Cashin, ed., *Our Common Affairs*, 275.

70. Ward, *Children of Bladensfield*, 44.

71. Anderson, ed., *Brokenburn*, 13, 17.

72. Frances Wallace Taylor, Catherine Taylor Matthews, and J. Tracy Power, eds., *The Leverett Letters: Correspondence of a South Carolina Family, 1851–1868* (Columbia: University of South Carolina Press, 2000), 97. Charles, who was twenty-eight at the time, died that same year.

73. Drago, *Confederate Phoenix*, 14, 16–18.

74. Fleet and Fuller, eds., *Green Mount*, 54, 61, 83, 211, 241, 243, 252–253, 274.

75. Ibid., 295, 298, 310–312. Ben was dressed in a Confederate uniform and scouting the retreat of Union Colonel Ulrich Dahlgren after a failed raid on Richmond when he unexpectedly encountered federal soldiers, who opened fire. Wounded in the arm, Benny attempted to flee to safety but bled to death in the woods. His horse was found grazing at Green Mount the following morning, and his dog led the searchers to his body. His friend and fellow scout William Taliaferro was also fired upon but escaped unharmed. See *Green Mount*, 312n5 and *Green Mount After the War*, 54n43.

76. Drago, *Confederate Phoenix*, 16.

77. Ward, *Children of Bladensfield*, 36.
78. Tracy J. Revels, *Grander in Her Daughters: Florida's Women During the Civil War* (Columbia: University of South Carolina Press, 2004), 52; see also Drago, *Confederate Phoenix*, 17, 24–25.
79. Drago, *Confederate Phoenix*, 15–16; Amy Murrell Taylor, *The Divided Family in Civil War America* (Chapel Hill: University of North Carolina Press, 2005), Chapter 1; Ward, *Children of Bladensfield*, 33.
80. Anderson, ed., *Brokenburn*, 327.
81. Andrews, *War-Time Journal*, 312.
82. Jabour, *Scarlett's Sisters*, 243.
83. James C. Bonner, ed., *The Journal of a Milledgeville Girl, 1861–1867* (Athens: University of Georgia Press, 1964), 9–10; Sally Munford to Jennie Munford, April 24, 1862, and Sally Munford to Lizzie Munford, April 30, 1862, Munford-Ellis Family Papers, Duke, quoted in Jabour, *Scarlett's Sisters*, 246–247; Sarah Wadley Diary, June 1, 1862. On "the politicization of the southern belle," see Ott, "When the Flower Blooms in Winter," Chapter 3, and Jabour, *Scarlett's Sisters*, Chapter 6.
84. Phyllis Jenkins Barrows, "History of Lucy Cobb Institute, 1858–1950," in Phinizy Spalding, ed., *Higher Education for Women in the South: A History of Lucy Cobb Institute, 1858–1994* (Athens: University of Georgia Press, 1994), 19, 57; Sarah "Sallie" Conley Clayton, *Requiem for a Lost City: A Memoir of Civil War Atlanta and the Old South*, ed. by Robert Scott Davis, Jr. (Macon, Ga.: Mercer University Press, 1999), 38.
85. John F. Marszalek, ed., *The Diary of Miss Emma Holmes, 1861–1866* (Baton Rouge: Louisiana State University Press, 1979, 1994), 264; Mary Lee Kemper, "Civil War Reminiscences at Danville Female Academy," *Missouri Historical Review* 62 (April 1968), 315.
86. Anderson, ed., *Brokenburn*, 17–18.
87. John W. Fields Interview, Indiana Narratives, Vol. 5, 80; King, *Stolen Childhood*, 131.
88. Marten, *The Children's Civil War*, 24.

Chapter Three. Play and Work

1. Alice Maury Parmalee, ed., *The Confederate Diary of Betty Herndon Maury, 1861–1863* (Washington, D.C.: privately printed, 1938), 89.
2. Rose P. Ravenel Reminiscences, ca. 1920, Ravenel Papers, South Carolina Historical Society; Elizabeth Preston Allan, *The Life and Letters of Margaret Junkin Preston* (Boston: Houghton Mifflin, 1903), 180.
3. Allan, *Life and Letters of Margaret Junkin Preston*, 158–159, 179.
4. Marten, *Children's Civil War*, 158–159; Monahon, *Children and Trauma*, 8.
5. Cross and Cross, eds., *Child of Glencoe*, 50; Jabour, *Scarlett's Sisters*, 20, 23; Wilma King, *Stolen Childhood: Slave Youth in Nineteenth-Century America*

(Bloomington: Indiana University Press, 1995), 46–47; see also Hannah Davidson Interview, Ohio Narratives, Vol. 12; Eda Harper Interview, Arkansas Narratives, Vol. 2, Part 3; Sally Murphy Interview, Alabama Narratives, Vol. 1; Wade Owens, Alabama Narratives, Vol. 1; and Ward, *Children of Bladensfield* 23, 24, 32, 93; Nagel, *Boy's Civil War Story*, 115–117 (quotation p. 116), 159. See also Robertson, *Small Boy's Recollections*, 9–10; Clinkscales, *On the Old Plantation*, 90.

6. Towers, ed., "Military Waif," 428; Ward, *Children of Bladensfield*, 21, 90, 93; Burton, *Memories of Childhood's Slavery Days*, 3; Nagel, *Boy's Civil War Story*, 146; and King, *Stolen Childhood*, Chapter 3 (quotation p. 46); Mississippi Narratives, Supplement Series 1, Vol. 10, Part 5, 2154. See also Cross and Cross, eds., *Child of Glencoe*, 24, 24, 101; John Van Hook Interview, Georgia Narratives, Vol. 4, Part 4; Sally Murphy Interview, Alabama Narratives, Vol. 1; and Wade Owens, Alabama Narratives, Vol. I.

7. King, *Stolen Childhood*, 45–46; Nagel, *Boy's Civil War Story*, 115, 160–161; Ward, *Children of Bladensfield*, 15, 24, 58, 89. See also "Aunt Adeline" Interview, Arkansas Narratives, Vol. 2, Part 1, 11; Hannah Davidson Interview, Ohio Narratives, Vol. 12; Sally Murphy Interview, Alabama Narratives, Vol. 1.

8. Howard P. Chudacoff, *Children at Play: An American History* (New York: New York University Press, 2007), 54.

9. For quotations, see Elias Thomas Interview, North Carolina Narratives, Vol. 11, Part 2, 345; and Ward, *Children of Bladensfield*, 14; Denham and Brown, eds., *Cracker Times and Pioneer Lives*, 103. See also Jabour, *Scarlett's Sisters*, 20; and Cross and Cross, eds., *Child of Glencoe*, 21, 24, 50, 101; Wilkins, *"War Boy,"* 39–40.

10. King, *Stolen Childhood*, 55.

11. Nagel, *Boy's Civil War Story*, 114–115; King, *Stolen Childhood*, 45, 55; "Aunt Adeline" Interview, Arkansas Narratives, Vol. 2, Part 1, 11; King, ed., *A Northern Woman*, 120.

12. Towers, ed., "Military Waif," 428; John F. Van Hook Interview, Georgia Narratives, Vol. 4, Part 4, 86. See also Nagel, *Boy's Civil War Story*, 30, 161–162, 172.

13. Jabour, *Scarlett's Sisters*, 21–22; "Aunt Adeline" Interview, Arkansas Narratives, Vol. 2, Part 1, 11; King, *Stolen Childhood*, 54; Virginia Ingraham Burr, ed., *The Secret Eye: The Journal of Ella Gertrude Clanton Thomas, 1848–1889* (Chapel Hill: University of North Carolina Press, 1990), 199; King, ed., *A Northern Woman*, 129.

14. Burr, ed., *Secret Eye*, 199; John Van Hook Interview, Georgia Narratives, Vol. 4, Part 4, 85.

15. Clinkscales, *On the Old Plantation*, 56, 100; King, *Stolen Childhood*, 54–55.

16. King, *Stolen Childhood*, 48–49; Eda Harper Interview, Arkansas Narratives, Vol. 2, Part 3, 167; Drago, *Confederate Phoenix*, 36.

17. Steven Mintz, *Huck's Raft: A History of American Childhood* (Cambridge, Mass.: Belknap/Harvard University Press, 2004), 107.

18. Chudacoff, *Children at Play*, 40, 55.

19. Burton, *Memories of Childhood's Slavery Days*, 4; Chudacoff, *Children at Play*, 54, 64; George Rawick, ed., *The American Slave: A Composite Autobiography* (Westport, Conn.: Greenwood Publishing, 1972–), Mississippi Narratives, Supplement Series 1, Vol. 10, Part 5, 2390; Mintz, *Huck's Raft*, 108. Thanks to Katie Knowles for supplying the reference about the grapevines.

20. Elias Thomas Interview, North Carolina Narratives, Vol. 11, Part 2, 345; Ward, *Children of Bladensfield*, 66.

21. Elias Thomas Interview, North Carolina Narratives, Vol. 11, Part 2, 345; Mintz, *Huck's Raft*, 107; see also King, *Stolen Childhood*, 52–53.

22. Werner, *Reluctant Witnesses*, 85; Hannah Davidson Interview, Ohio Narratives, Vol. 12, 31; Ward, *Children of Bladensfield*, 66; Berlin, et al., eds., *Remembering Slavery*, 216–217. See also Wylie Nealy Interview, Arkansas Narratives, Vol. 2, Part 5, 279–280.

23. King, *Stolen Childhood*, 130–131.

24. Frank A. Patterson Interview, Arkansas Narratives, Vol. 2, Part 5, 279.

25. Berlin, et al., eds., *Remembering Slavery*, 216–217. See also Wylie Nealy Interview, Arkansas Narratives, Vol. 2, Part 5, 279–280; King, *Stolen Childhood*, 130.

26. Eda Harper Interview, Arkansas Narratives, Vol. 2, Part 3, 164.

27. Berlin, et al., eds., *Remembering Slavery*, 216–217.

28. Towers, ed., "Military Waif," 429.

29. Baer, *Shadows on My Heart*, 47; Gordon A. Cotton, ed., *From the Pen of a She-Rebel: The Civil War Diary of Emilie Riley McKinley* (Columbia: University of South Carolina Press, 2001), 30, 61.

30. Drago, *Confederate Phoenix*, 10; Virginia Clay-Clopton, *A Belle of the Fifties: Memoirs of Mrs. Clay of Alabama* (1905; reprinted Tuscaloosa: University of Alabama Press, 1999), 276.

31. Drago, *Confederate Phoenix*, 9, 11; Cornelia Peake McDonald, *A Woman's Civil War: A Diary, with Reminiscences of the War, from March 1862*, ed. by Minrose C. Gwin (Madison: University of Wisconsin Press, 1992), 120.

32. Bardaglio, "On the Border," 317; McDonald, *Woman's Civil War*, 120; Drago, *Confederate Phoenix*, 10; "Lucy Ann" Caption, in *A Woman's War: Southern Women, Civil War, and the Confederate Legacy*, ed. by Edward D. C. Campbell, Jr., and Kym S. Rice (Charlottesville: University Press of Virginia, 1996), 123.

33. McDonald, *Woman's Civil War*, 31, 35–36, 132–133, 148.

34. Marten, *Children's Civil War*, 158–159, and McDonald, *Woman's Civil War*, 133; see also Robertson, *Small Boy's Recollections*, 19–20; Wilkins, "War Boy," 23.

35. Towers, ed., "Military Waif," 428.

36. Marten, *Children's Civil War*, 161; Bardaglio, "Children of Jubilee," 220.
37. Sarah "Sallie" Conley Clayton, *Requiem for a Lost City: A Memoir of Civil War Atlanta and the Old South* (Macon, Ga.: Mercer University Press, 1999), 60; Ward, *Children of Bladensfield*, 32, 77; Marten, *Children's Civil War*, 160.
38. Marten, *Children's Civil War*, 165; Drago, *Confederate Phoenix*, 96.
39. Burr, ed., *Secret Eye*, 187.
40. Ward, *Children of Bladensfield*, 33; Bardaglio, "Children of Jubilee," 220. See also Marten, *Children's Civil War*, 161.
41. Ward, *Children of Bladensfield*, 57–58; Bardaglio, "Children of Jubilee," 220.
42. McDonald, *Woman's War*, 96; Drago, *Confederate Phoenix*, 100; Robertson, *Small Boy's Recollections*, 73; Faust, *Mothers of Invention*, 130. See also Wilkins, "War Boy," 41.
43. Werner, *Reluctant Witnesses*, 85; Baer, ed., *Shadows on My Heart*, 169; Drago, *Confederate Phoenix*, 100.
44. Ward, *Children of Bladensfield*, 13, 61, 67, 69; Nagel, *Boy's Civil War Story*, 123, 130, 161–162, 172.
45. Marie Jenkins Schwartz, *Born in Bondage: Growing Up Enslaved in the Antebellum South* (Cambridge, Mass.: Harvard University Press, 2000), 3.
46. King, ed., *A Northern Woman*, 67, 89. See also 81, 87.
47. Hannah Davidson Interview, Ohio Narratives, Vol. 12, 26; Margaret Hulm Interview, Arkansas Narratives, Vol. 2, Part 3, 357; Schwartz, *Born in Bondage*, 26–27.
48. Anderson, ed., *Brokenburn*, 10–11; Andrews, *War-Time Journal*, 293; King, ed., *A Northern Woman*, 120; Ward, *Children of Bladensfield*, 61, 69.
49. Anderson, ed., *Brokenburn*, 10; Schwartz, *Born in Bondage*, 26–27.
50. Douglass, *Narrative*, 34, 43; Anderson, ed., *Brokenburn*, 9, 10.
51. Schwartz, *Born in Bondage*, 134–147.
52. Schwartz, *Born in Bondage*, 23, 33; Hannah Davidson Interview, Ohio Narratives, Vol. 12, 26.
53. Nagel, *Boy's Civil War Story*, 75, 78, 80–81, 121–122 (quotations), 123, 125, 127.
54. Ward, *Children of Bladensfield*, 90; Denham and Brown, eds., *Cracker Times and Pioneer Lives*, 103–104.
55. King, ed., *A Northern Woman*, 90, 120, 126; Ward, *Children of Bladensfield*, 65–66; Fleet and Fuller, eds., *Green Mount*, 26, 27–28. See also Jabour, *Scarlett's Sisters*, 23; Clinkscales, *On the Old Plantation*, 73–74, 105.
56. Baer, ed., *Shadows on My Heart*, 203; S. A. Steel, *The Sunny Road: Home Life in Dixie During the War*, Vol. 2 ([Memphis: Latsch & Arnold, 1925]), 47–48.
57. Ward, *Children of Bladensfield*, 77.
58. McDonald, *Woman's Civil War*, 101.
59. Steel, *Sunny Road*, 37–41; Clinkscales, *On the Old Plantation*, 67; and Fleet and Fuller, eds., *Green Mount*, 165, 170, 283–284, 289–292, 298.
60. Fleet and Fuller, eds., *Green Mount*, 77, 95. See also 90–91, 98–99, 197–198.

61. John Rozier, ed., *The Granite Farm Letters: The Civil War Correspondence of Edgeworth and Sallie Bird* (Athens: University of Georgia Press, 1988), 239–240.
62. Rose P. Ravenel Reminiscences; Anderson, ed., *Brokenburn*, 146; Sally Munford to Jennie Munford, September 2, 1863, quoted in Jabour, *Scarlett's Sisters*, 266; Clayton, *Requiem for a Lost City*, 84; Werner, *Reluctant Witnesses*, 107, 112. See also Cross and Cross, eds., *Child of Glencoe*, 92–93.
63. Cross and Cross, eds., *Child of Glencoe*, 98; Marszalek, ed., *Diary of Miss Emma Holmes*, 289; Werner, *Reluctant Witnesses*, 110, 115; Baer, ed., *Shadows on My Heart*, 208; see also 209–215.
64. Frances Wallace Taylor, Catherine Taylor Matthews, and J. Tracy Power, eds., *The Leverett Letters: Correspondence of a South Carolina Family, 1851–1868* (Columbia: University of South Carolina Press, 2000), 407; McDonald, *Woman's Civil War*, 154.
65. Nagel, *Boy's Civil War Story*, 126–127.
66. Revels, *Grander in Her Daughters*, 52, 56; Daniel W. Stowell, "'A family of women and children': The Fains of East Tennessee During Wartime," in Catherine Clinton, ed., *Southern Families at War: Loyalty and Conflict in the Civil War South* (New York: Oxford University Press, 2000), 164.
67. Drago, *Confederate Phoenix*, 24–26, 44.
68. Revels, *Grander in Her Daughters*, 59; Mintz, *Huck's Raft*, 112; Berlin et al., eds., *Remembering Slavery*, 245; Anderson, ed., *Brokenburn*, 203, 207.

Chapter Four. Refugees and Runaways

1. Baer, ed., *Shadows on My Heart*, 36. T. J. "Stonewall" Jackson's Confederate forces were victorious in the Battle of Front Royal on May 23, 1862. Fighting in the Front Royal area began in March and continued through June.
2. Ibid., 51.
3. Marten, *Children's Civil War*, 10.
4. Margaret Hulm Interview, Arkansas Narratives, Vol. 2, Part 3, 358; Bardaglio, "Children of Jubilee," 223; Anderson, ed., *Brokenburn*, 181; McDonald, *Woman's Civil War*, 35, 73; Taylor, *Black Woman's Civil War Memoirs*, 87; Marten, *Children's Civil War*, 106; McDonald, *Woman's Civil War*, 160.
5. Werner, *Reluctant Witnesses*, 15; Adeline Blakeley Narrative, Arkansas Narratives, Vol. 2, Part 1, 187; Faust, *This Republic of Suffering*, 137, 142; Bardaglio, "Children of Jubilee," 223.
6. Mary D. Roberts, ed., *Lucy Breckinridge of Grove Hill: The Journal of a Virginia Girl, 1862-1864* (Columbia: University of South Carolina Press, 1994), 162; Fleet and Fuller, eds., *Green Mount*, 127, 130, 189, 238.
7. Anderson, ed., *Brokenburn*, 179; Bardaglio, "On the Border," 321.
8. Sue Chancellor, "Personal Recollections of the Battle of Chancellorsville," *Register of the Kentucky Historical Society*, 66 (April 1968), 139.

9. Drago, *Confederate Phoenix*, 5; Revels, *Grander in Her Daughters*, 123.
10. Fleet and Fuller, eds., *Green Mount*, 153; Mary D. Robertson, ed., *A Confederate Lady Comes of Age: The Journal of Pauline DeCaradeuc Heyward, 1863–1888* (Columbia: University of South Carolina Press, 1992), 23.
11. Joan E. Cashin, "Into the Trackless Wilderness: The Refugee Experience in the Civil War," in *A Woman's War*, 48.
12. Andrews, *War-Time Journal*, 67, 149.
13. Steel, *Sunny Road*, 16, 45.
14. Anderson, ed., *Brokenburn*, 182; Stowell, "'A family of women and children,'" 160.
15. Drago, *Confederate Phoenix*, 11; Andrews, *War-Time Journal*, 305; Burr, ed., *Secret Eye*, 286.
16. Anderson, ed., *Brokenburn*, 212; Baer, ed., *Shadows on My Heart*, 218–219, see also 143; Revels, *Grander in Her Daughters*, 131.
17. Ward, *Children of Bladensfield*, 49; Revels, *Grander in Her Daughters*, 116.
18. Lisa Tendrich Frank, "Bedrooms as Battlefields: The Role of Gender Politics in Sherman's March," in LeeAnn Whites and Alecia P. Long, eds., *Occupied Women: Gender, Military Occupation, and the American Civil War* (Baton Rouge: Louisiana State University Press, 2009), 34.
19. Drago, *Confederate Phoenix*, 95–97; Robertson, ed., *Confederate Lady Comes of Age*, 66; Fleet and Fuller, eds., *Green Mount*, 328, 354.
20. Smedes, *Memorials*, 192–193; Baer, ed., *Shadows on My Heart*, 181; Frank, "Bedrooms as Battlefields," 43.
21. Drago, *Confederate Phoenix*, 95–97.
22. Smedes, *Memorials*, 193.
23. E. Susan Barber and Charles F. Ritter, "'Physical Abuse . . . and Rough Handling': Race, Gender, and Sexual Justice in the Occupied South," in Whites and Long, eds., *Occupied Women*, 51, 59.
24. Robertson, ed., *Confederate Lady Comes of Age*, 67–69. The phrase "symbolic rape" comes from Michael Fellman, *Inside War: The Guerrilla Conflict in Missouri During the American Civil War* (New York: Oxford University Press, 1989), 207–208.
25. Barber and Ritter, "Physical Abuse," 61.
26. Michael Fellman, "Women and Guerrilla Warfare," in Clinton and Silber, eds., *Divided Houses*, 151–152.
27. Anderson, ed., *Brokenburn*, 196.
28. Fleet and Fuller, eds., *Green Mount*, 328, 331, 354.
29. Drago, *Confederate Phoenix*, 49; Baer, ed., *Shadows on My Heart*, 92, 95–98.
30. Virginia Clay-Clopton, *A Belle of the Fifties: Memoirs of Mrs. Clay of Alabama* (1905; reprint Tuscaloosa: University of Alabama Press, 1999), 262.
31. Smedes, *Memorials*, 193–196.
32. Robertson, *Small Boy's Recollections*, 98–100.
33. Baer, ed., *Shadows on My Heart*, 73, 77; see also 102.

34. McDonald, *Woman's Civil War*, 24, 40, 44, 149.
35. Ibid., 47.
36. Ward, *Children of Bladensfield*, 84–88.
37. Baer, ed., *Shadows on My Heart*, 70, 94, 97; see also 95.
38. Bardaglio, "Children of Jubilee," 222.
39. Hannah Davidson Interview, Ohio Narratives, Vol. 12, 31; Henry Cheatham Interview, Alabama Narratives, Vol. 1, 67. See also Berlin, et al., eds., *Remembering Slavery*, 211–212, 240.
40. Barney A. Laird Interview, Arkansas Narratives, Vol. 2, Part 4, 225–226.
41. Cornelia Robinson Interview, Alabama Narratives, Vol. 1, 331.
42. Eda Harper Interview, Arkansas Narratives, Vol. 2, Part 3, 164; Cornelia Robinson Interview, Alabama Narratives, Vol. 1, 331.
43. Barber and Ritter, "Physical Abuse," 63.
44. Marten, *Children's Civil War*, 139; Fellman, "Women and Guerrilla Warfare," 153; Barber and Ritter, "Physical Abuse," 59.
45. Clayton, *Requiem for a Lost City*, 127, 176.
46. Fleet and Fuller, eds., *Green Mount*, 118.
47. Bardaglio, "Children of Jubilee," 222. For another account of "hanging" a master, see Margaret Hulm Interview, Arkansas Narratives, Vol. 2, Part 3, 358.
48. Hannah Davidson Interview, Ohio Narratives, Vol. 12, 31.
49. Faust, *This Republic of Suffering*, 141.
50. Ward, *Children of Bladensfield*, 78.
51. Ibid., 53–57.
52. Ibid., 57–58.
53. Ibid., 55.
54. Anderson, ed., *Brokenburn*, 168–169, 171, 180; Marten, *Children's Civil War*, 128.
55. Anderson, ed., *Brokenburn*, 190–191.
56. Ibid., 193–194, 221, 227.
57. Ibid., 221, 249–251.
58. Cashin, "Into the Trackless Wilderness," 45; Faust, *This Republic of Suffering*, 139; McDonald, *Woman's Civil War*, 99.
59. Baer, ed., *Shadows on My Heart*, 157–158.
60. Rozier, ed., *Granite Farm Letters*, 224–227.
61. Anderson, ed., *Brokenburn*, 243.
62. Michael P. Johnson, "Looking for Lost Kin: Efforts to Reunite Free Families after Emancipation," in Clinton, ed., *Southern Families at War*, 15–34, quotation p. 16.
63. Werner, *Reluctant Witnesses*, 80–81.
64. Ibid., 82–84.
65. Ibid., 81, 84, 87, 89, 91.
66. Ibid., 106.

67. Ibid., 107.
68. Ibid., 130.
69. Ibid., 113–114.
70. Ibid., 110, 113.
71. Anderson, ed., *Brokenburn*, 183; Marten, *Children's Civil War*, 129.
72. Berlin, et al., eds., *Remembering Slavery*, 227–228.
73. McDonald, *Woman's Civil War*, 82–84.
74. Ibid., 65.
75. Baer, ed., *Shadows on My Heart*, 228.
76. Anderson, ed., *Brokenburn*, 180; Roberts, ed., *Lucy Breckinridge of Grove Hill*, 194.
77. Thavolia Glymph, "'This species of property': Female Slave Contrabands in the Civil War," in *A Woman's War*, 57–58, 68; Werner, *Reluctant Witnesses*, 47.
78. King, *Stolen Childhood*, 136.
79. Fellman, "Women and Guerrilla Warfare," 153–154; Glymph, "'This species of property,'" 68.
80. Gordon A. Cotton, ed., *From the Pen of a She-Rebel: The Civil War Diary of Emilie Riley McKinley* (Columbia: University of South Carolina Press, 2001), 69.
81. Werner, *Reluctant Witnesses*, 119; Michael P. Johnson, "Looking for Lost Kin: Efforts to Reunite Free Families After Emancipation," in Clinton, ed., *Southern Families at War*, 15–34.
82. Faust, *This Republic of Suffering*, 141.
83. Kym S. Rice and Edward D. C. Campbell, Jr., "Voices from the Tempest: Southern Women's Wartime Experiences," in *A Woman's War*, 83.
84. Roberts, ed., *Lucy Breckinridge*, 194; McDonald, *Woman's Civil War*, 65.
85. Mintz, *Huck's Raft*, 113; Marten, *Children's Civil War*, 129; and Fellman, "Women and Guerrilla Warfare," 163. See also Glymph, "'This species of property,'" 58.
86. Marten, *Children's Civil War*, 130; Faust, *This Republic of Suffering*, 139.
87. Marten, *Children's Civil War*, 131–132.
88. Berlin, et al., eds., *Remembering Slavery*, 242–243.
89. King, *Stolen Childhood*, 139.

Chapter Five. Defeat and Freedom

1. Bonner, ed., *Journal of a Milledgeville Girl*, 73–74.
2. Berlin, et al., eds., *Remembering Slavery*, 238–240.
3. Charles M. McGee, Jr., and Ernest M. Lander, Jr., eds., *A Rebel Came Home: The Diary and Letters of Floride Clemson, 1863–1866* (Columbia: University of South Carolina Press, 1989), 75, 83, 92.

4. Berlin, et al., eds., *Remembering Slavery*, 270.
5. Rozier, ed., *Granite Farm Letters*, 248n1.
6. Berlin, et al., eds., *Remembering Slavery*, 233–234. All spellings as in original.
7. Ibid., 265.
8. Charlie Moses Interview, Mississippi Narratives, Vol. 9, 116.
9. Berlin, et al., eds., *Remembering Slavery*, 267.
10. Wilkins, *"War Boy,"* 43–44.
11. Eppes, *Through Some Eventful Years*, 270; Andrews, *War-Time Journal*, 153–154, 171.
12. Anderson, ed., *Brokenburn*, 339–340.
13. Wilkins, *"War Boy,"* 44; Andrews, *War-Time Journal*, 193, 198, 210; McGee and Lander, eds., *Rebel Came Home*, 92.
14. Berlin, et al., eds., *Remembering Slavery*, 240.
15. Taylor, *Black Woman's Civil War*, 33; Willie Lee Rose, *Rehearsal for Reconstruction: The Port Royal Experiment* (1964; reprinted Athens: University of Georgia Press, 1999).
16. Wayne E. Reilly, ed., *Sarah Jane Foster: Teacher of the Freedmen* (Charlottesville: University of Virginia Press, 1990), 98.
17. Taylor, *Black Woman's Civil War*, 37–38; Henry L. Swint, ed., *Dear Ones at Home: Letters from Contraband Camps* (Nashville: Vanderbilt University Press, 1966), 62; Reilly, ed., *Sarah Jane Foster*, 171.
18. Mary Niall Mitchell, *Raising Freedom's Child: Black Children and Visions of the Future After Slavery* (New York: New York University Press, 2008), 95, 98.
19. Rose, *Rehearsal for Reconstruction*, 81–82.
20. Catherine Clinton, "Reconstructing Freedwomen," in Clinton and Silber, eds., *Divided Houses,* 309; Swint, ed., *Dear Ones at Home*, 203–204.
21. Charlie Moses Interview, Mississippi Narratives, Vol. 9, 116–117; Samuel Watson Interview, Indiana Narratives, Vol. 5, 206–207.
22. Karin L. Zipf, *Labor of Innocents: Forced Apprenticeship in North Carolina, 1715–1919* (Baton Rouge: Louisiana State University Press, 2005); Mitchell, *Raising Freedom's Child*, Chapter 4; and Mintz, *Huck's Raft*, 113.
23. Zipf, *Labor of Innocents*, 44.
24. Ibid., 2, 69, 73.
25. Mitchell, *Raising Freedom's Child*, 154.
26. Gutman, *Black Family*, 410; Zipf, *Labor of Innocents*, 57.
27. Mitchell, *Raising Freedom's Child*, 145, 159; Bardaglio, "Children of Jubilee," 227.
28. Bardaglio, "Children of Jubilee," 226.
29. Ibid., 227; Berlin, et al., eds., *Remembering Slavery*, 161–163.
30. Burton, *In My Father's House*, 262; Belinda Hurmence, ed., *My Folks Don't Want Me to Talk About Slavery* (Winston-Salem, N.C.: John F. Blair, 1984), 28–29.

31. Jacqueline Jones, "The Political Economy of Sharecropping Families: Blacks and Poor Whites in the Rural South, 1865–1915," in Bleser, ed., *In Joy and in Sorrow*, 197.

32. Jones, *Labor of Love, Labor of Sorrow*, 64; Burton, *In My Father's House*, 234; Jones, "Political Economy of Sharecropping Families," 64.

33. Jones, *Labor of Love, Labor of Sorrow*, 78; Jones, "Political Economy of Sharecropping Families," 200–211.

34. Jones, *Labor of Love, Labor of Sorrow*, 77.

35. Williams, *Self-Taught*, 67.

36. Mitchell, *Raising Freedom's Child*, 200, 211, 205.

37. Reilly, ed., *Sarah Jane Foster*, 96; Mitchell, *Raising Freedom's Child*, 200, 204; Swint, ed., *Dear Ones at Home*, 202; King, ed., *A Northern Woman*, 152.

38. Williams, *Self-Taught*, 194; Mitchell, *Raising Freedom's Child*, 200–201.

39. Reilly, ed., *Sarah Jane Foster*, 95; Mitchell, *Raising Freedom's Child*, 214; King, *Essence of Liberty*, 191.

40. Reilly, ed., *Sarah Jane Foster*, 118; Marten, *Children's Civil War*, 194.

41. Marinda Branson Moore, *The First Dixie Reader: Designed to Follow the Dixie Primer* (Raleigh, N.C.: Branson, Farrar & Co., 1863), 22, 38–40, 50–51.

42. Marinda Branson Moore, *The Geographical Reader, for the Dixie Children* (Raleigh, N.C.: Branson, Farrar & Co., 1863), 9–11.

43. Ibid., 11, 13–15.

44. Andrews, *War-Time Journal*, 373.

45. Lee Ann Whites, *The Civil War as a Crisis in Gender: Augusta, Georgia, 1860–1890* (Athens: University of Georgia Press, 1995), 96.

46. Anderson, ed., *Brokenburn*, 340, 362–363; Frances Butler Leigh, *Ten Years on a Georgia Plantation Since the War*, in Dana D. Nelson, ed., *Principles and Privilege: Two Women's Lives on a Georgia Plantation* (Ann Arbor: University of Michigan Press, 1995), 2–3.

47. Smedes, *Memorials*, 223.

48. Wilkins, *"War Boy,"* 33; Eppes, *Through Some Eventful Years*, 273.

49. Rozier, ed., *Granite Farm Letters*, 126.

50. Burr, ed., *Secret Eye*, 311, 342, 374. See also Marten, *Children's Civil War*, 204–207; and Marten, "Fatherhood in the Confederacy: Southern Soldiers and Their Children," *Journal of Southern History* 63 (May 1997), 269–292.

51. Betsy Fleet, ed., *Green Mount After the War: The Correspondence of Maria Louisa Wacker Fleet and Her Family, 1865–1900* (Charlottesville: University Press of Virginia, 1978), 104–105; Burr, ed., *Secret Eye*, 311, see also 277–278, 350.

52. Anya Jabour, "Marriage and Family in the Nineteenth-Century South," in Jabour, ed., *Major Problems in the History of American Families and Children* (Boston: Houghton Mifflin, 2005), 121–130 (quotation).

53. Rozier, ed., *Granite Farm Letters*, 57; McDonald, *Woman's Civil War*, 97, 148.

54. Smedes, *Memorials*, 225; King, ed., *A Northern Woman*, 143 and *passim*; Burr, ed., *Secret Eye*, 309; Miers, ed., *When the World Ended*, 100.

55. Fleet, ed., *Green Mount After the War*, 140; Jane H. Pease and William H. Pease, *A Family of Women: The Carolina Petigrus in Peace and War* (Chapel Hill: University of North Carolina Press, 1999), 217 and *passim*; Burr, ed., *Secret Eye*, 321.
56. Miers, ed., *When the World Ended*, 110; Fleet, ed., *Green Mount After the War*, 88.
57. Gould, ed., *Chained to the Rock of Adversity*, 85, 87.
58. Miers, ed., *When the World Ended*, 22.
59. Grace Elmore Diary, September 21, 1865, quoted in Jabour, *Scarlett's Sisters*, 278; Fleet, ed., *Green Mount After the War*, 101, 111.
60. Wilkins, "War Boy," 54; Burr, ed., *Secret Eye*, 311; King, ed., *A Northern Woman*, 157 and *passim*.
61. Wilkins, "War Boy," 54–60.
62. Eppes, *Through Some Eventful Years*, 302; Ward, *Children of Bladensfield*, 111.
63. Burr, ed., *Secret Eye*, 366–367.
64. Rozier, ed., *Granite Farm Letters*, 285; King, *Essence of Liberty*, 191.
65. Robertson, *Small Boy's Recollections*, 115.

Chapter Six. Memory and Meaning

1. Steel, *Sunny Road*, 71–72.
2. Sarah E. Gardner, *Blood and Irony: Southern White Women's Narratives of the Civil War, 1861–1937* (Chapel Hill: University of North Carolina Press, 2004), 93; see also Marten, *Children's Civil War*, 221–222.
3. Clinkscales, *On the Old Plantation*, 5, 8.
4. Steel, *Sunny Road*, 17, 21–23.
5. Clayton, *Requiem for a Lost City*, 169; Wilkins, "War Boy," 79.
6. Clinkscales, *On the Old Plantation*, 9; Steel, *Sunny Road*, 14; Robertson, *Small Boy's Recollections*, 104; Clayton, *Requiem for a Lost City*, 171.
7. Gardner, *Blood and Irony*, 86, 103–104.
8. Miers, *When the World Ended*, 4. This entry is dated December 31, 1864.
9. Steel, *Sunny Road*, 16, 73; Andrews, *War-Time Journal*, 1, 254.
10. A notable exception is Benjamin Wilkins, who emphasized the "sorrow and the suffering" of the war years and hoped to convey "the ruin, suffering and horrors of war" to a new generation as a way to prevent future wars. See "War Boy," 3–4.
11. Miers, *When the World Ended*, 21–22.
12. Steel, *Sunny Road*, 41–42, 140–141.
13. Henry Cheatam Interview, Alabama Narratives, Vol. 1, 70; Hurmence, ed., *My Folks Don't Want Me to Talk About Slavery*.
14. John W. Fields Interview, Indiana Narratives, Vol. 5, 79; Henry Cheatam Interview, Alabama Narratives, Vol. 1, 66–67; Berlin, et al., eds., *Remembering Slavery*, 8.

15. Charlie Moses Interview, Mississippi Narratives, Vol. 9, 117; Berlin, et al., eds., *Remembering Slavery*, 8, 21, 30, 129.
16. Henry Cheatam Interview, Alabama Narratives, Vol. 1, 67; Bardaglio, *Reconstructing the Family*, 226–227; Bardaglio, "Children of Jubilee," 227.
17. Berlin, et al., eds., *Remembering Slavery*, 265.
18. Hannah Davidson Interview, Ohio Narratives, Vol. 12, 31; Charlie Moses Interview, Mississippi Narratives, Vol. 9, 116.
19. Margaret Hulm Interview, Arkansas Narratives, Vol. 2, Part 3, 358; Wade Owens Interview, Alabama Narratives, Vol. 1, 308; Frank A. Patterson Interview, Arkansas Narratives, Vol. 2, Part 5, 278.
20. Gardner, *Blood and Irony*, 180.
21. Berlin, et al., eds., *Remembering Slavery*, 262; Andrews, *War-Time Journal*, 1, 254.
22. Marten, *Children's Civil War*, 207.

A Note on Sources

MATERIAL FOR THIS STUDY is both abundant and uneven. Wealthy white Southerners, blessed with both literacy and leisure, maintained extensive correspondence with and about their children, kept detailed diaries regarding child care and child-rearing, and wrote lengthy memoirs of their lives. Cognizant of the historical importance of the Civil War era and convinced of the significance of their own prominent family networks, planter-class Southerners also preserved family records and published wartime writings. Quoted letters, diaries, and memoirs are cited in the footnotes, but some deserve special mention here.

The unpublished diaries of Fannie Page Hume, C. Alice Ready, and Sarah Lois Wodley, located in the Southern Historical Collection at the University of North Carolina at Chapel Hill, offer teenagers' and young adults' perspective on the secession crisis and the coming of the Civil War. Elizabeth Preston Allan, *The Life and Letters of Margaret Junkin Preston* (Boston: Houghton Mifflin, 1903), includes the comments of a Civil War mother on her children's wartime play. Both John Q. Anderson, ed., *Brokenburn: The Journal of Kate Stone, 1861–1868* (1955, reprinted Baton Rouge: Louisiana State University Press, 1995) and Eliza Frances Andrews, *The War-Time Journal of a Georgia Girl, 1864–1865*, edited by Spencer Bidwell King, Jr. (Macon, Ga.: Ardivan Press, 1960) reveal the process of refugeeing from the perspective of young adults. Elizabeth R. Baer, ed., *Shadows on My Heart: The Civil War Diary of Lucy Rebecca Buck of Virginia* (Athens: University of Georgia Press, 1997) sheds light on the terrors of living in a war zone. Virginia Ingraham Burr, ed., *The Secret Eye: The Journal of Ella Gertrude Clanton Thomas, 1848–1889* (Chapel Hill:

University of North Carolina Press, 1990) contains a mother's comments on her children, including commentary on wartime Christmas celebrations. Gordon A. Cotton, ed., *From the Pen of a She-Rebel: The Civil War Diary of Emilie Riley McKinley* (Columbia: University of South Carolina Press, 2001) contains the reflections of a governess to children ranging from ten to fifteen years of age at the war's beginning on a plantation near the occupied city of Vicksburg, Mississippi. Eleanor P. Cross and Charles B. Cross, Jr., eds., *Child of Glencoe: Civil War Journal of Katie Darling Wallace* (Chesapeake, Va.: Norfolk County Historical Society, 1983) is a brief diary by an eleven-year-old living on a plantation in Virginia and attending school in Portsmouth during the Civil War. Susan Bradford Eppes, *Through Some Eventful Years* (1926; reprinted Gainesville: University of Florida Press, 1968) is an especially useful memoir-diary by a Florida planter's daughter, containing her early reflections on slavery and secession as well as on the Civil War (some of which may have been revised at a later date).

An extensive collection of family papers is Betsy Fleet and John D. P. Fuller, eds., *Green Mount: A Virginia Plantation Family During the Civil War: Being the Journal of Benjamin Robert Fleet and Letters of His Family* (Charlottesville: University Press of Virginia, 1962); and its sequel, Betsy Fleet, ed., *Green Mount After the War: The Correspondence of Maria Louisa Wacker Fleet and Her Family, 1865–1900* (Charlottesville: University Press of Virginia, 1978). Wilma King, ed., *A Northern Woman in the Plantation South: Letters of Tryphena Blanche Holder Fox, 1856–1876* (Columbia: University of South Carolina Press, 1993) contains wonderful information about both a young planter's daughter and her slave attendant in the Civil War years. Cornelia Peake McDonald, *A Woman's Civil War: A Diary, with Reminiscences of the War, from March 1862*, edited by Minrose C. Gwin (Madison: University of Wisconsin Press, 1992) has extensive commentary on children in the occupied city of Winchester, Virginia. Earl Schenck Miers, ed., *When the World Ended: The Diary of Emma LeConte* (New York: Oxford University Press, 1957); Mary D. Roberts, ed., *Lucy Breckinridge of Grove Hill: The Journal of a Virginia Girl, 1862–1864* (Columbia: University of South Carolina Press, 1994); and Mary D. Robertson, ed., *A Confederate Lady Comes of Age: The Journal of Pauline DeCaradeuc Heyward, 1863–1888* (Columbia: University of South Carolina Press, 1992) are especially useful diaries of teenage girls in the

Civil War South. Another excellent collection of wartime family letters is John Rozier, ed., *The Granite Farm Letters: The Civil War Correspondence of Edgeworth and Sallie Bird* (Athens: University of Georgia Press, 1988). Several girls' wartime accounts are included in Joan E. Cashin, ed., *Our Common Affairs: Texts from Women in the Old South* (Baltimore: Johns Hopkins University Press, 1996). Charles M. McGee, Jr., and Ernest M. Lander, Jr., eds., *A Rebel Came Home: The Diary and Letters of Floride Clemson, 1863–1866* (Columbia: University of South Carolina Press, 1989) has especially good material on the end of the war.

White Southerners wrote memoirs after the fact as well as kept diaries during the war. Lucy Paxton Scarborough, "So It Was When Her Life Began: Reminiscences of a Louisiana Girlhood," *Louisiana Historical Quarterly*, 13 (July 1930), 428–444, and Lily Logan Morrill, ed., *My Confederate Girlhood: The Memoirs of Kate Virginia Cox Logan* (Richmond: Garrett and Massie, 1932) both offer children's recollections of the secession crisis. Sophia Haskell Cheves's unpublished memoirs, located in the South Carolina Historical Society in Charleston, offer a firsthand child's description of the first shots of the Civil War.

Sue Chancellor, "Personal Recollections of the Battle of Chancellorsville," *Register of the Kentucky Historical Society*, 66 (April 1968), 137–146, offers a vivid description of battle many decades later while [Constance Cary Harrison], "A Virginia Girl in the First Year of the War," *Century Magazine* 30 (1885), 606–614, provides another youthful perspective on the war from the vantage point of a later era. J. G. Clinkscales, *On the Old Plantation; Reminiscences of His Childhood* (Spartanburg, S.C.: Band & White Publishers, 1916); George F. Robertson, *A Small Boy's Recollections of the Civil War* (Clover, S.C.: George F. Robertson, 1932); S. A. Steel, *The Sunny Road: Home Life in Dixie During the War*, vol. 2 ([Memphis: Latsch & Arnold, 1925]); and B. H. [Benjamin Hawkins] Wilkins, *"War Boy": A True Story of the Civil War and Reconstruction Days* (Tullahoma, Tenn.: Wilson Brothers, 1938), all offer an amalgam of fond boyhood reminiscing, excoriations of Yankee depredations, and defenses of slavery. Similar accounts from a female perspective include Sarah "Sallie" Conley Clayton, *Requiem for a Lost City: A Memoir of Civil War Atlanta and the Old South* (Macon, Ga.: Mercer University Press, 1999); and Susan Dabney Smedes, *Memorials of a Southern Planter* (1887; reprinted Jackson: University Press of Mississippi, 1981). Frances A.

Kemble and Frances A. Butler Leigh, *Principles and Privilege: Two Women's Lives on a Georgia Plantation*, edited by Dana D. Nelson (Ann Arbor: University of Michigan Press, 1995) contains both the diaries of plantation mistress Frances Kemble Butler and the memoirs of her daughter, Frances A. Butler Leigh.

*

Historians of Southern women, families, and children have built upon this basis by editing and publishing numerous memoirs, diaries, and collections of family correspondence (as indicated above) as well as by producing a vast body of scholarship on Southern white family life and elite child-rearing practices. Representative scholarship includes Peter Bardaglio, *Reconstructing the Household: Families, Sex, and the Law in the Nineteenth-Century South* (Chapel Hill: University of North Carolina Press, 1995); Joan E. Cashin, *A Family Venture: Men and Women on the Southern Frontier* (New York: Oxford University Press, 1991); Jane Turner Censer, *North Carolina Planters and Their Children, 1800–1860* (Baton Rouge: Louisiana State University Press, 1984); Anya Jabour, *Marriage in the Early Republic: Elizabeth and William Wirt and the Companionate Ideal* (Baltimore: Johns Hopkins University Press, 1998); Jan Lewis, *The Pursuit of Happiness: Family and Values in Jefferson's Virginia* (New York: Cambridge University Press, 1983); Sally McMillen, *Motherhood in the Old South: Pregnancy, Childbirth, and Infant Rearing* (Baton Rouge: Louisiana State University Press, 1990); and Daniel Blake Smith, *Inside the Great House: Planter Family Life in Eighteenth-Century Chesapeake Society* (Ithaca: Cornell University Press, 1980). An excellent collection of essays that includes case studies of child-rearing is Carol Bleser, ed., *In Joy and in Sorrow: Women, Family, and Marriage in the Victorian South, 1830–1900* (New York: Oxford University Press, 1991). Craig Thompson Friend and Anya Jabour, eds., *Family Values in the Old South* (Gainesville: University Press of Florida, 2010), includes essays on poor white orphans and slave family life as well as elite white Southerners.

Enslaved African Americans, though usually deprived of either literacy or leisure, nonetheless also left a rich record of their lives before and during the Civil War. Decades after emancipation, during the Great Depression, the Works Progress Administration recruited writers—both black and white—to conduct interviews with former slaves. The elderly

African Americans who participated in this New Deal project were children and adolescents at the time of the Civil War. Thus the WPA oral histories—filling scores of typescript volumes—offer valuable insights into slaves' childhood experiences. George Rawick compiled and edited these oral histories in the multi-volume collection *The American Slave: A Composite Autobiography* (Westport, Conn.: Greenwood Publishing, 1972–). A useful selection of WPA interviews is Ira Berlin, Marc Favreau, and Steven F. Miller, eds., *Remembering Slavery: African Americans Talk About Their Personal Experiences of Slavery and Emancipation* (New York: New Press, 1998); other excellent selected interviews are included in Charles L. Perdue, Jr., Thomas E. Barden, and Robert K. Phillips, eds., *Weevils in the Wheat: Interviews with Virginia Ex-Slaves* (Charlottesville: University Press of Virginia, 1976) and Belinda Hurmence's several edited volumes, including *My Folks Don't Want Me to Talk About Slavery: Twenty-One Oral Histories of Former North Carolina Slaves* (Winston-Salem, N.C.: J. F. Blair, 1984). The WPA interviews have recently become available in on-line, searchable format through the Library of Congress's "American Memory" website: http://memory.loc.gov. Unless otherwise indicated in the notes, all interviews with former slaves are found in "Born in Slavery: Slave Narratives from the Federal Writers' Project, 1936–1938" at this URL.

Historians of Southern slavery have combined these firsthand accounts with plantation records and fugitive slaves' autobiographies to produce a rich collection of scholarly work on slave family life—and, more recently, on slave childhood as well. Following in the footsteps of the pioneering essay by Willie Lee Rose, "Childhood in Bondage," in William W. Freehling, ed., *Slavery and Freedom* (New York: Oxford University Press, 1982), 37–48, there are two fine books on slave children: Wilma King, *Stolen Childhood: Slave Youth in Nineteenth-Century America* (Bloomington: Indiana University Press, 1995); and Marie Jenkins Schwartz, *Born in Bondage: Growing Up Enslaved in the Antebellum South* (Cambridge, Mass.: Harvard University Press, 2000). These should be read in combination with the vast—and growing—literature on slave family life. See especially Herbert G. Gutman, *The Black Family in Slavery and Freedom, 1750–1925* (New York: Pantheon Books, 1976); Jacqueline Jones, *Labor of Love, Labor of Sorrow: Black Women, Work, and the Family, from Slavery to the Present* (1985; rev. ed., New York: Vintage

Books, 1995); Ann Patton Malone, *Sweet Chariot: Slave Family and House-hold Structure in Nineteenth-Century Louisiana* (Chapel Hill: University of North Carolina Press, 1992); and Emily West, *Chains of Love: Slave Couples in Antebellum South Carolina* (Urbana: University of Illinois Press, 2004). Useful comparative works that address both black and white family life include Orville Vernon Burton, *In My Father's House Are Many Mansions: Family and Community in Edgefield, South Carolina* (Chapel Hill: University of North Carolina Press, 1985); and Brenda E. Stevenson, *Life in Black and White: Family and Community in the Slave South* (New York: Oxford University Press, 1996).

A few former slaves published their memoirs. The best-known of these were written by fugitive slaves—one male, one female—intent on arousing abolitionist sentiment: Frederick Douglass, *Narrative of the Life of Frederick Douglass, an American Slave, Written by Himself* (1845; reprinted New York: Signet Books, 1968); and Harriet A. Jacobs, *Incidents in the Life of a Slave Girl, Written by Herself*, edited by Jean Fagan Yellin (Cambridge, Mass.: Harvard University Press, 1987). Other useful memoirs by former slaves include Annie L. Burton, *Memories of Childhood's Slavery Days* (Boston: Ross Publishing Company, 1909), a nostalgic narrative, and Susie King Taylor, *A Black Woman's Civil War Memoirs*, ed. by Patricia W. Romero and Willie Lee Rose (1902; reprinted Princeton, N.J.: Markus Wiener Publishers, 1988), the memoirs of a slave who participated in the experimental emancipation on the Sea Islands.

While both primary and secondary source materials are readily available for slaves and slaveholders, evidence about the lives of less privileged whites and free people of color is scant. Much of the limited research that has been done on these groups is based on the decennial census and on tax records. While such evidence is valuable in terms of determining household membership and land ownership, it is comparatively—even frustratingly—silent on issues such as child care and child-rearing. A representative study of nonslaveholding whites before the war is Frank Lawrence Owsley, *Plain Folk of the Old South* (Baton Rouge: Louisiana State University Press, 1949). Stephanie McCurry's monograph, *Masters of Small Worlds: Yeoman Households, Gender Relations, and the Political Culture of the Antebellum South Carolina Low Country* (New York: Oxford University Press, 1995), offers more insight into the power relations of antebellum plain-folk families while useful details about these families during the war years can be found in James M. Denham, "Cracker Women and Their Families in Nineteenth-Century Florida," in Mark I. Greenberg, William Warren Rogers, and Canter Brown, Jr., eds., *Florida's Heritage of Diversity: Essays in Honor of Samuel Proctor* (Tallahassee, Fla.: Sentry Press, 2007) and Tracy J. Revels, *Grander in Her Daughters: Florida's Women During the Civil War* (Columbia: University of South Carolina Press, 2004).

Scholarship on free blacks includes Ira Berlin, *Slaves Without Masters: The Free Negro in the Antebellum South* (New York: Vintage Books, 1974) and Michael P. Johnson and James L. Roark, *Black Masters: A Free Family of Color in the Old South* (New York: W. W. Norton, 1984). See also Adele Logan Alexander, *Ambiguous Lives: Free Women of Color in Rural Georgia, 1789–1879* (Fayetteville: University of Arkansas Press, 1991). Wilma King, *The Essence of Liberty: Free Black Women During the Slave Era* (Columbia: University of Missouri Press, 2006) is a good synthetic work that pulls together research on free black women and their children from a variety of primary and secondary sources.

Scattered information on these groups comes from the observations of outsiders (Northern tourists and Southern planters) and from a small number of published family documents, such as those contained in Virginia Meacham Gould's edited volume, *Chained to the Rock of Adversity: To Be Free, Black, and Female in the Old South* (Athens: University of Georgia Press, 1998), and personal memoirs, such as those included in James M. Denham and Canter Brown, Jr., eds., *Cracker Times and Pioneer Lives: The Florida Reminiscences of George Gillett Keen and Sarah Pamela Williams* (Columbia: University of South Carolina Press, 2000). Evelyn D. Ward, *The Children of Bladensfield* (New York: Viking Press, 1978) is a particularly rich memoir about life on a small Virginia plantation before and during the Civil War while Charles Nagel, *A Boy's Civil War Story* (St. Louis: [Eden Publishing House], 1934) is one of the few memoirs authored by a plain-folk child. Frank Towers, ed., "Military Waif: A Sidelight on the Baltimore Riot of 19 April 1861," *Maryland Historical Magazine*, 89 (Winter 1994), 427–446, also includes the observations of a boy from a nonslaveholding family. Information on nonslaveholding whites and free blacks is far more scarce than that on either slaveholding whites or enslaved blacks; thus while this study incorporates the experiences of plain folk and free black children wherever possible, it necessarily devotes less space to these groups than to the much better documented and more extensively researched lives of slaves and slaveholders.

Sources on Southern families and children in general are augmented by a small but growing body of literature on Southern families and children in the Civil War era, mostly in the form of collections of essays rather than monographs. Nina Silber and Catherine Clinton included some of the earliest explorations of the private sides of the military conflict in their edited volume, *Divided Houses: Gender and the Civil War* (New York: Oxford University Press, 1992), which includes an excellent essay by Peter Bardaglio, "The Children of Jubilee: African American Childhood in Wartime," pp. 213–229. Other useful collections are *A Woman's War: Southern Women, Civil War, and the Confederate Legacy*, edited by Edward D. C. Campbell, Jr., and Kym S. Rice (Charlottesville: University Press of Virginia, 1996), which includes Thavolia Glymph, "'This species of property': Female Slave Contrabands in the Civil War," 55–71; and Kym S. Rice and Edward D. C. Campbell, Jr., "Voices from the Tempest: Southern Women's Wartime Experiences," 73–111. Catherine Clinton, ed., *Southern Families at War: Loyalty and Conflict in the Civil War South* (New York: Oxford University Press, 2000), includes an essay on a plain-folk family, Daniel W. Stowell, "'A family of women and children': The Fains of East Tennessee During Wartime," pp. 155–173. Joan E. Cashin, ed., *The War Was You and Me: Civilians in the American Civil War* (Princeton, N.J.: Princeton University Press, 2002) includes Peter W. Bardaglio, "On the Border: White Children and the Politics of War in Maryland," pp. 313–331. Essays in Stephen Berry, ed., *Weirding the War*, forthcoming from the University of Georgia Press, address issues such as post-traumatic stress disorder among Confederate veterans (Diane Sommerville), hunger and starvation (Joan Cashin), and civilians' interest in Civil War ruins and souvenirs (Michael de Gruccio and Megan Nelson).

While focusing on the Union, James Marten's study, *The Children's Civil War* (Chapel Hill: University of North Carolina Press, 1998) includes a good deal of information about children in the Confederate South, as do Howard Chudacoff, *Children at Play: An American History* (New York: New York University Press, 2007) and Steven Mintz, *Huck's Raft: A History of American Childhood* (Cambridge, Mass.: Harvard University Press, 2004). Emmy E. Werner, *Reluctant Witnesses: Children's*

Voices from the Civil War (Boulder, Colo.: Westview Press, 1998) is a rich resource of detailed firsthand accounts of the Civil War. Catherine Clinton's *Civil War Stories* (Athens: University of Georgia Press, 1998) contains useful information about children, including orphans in the Civil War South. A recent volume on Southern children and families during the Civil War is Edmund L. Drago, *Confederate Phoenix: Rebel Children and Their Families in South Carolina* (New York: Fordham University Press, 2008). Donald E. Reynolds, *Texas Terror: The Slave Insurrection Panic of 1860 and the Secession of the Lower South* (Baton Rouge: Louisiana State University Press, 2007), while not focused on children, nonetheless indicates how prominently children featured in newspaper coverage of the secession crisis.

Scholarship on women in the Civil War era also offers useful insights into children's wartime experiences. See especially Drew Gilpin Faust, *Mothers of Invention: Women of the Slaveholding South in the American Civil War* (Chapel Hill: University of North Carolina Press, 1996) and Anya Jabour, *Scarlett's Sisters: Young Women in the Old South* (Chapel Hill: University of North Carolina Press, 2007), Chapter 6. Drew Gilpin Faust's recent study of mortality and morbidity in the Civil War era also provides a window into wartime; see *This Republic of Suffering: Death and the American Civil War* (New York: Alfred A. Knopf, 2008). LeeAnn Whites and Alecia P. Long, eds., *Occupied Women: Gender, Military Occupation, and the American Civil War* (Baton Rouge: Louisiana State University Press, 2009) contains several useful essays on Union invasions in Confederate territory, including Lisa Tendrich Frank, "Bedrooms as Battlefields: The Role of Gender Politics in Sherman's March," pp. 33–48; and E. Susan Barber and Charles F. Ritter, "'Physical Abuse . . . and Rough Handling': Race, Gender, and Sexual Justice in the Occupied South," pp. 49–64. Stories of Southern youth shed light on young men's responses to secession and war. See Peter S. Carmichael, *The Last Generation: Young Virginians in Peace, War, and Reunion* (Chapel Hill: University of North Carolina Press, 2009) and Lorri Glover, *Southern Sons: Becoming Men in the New Nation* (Baltimore: Johns Hopkins University Press, 2007).

Remarkably little work has been done on Unionism in the Confederacy, especially as regards the experiences of women and children. For more on this subject, see Victoria E. Bynum, *Unruly Women: The Politics of Social and Sexual Control in the Old South* (Chapel Hill: University of North

Carolina Press, 1992) and Tracy J. Revels, *Grander in Her Daughters: Florida's Women During the Civil War* (Columbia: University of South Carolina Press, 2004), Chapter 5. The best analysis of competing politics within families is Amy Murrell Taylor, *The Divided Family in Civil War America* (Chapel Hill: University of North Carolina Press, 2005). A recent case study is Stephen Berry, *House of Abraham: Lincoln and the Todds, A Family Divided by War* (Boston: Houghton Mifflin Harcourt, 2007). A good primary source is John David Smith and William Cooper, Jr., *Window on the War: Frances Dallam Peter's Lexington Civil War Diary* (Lexington, Ky.: Lexington-Fayette County Historic Commission, 1976). On Southern unionism more generally, see Daniel W. Crofts, *Reluctant Confederates: Upper South Unionists in the Secession Crisis* (Chapel Hill: University of North Carolina Press, 1989) and John C. Inscoe and Robert C. Kenzer, eds., *Enemies of the Country: New Perspectives on Unionists in the Civil War South* (Athens: University of Georgia Press, 2001).

For black children and education in the postwar era, an especially important source is Mary Niall Mitchell, *Raising Freedom's Child: Black Children and Visions of the Future After Slavery* (New York: New York University Press, 2008) and the classic and still-useful study by Willie Lee Rose, *Rehearsal for Reconstruction: The Port Royal Experiment* (Athens: The University of Georgia Press, 1964). Relevant to both the slavery and the postwar eras, Heather Andrea Williams, *Self-Taught: African American Education in Slavery and Freedom* (Chapel Hill: University of North Carolina Press, 2005) argues that African Americans themselves fought for and developed a system for educating blacks. On Northern white teachers in freedmen's schools, see Jacqueline Jones, *Soldiers of Light and Love: Northern Teachers and Georgia Blacks, 1865–1873* (Chapel Hill: University of North Carolina Press, 1980). Published correspondence by Northern schoolteachers in the Civil War and postwar South includes Wayne E. Reilly, ed., *Sarah Jane Foster: Teacher of the Freedmen* (Charlottesville: University Press of Virginia, 1990) and Henry L. Swint, ed., *Dear Ones at Home: Letters from Contraband Camps* (Nashville: Vanderbilt University Press, 1966).

On whites' education and teaching in the postwar South, see Jane Turner Censer, *The Reconstruction of White Southern Womanhood, 1865–1895* (Baton Rouge: Louisiana State University Press, 2003); Ann Short Chirhart, *Torches of Light: Georgia Teachers and the Coming of the Modern*

South (Athens: University Press of Georgia, 2005); and Rebecca S. Montgomery, *The Politics of Education in the New South: Women and Reform in Georgia, 1890–1930* (Baton Rouge: Louisiana State University Press, 2006). Useful primary sources on white children's wartime and postwar education include Marinda Branson Moore, *The First Dixie Reader: Designed to Follow the Dixie Primer* (Raleigh, N.C.: Branson, Farrar & Co., 1863) and Marinda Branson Moore, *The Geographical Reader, for the Dixie Children* (Raleigh, N.C.: Branson, Farrar & Co., 1863).

In addition to Herbert Gutman, *The Black Family in Slavery and Freedom*, and Jacqueline Jones, *Labor of Love, Labor of Sorrow*, important scholarship on the apprenticeship of black children after the war may be found in Karin L. Zipf, *Labor of Innocents: Forced Apprenticeship in North Carolina, 1715–1919* (Baton Rouge: Louisiana State University Press, 2005).

Because so much of this book is based on subjective and sometimes after-the-fact accounts, I have benefited from the insights of the historian Jennifer Ritterhouse, who suggests that because memoir and autobiography are the record of self-fashioning, such documents are excellent sources on identity formation even when (sometimes especially when) they do not reflect empirical facts. Ritterhouse's work on racial identity in the twentieth-century South also offers valuable insights and comparisons to children's identity formation in the slaveholding South. See Jennifer Ritterhouse, *Growing Up Jim Crow: How Black and White Southern Children Learned Race* (Chapel Hill: University of North Carolina Press, 2006). Also useful in interpreting diaries as well as memoirs of the Civil War South is the work of the literary scholar Sarah E. Gardner, who examines white women's writings about the Civil War both during and after the war. See *Blood and Irony: Southern White Women's Narratives of the Civil War, 1861–1937* (Chapel Hill: University of North Carolina Press, 2004).

Index

Illustrations are indicated by page numbers in *italics*.

A NOTE ON THE AUTHOR

Anya Jabour was born in Atlanta and studied history at Oberlin College and Rice University, where she received a Ph.D. Her other books include *Family Values in the Old South* (co-edited with Craig Thompson Friend); *Marriage in the Early Republic: Elizabeth and William Wirt and the Companionate Ideal*; *Major Problems in the History of American Families and Children*; and *Scarlett's Sisters: Young Women in the Old South*. Dr. Jabour is professor of history at the University of Montana. She lives in Missoula.